A Life in the Shadows

Celebrating
30 Years of Publishing
in India

Praise for *Kashmir: The Vajpayee Years* and *The Spy Chronicles*

'Dulat was, perhaps, the best man for the job of handling and winning over the Kashmiris. There was no one else in India's serving bureaucracy who understood and empathized with the Kashmiris more than he did. He was genuinely committed to trying and solving the issue even though at times one disagreed with his approach. Perhaps, Prime Minister Manmohan Singh made a mistake in letting Dulat go in 2004. Maybe history would have been different had he been asked to stay on.'

—Vikram Sood, *The Asian Age*

'For years, Dulat was a mysterious character from a spy thriller, who seemed to be everywhere in Kashmir, trying to win over separatist leaders and elected officials for New Delhi ... Dulat's account of his "mission" doesn't disappoint ... [T]he larger truth about Kashmir clearly comes out.'

—Muzamil Jaleel, *The Indian Express*

'Dulat's book ... provides an insight into how the intelligence agencies and government functionaries work ... His observations about the Kashmiri thought process is both revealing as also depict his expertise on the subject.'

—Pankaj Vohra, *Sunday Guardian*

'*The Spy Chronicles* has created publishing history. It is a bit like the heads of the CIA and KGB cobbling together a book on espionage in the middle of the Cold War ... It marks an interesting turn in the history of books on espionage written by former practitioners of what is called the second oldest profession.'

—Dipankar De Sarkar, *Mint*

'Most books have value because of what is written in them, some rare ones are valued simply because of the idea that became the book. *The Spy Chronicles* falls neatly in the second category ... The strength of the book is its format, where Dulat and Durrani are in a dialogue, mediated by Sinha. It allows the two distinct voices to come through, with their agreements and disagreements coming to the fore.'

—Sushant Singh, *The Indian Express*

'Sometimes, books take on a life of their own because of the way they capture the zeitgeist or tap into a subject that is central to the lives of millions of people. In the case of *The Spy Chronicles*, it is a bit of both.'

—Rezaul H. Laskar, *Hindustan Times*

A Life in the Shadows

A MEMOIR

A.S. Dulat

HarperCollins *Publishers* India

First published in India by
HarperCollins *Publishers* 2023
4th Floor, Tower A, Building No. 10, Phase II, DLF Cyber City,
Gurugram, Haryana—122002
www.harpercollins.co.in

2 4 6 8 10 9 7 5 3 1

Copyright © A.S. Dulat 2023

P-ISBN: 978-93-5629-596-4
E-ISBN: 978-93-5629-597-1

The views and opinions expressed in this book are the author's own
and the facts are as reported by him, and the publishers
are not in any way liable for the same.

A.S. Dulat asserts the moral right
to be identified as the author of this work.

All rights reserved. No part of this publication may be reproduced,
stored in a retrieval system, or transmitted, in any form or by any means,
electronic, mechanical, photocopying, recording or otherwise,
without the prior permission of the publishers.

Typeset in 11/16 Sabon LT Std at
Manipal Technologies Limited, Manipal

Printed and bound at
Thomson Press (India) Ltd

This book is produced from independently certified FSC® paper
to ensure responsible forest management.

*To the intelligence services, whose heroes remain
unknown and unsung*

'I am my own messenger.
So, ask my heart
No pen, no message will carry my tale.'

—Rasul Mir, nineteenth-century Kashmiri poet

Contents

1. Beginnings — 1
2. Wilderness of Mirrors — 33
3. Nepal — 84
4. A Handful of Greats — 98
5. Travels with a President — 123
6. Bhopal — 152
7. Doctor Sahib — 172
8. Kashmiriyat: The Kashmiri and Delhi — 203
9. Spooks as Friends: A Tale of Two Spymasters — 221

Epilogue — 237
Acknowledgements — 241
Index — 243

1
Beginnings

WHERE DID IT ALL BEGIN?

That's the question I've been asking myself while writing this book. Each time I think of this question, it leaves me with a different answer. I was never a compulsive diarist or journal-keeper, so really, I don't have much beyond my memory to tell you where it might have begun. Life doesn't wait for you to fill the pages sometimes. But what I *can* do is give you some of the answers I found while I was putting this book together.

For me, then, it all began in Chandigarh. It is a city that is tied up, for me, in all kinds of emotions, and in many ways, it is home. For my family, however, it began far away—in terms of both geography and time.

The Dulat family's history is one that is shrouded in the mists of the past. The closest that I have been able to uncover is a charming little story told by a brilliant administrator and historian of colonial Punjab, Sir Lepel Griffin, KCSI. According to Griffin, our family belongs to a good-looking Rajput clan from Bikaner, the men of which wore their hair long and in two plaits. Two plaits, in the vernacular, means *do latt*—and from there, we have Dulat. Is this true? Who can say—but it makes for quite a nice little anecdote. From Bikaner, my family shifted—I can't tell you when—to Longowal, and thence to Nabha. That is why anyone from my family will tell you, should you ask, that they belong to Nabha. But the trajectory really began from Bikaner, many, many years ago.

My grandfather, Gurdial Singh Dulat, served the court of Nabha for some years. In the early 1920s, the Maharaja of Nabha, Ripudaman Singh, and the Maharaja of Patiala fell out on some issue or other which is lost to history. The Government of India appointed Sir Louis Stuart as the commissioner to inquire into the quarrel. Sir Louis submitted a report sometime in April 1923, according to which the Maharaja of Nabha was removed from Nabha, and came to live in Dehra Dun. He was, however, allowed to retain his title and the privileges of a privy purse and a gun salute. Later, even that would be snatched away from Ripudaman Singh, and he would be deported to—of all places—Kodaikanal. Meanwhile, the regency of Nabha was handed to the minor son of the erstwhile maharaja. The administration of the state was placed under an administrator and an assistant administrator, with a Council of Regency keeping watch. Why do I tell you this story? Because the assistant administrator in question was my grandfather, Sardar Bahadur Gurdial Singh Dulat. In our family, he was always referred to as the Home Minister of Nabha, for that was what the duties of his post entailed.

I don't remember much about old Gurdial Singh, or, indeed, about my maternal grandfather, Shiv Ram Sawhney (in the family, he was called Shyam). But I do know they were good men, large-hearted and kind, and they got along excellently. Sawhney was a barrister, who joined Sir Sikander Hayat Khan's Unionist Party, but sadly, just like Sir Sikander, who died in 1942, both my grandfathers also passed

Beginnings

away before the partition of India took place. Still, while he was alive, the Sawhney home on Temple Road and, subsequently, at 4 Zafar Ali Road, Lahore, was said to be an open, welcoming house. Gurdial Singh must have been an open-minded person too, because he sent his son, Shamsher (my father), abroad to the University of Cambridge. Young Shamsher grew up in Lahore, in an atmosphere that was clearly conducive to the ideas of government and administrative service. He finished both his schooling—from DAV School—and his college—from Government College—in Lahore, before he set off overseas.

His relationship with Gurdial—as was the wont of those days—was fairly formal, particularly since he grew up without a mother. Gurdial's first wife, Shamsher's mother, died fairly young, and the boy was brought up by Gurdial's sister. This is where it gets interesting, because when I was older, I discovered that the Dulat family is also connected to the Patiala family. My father's first cousin, Jaswant Kaur, was married to Maharaja Bhupendra Singh. She was the second of his wives, known formally as Maharani Jaswant Kaur of Rare. Here, I must digress just a little to tell you an even more interesting connection. Jaswant Kaur's half-brother and father's cousin as well, Sardar Gian Singh Rarewala, was the first chief minister of the Patiala and East Punjab States Union (PEPSU) in 1948, where he continued until he joined the government of Sardar Partap Singh Kairon in 1957.

Jaswant Kaur's son, Raja Bhalindra Singh (1919–92) grew up to become a first-class cricketer, a middle order batsman and a slow bowler (aside from being the Maharajkumar of Patiala). He, too, went abroad to study—at Magdalene College, in Cambridge University. Bhalindra played just one first class match in England, for Cambridge University in 1939, and much later, he became member of the International Olympic Committee (1947–92) and president of the Indian Olympic Association twice, from 1960 to 1975 and from

1980 to 1984. In 1982, Bhalindra was instrumental in organizing and bringing the Asian Games to India.

In fact, sports seems to have run through my family. Bhalindra's son, Randhir, for instance, grew up to become an Olympic-level trap and skeet shooter. He was only about eighteen years old when he debuted as part of the winning trap shooting team at the Indian National Championships in 1964, and he went on to become, I am proud to say, the first Indian shooter to win a continental gold at the 1978 Asian Games in Bangkok. It would be the first of many accolades in the field. Today, Randhir is one of India's most influential sports administrators, having won the Arjuna Award in 1979 and holds the post of the acting president of the Olympic Council of Asia (OCA). Small wonder, then, that cricket—which I played until my career and my age intervened—has been one of my abiding passions!

Of course, all these stories of Bhalindra and Randhir came much later. In the early days, as I was to discover, nobody paid that much attention to what was due to the family name or our faith. We were an irreligious, irreverent lot right from the start. My father grew up with the understanding that he would eventually train for the Indian Civil Service (ICS), and as part of his training, he was sent abroad to King's College at the University of Cambridge, to take his Tripos in History. Those were days when upper-caste Indians of good families didn't really go overseas, unless they were of both means and privilege. Shamsher arrived in England sometime in 1924, and almost as soon as he arrived, not only did he cut off his long hair, but he lost no time in falling in love with an Englishwoman by the name of Eileen Margaret Lawrence. They were married in 1926. None of us ever met her. She passed away in childbirth, having given birth to my brother, Jugjeet Barnaby (yes, Barnaby!) Dulat, in 1928.

I have often wondered whether Sardar Bahadur Gurdial Singh Dulat minded what his son had done, because though Shamsher

Beginnings

returned to India once his Tripos was done, Eileen—by then pregnant with Jugjeet—stayed behind in England. Jugjeet was brought up by suitable nannies and Eileen's mother until he was seven years old. By this time, of course, my father had joined the ICS in Punjab. He was one of the eleven Sikh officers to be selected for the ICS, and one of the three officers who were nominated (the others had to unfortunately sit for the examinations!). My father was, in fact, doing very well for himself by the time Jugjeet came out to India. Shortly after he arrived, however, Shamsher felt the need to marry again. It was a late second marriage as it was, because there is a twelve-year gap between Jugjeet and me. He had seemed in no hurry to marry, but his second marriage proved to be a happy one. This was to a Hindu woman, my mother. In those days, there were many Sikh and Hindu inter-caste marriages, but in our family, there was no real talk of religion or caste. It didn't seem to matter to either my parents or to us later.

Curiously, though, it mattered much more to Jugjeet. He was very deeply conscious of his identity as a Sikh—much more so than his other half, English. Indeed, soon after he came to India, Jugjeet Barnaby went by the wayside and my brother became plain old Jagjit Singh Dulat. He was a bright boy, and went on to study Physics at Government College, Ludhiana. My father steadfastly refused to send him abroad. Jagjit never stopped looking for his other family though, and when I went to England for a year's training, Jagjit asked me to see if I could find out anything about his mother's side of the family. Unfortunately, in those days, I had no idea of how to go about getting this kind of information, and so I was eventually unable to help my brother. Perhaps that's why I've always been so keen to track down as many of my forefathers as I possibly can.

Now this is all very well, but where, you might demand, does *my* story begin? According to my mother, it began at Sialkot in the Sessions Judges' Bungalow, at 11.15 a.m. on a cold December morning in 1940. I was born there because my father was, at the time, the sessions judge at Sialkot. From Sialkot, our family travelled to Hoshiarpur for my father's next posting. In those days, Hoshiarpur was a sprawling district, encompassing Dharamshala, Kullu and Manali. My earliest childhood years were spent there, until I was about five years old in 1946. From Hoshiarpur, my father was posted to Rawalpindi. We transited through Lahore on the way to Pindi, and it was in Lahore that we had to pause for a while, because my sister, Poma, decided to make her entry into this world at that point. It was July, the summer of 1946, and my father was obviously in a happy, hopeful mood, because he bought a shiny, new navy blue Ford. Poma would grow up to become Father's favourite, and my pillar of strength, the person I often turned to when I needed support.

I often think about that moment in the summer of 1946, which prompted Father to buy a new car. After all, it was barely a year away from Independence. But clearly, he had no idea that Partition was in the offing. When I think back to those lost days, I wonder to myself if the British at the time knew that Partition was happening, and that Punjab was going to be divided, why weren't the officers from India—or who would eventually choose India—posted back here? Why did the Raj keep them on in what would become modern Pakistan? But then, retrospect is a convenient thing.

To continue with my story, Father was posted to Rawalpindi—then part of undivided Punjab and a predominantly Muslim district. He made some excellent friends there. I remember one A.R. Fletcher, who became the chief secretary of Haryana and the vice chancellor of the Agricultural University in Hissar. He was a favourite of Bansi Lal. There was also General Kulwant Singh, who would go on to fight the Pakistanis in Kashmir in 1947. I remember these people, because they would often meet with my father.

Beginnings

Father was God's good man and God was good to him. He was a man of few words, an individual whom I held in the deepest respect and awe. Not once in all his life did I hear him utter a swear word. Neither did he need to visit a hospital, except on the couple of occasions when Mother underwent minor surgeries. I don't even remember him ever being sick, until he finally did fall sick with leukaemia in the last few years of his life. But even leukaemia couldn't defeat him. He passed away when his time was up, without troubling anyone. Father had the strongest principles; a very basic, down-to-earth human being. In my life, there is nobody I have wanted to emulate more—in terms of his integrity and his fairness—than my father. He was a likeable person, and rarely did one hear anyone speak ill of him. As a judge, he had an unblemished reputation. The younger members of the bar—S.S. Sodhi, Rajinder Sachar, Rajendra Nath Aggarwal, Brij Khanna—among others—venerated him because of the encouragement he provided them.

Justice S.S. Sodhi, who retired as Chief Justice of the Allahabad High Court, recalls: 'Justice Dulat, though not the chief justice, was a towering personality, whom everyone looked up to, not only in the High Court, but throughout Punjab. His ways as a judge were simple and straightforward and you always knew you would get justice in his court.' Once sitting in his court, which I did off and on, an elderly lady reached out to Father, pleading for mercy for her son, accused in a murder case. I remember Father saying that he was not God, but a lowly judge, duty-bound to interpret the law. Nonetheless, to me, the incident demonstrated the faith that people had in him in seeking justice. He was also only one of the two judges in the high court who dictated his judgment in court. The only other I can remember was Donald Falshaw who did so in keeping with the British tradition, which is completely lost now. My father would hear the arguments and dictate his verdict on the spot—a rare talent.

I had a formal relationship with Father. He understood human frailties and did not believe in lecturing anyone, yet his word was command for all three of his children. I respected his opinion and that's how I landed up in government service. Father liked the good things in life. He enjoyed a drink until his very last night. He would often remark that there was much to learn from the British other than wearing a coat and tie. Sometimes, I think I have spent a lifetime trying to be my father, but I could never be so, considering the legend that Mother built around him. I like to think that towards the end perhaps Father saw something of himself in me, which is consolation enough.

When he retired, Father decided to settle in Delhi, largely due to Mother, who found Chandigarh too dull. He spent two terms with the Union Law Commission, then headed by K.V.K. Sundaram, a year senior to Father in service and a good friend. Books were his constant companion in his retirement. He had a fabulous library, reckoned to be among the best in Chandigarh. It was inherited by Jagjit, considered to be the most learned of us all. Unfortunately, Jagjit himself passed away at the age of sixty-four. But that is another story.

Mother was much harder than Father was, but she loved me immensely, as mothers often love their sons. She could be tough and she was unafraid of voicing her opinions, no matter how they might be received. She was also very different from Father. Born into a sporting family herself, she played every game—tennis, badminton and cricket. Her brother, S.L.R. (Shubh) Sawhney was India's tennis champion in 1939–40 played at Wimbledon and represented India at the Davis Cup.

But Mother was also an example for how little we truly understand people, even when they are people we love. This is digressing a little, but I'd like to give you an example. Here was a woman who did little without her husband. Mother rarely ventured out if Father was not with her. She appeared totally dependent on him. So, when my father suddenly died at the relatively young age of seventy-eight in 1982, I was very worried about her. She used to live in New Delhi in those days, on Tilak Marg. I was married by then, and I took it for granted that we would have to shift in with her, because I didn't think she would be able to live alone. To my shock, she wouldn't hear of it. She refused point-blank, insisting that she was fine on her own. 'And if I am not fine on my own, I will come to your place. You don't have to come to my place.' She was making a definite point, which I understood—*you can't come and occupy my space.*

You think you know your mother—and then something happens to prove to you just how little you know her after all. If ever I saw a metaphor for life, it was my mother! She went on to surprise us all with her newfound independence, living alone in her flat and driving to and from the Gymkhana Club every evening. Mother never drank while Father was alive, but after his death, she had a permanent spot at the bar in the Gymkhana Club, where she would invariably have a drink after her game of bridge. This went on until she was around eighty-six.

She was notorious in the family for her thrift, but if it were not for that, we would not be as comfortable as we are today. Father, you see, had no interest in worldly affairs. Yet, in that typical way that mothers have, Mother never lost her ability to cut me down to size if she felt I was getting too big for my boots. When I suggested once to her that she might like a driver now that she was getting on, she snubbed me, telling me that she could take care of herself. On yet another occasion, I remember, once she had come to stay with us, and I made some remark which I now forget. But it offended her. She said coldly: 'So you've become a big police officer now. You want to teach *me* things now?'

We never stop learning things from our parents, do we?

For both my parents, Partition was a shock. There was no talk of Partition or what it might mean in the Lahore and Rawalpindi of 1946 and 1947. Only when it finally happened, in the summer of 1947, I remember seeing fires burning brightly against the night skies of Rawalpindi, with screams and wails echoing in the distance. It was only later that I realized that the main sufferers of Partition in Pindi were Sikhs. And so, there were unending delegations of people—often harassed, upset Sikh women—who would come to meet Father. My mother, I remember, would be terribly worried for him. Often, she begged him not to meet these strangers: 'You don't know who these people are,' she would plead. But my father wouldn't hear of it. 'It's my duty to go,' he would say. 'How can I refuse?'

The atmosphere changed as the full implications of Partition dawned on all of us. What was happening across Punjab made it untenable for us to stay on in Rawalpindi. But even then, we had to wait. My father's orders to leave came only after independence had been declared, and after the rioting and killings had begun. Our belongings were packed and put on board one of the slow goods trains which would carry them to Delhi. We left the shiny Ford behind in Rawalpindi, and in September 1947, boarded a Dakota, which carried us to Lahore and thence to Delhi.

My parents would never return to Pakistan, and when I went back, decades later, it was as a former intelligence official. The aftermath of Partition was deeply emotional—or it was for my mother, who was vocal about that, as she was vocal about everything else. Often, when I was young, I heard her talking in strange paradoxes: endless stories of how her father's friends were Muslims, but that Muslims in general were unreliable. It was only much later, when I was more grown up, that I challenged her on this. But it might have had something to do with the fact that her uncle (her *chacha*), S.P.R. Sawhney, had been hacked to death in his office by his peons. Sawhney, the district engineer of Lahore, was on vacation in Dalhousie when Partition occurred. He returned to Lahore on 11 September 1947, only to be advised by his Muslim colleagues and friends to leave immediately—for there were no Hindus or Sikhs to be seen in Lahore. The next day, Sawhney went to office to hand over charge—and that was the end of him.

My father, true to form, rarely spoke of how Partition might have affected him. If I had to take a guess, I'd say that for him it was merely a shift back home, because he was, after all, from East Punjab. The jumbled, chaotic fallout of Partition still reverberates today. I recall an elderly Muslim family—I think we called the old gentleman Bakshi sahib—from Nabha coming to visit us often after Partition. Many years later, I bumped into the descendants of that same family at a dinner in, of all places, Gulmohar Park!

When we arrived in Delhi, it was to mixed news. On a happy note, Father had been appointed to the post of district and sessions judge, the first in Delhi and in independent India. He succeeded Amar Nath Bhandari, who was elevated to the Bench and eventually ended up as chief justice. With a bit of luck, Father, too, should have been chief justice, but for the fact that Donald Falshaw of the same batch was senior to him, and in independent India, Englishmen could still be chief justices of high courts, but could not join the Supreme Court.

Father had been allotted a house in Civil Lines: 2 North End Road. Immediately after Partition, it looked more like a refugee camp than a home. All the relatives who had fled Lahore after Partition had nowhere else to stay, except with us. So the house was full of people: my family, my maternal uncle's family, his uncle's family and my mother's two uncles. It was a sticky, humid time of year and large cots were put in the courtyard at the back of the house so that we could sleep outside, in the cool of the night.

But Delhi was no different, atmospherically, from Rawalpindi. It was still very tense, and shortly after we arrived, rioting broke out across the city. One morning, a German—whom I remember only by the name of Karl Heinz, who would, later, become one of the most sought after architects in Delhi, post Partition—came running into the garden, through to the verandah where my uncles and my father were sipping their morning tea. 'I have disturbing news,' he blurted out without preamble. 'We're going to be attacked tonight. I live all by myself. If there is trouble tonight, may I come to your house?'

Sure enough, there was trouble that night.

A squad led by a Muslim station house officer (SHO) of the Civil Lines Police Station began firing right outside the gates of 2 North End Road. There was instant commotion. My grandmother took me and my cousins into the drawing room and hid us under the bed. The men of the house—along with Heinz—crept up the open staircase that wound around the back of the house to the roof. Bullets were ricocheting everywhere and the noise was deafening. One of our Muslim cooks—a 'Mug cook' from Dhaka—had been shot in the stomach as he tried to hide in the bushes outside. He was now sprawled where he had been shot, bleeding profusely. Eventually, the men kicked down the front door. They were now inside the house, and we were staring down the barrels of guns. Father, who had come back down, stood in front of us, and demanded: 'What is the meaning of this?' Such was the authority in his tone that the policemen lowered their arms.

For a while afterwards, we had to shift out of 2 North End Road. The walls were riddled with bullet holes and my mother was terrified for days after the event. We stayed temporarily at the nearby Maidens Hotel, and my father—then sessions judge—went to see the superintendent of police (SP), an officer by the name of Donald Lall. The grown-ups in the family felt that the SHO had obviously been looking for Muslims. But we were wrong. He was looking, we would learn, for Hindus. 'I've heard of what happened,' Lall told my father. 'I'm very sorry about it, but the SHO of Civil Lines had received word that his family had been murdered in Pakistan. He was out to take revenge.' Father understood that Lall was protecting his officers, but Mother was livid that the SP had allowed a murderer to go back home.

Revenge and bloodshed were the themes of those days. People were doing ghastly things to each other, in the name of religion. In Daryaganj one evening, there was an uproar in the narrow streets that connected the busy main square with the nearby Neel Masjid. We didn't wait to see what was happening. We fled as soon as we heard the shouts. On another evening, my family and I were going towards Kashmeri Gate when a tonga passed us, moving quickly. It had but one passenger. Things happened so fast that I could hardly believe what I was seeing. As I watched, the passenger leaned coolly forward and sliced the driver's throat. As the tonga veered crazily across the road, he jumped off and ran away. The tongawala, I'm willing to bet, was Muslim.

But for every horrific memory, I have three beautiful memories. One of them was of days spent at the pretty Roshanara Club in Old Delhi, which could be accessed through the serene Roshanara Garden. My parents were regulars at the club, playing tennis and bridge. On Sundays in winter, I was taken to watch cricket matches. We spent the entire day there, basking in the sun, watching cricket and eating delicious lunches on the little terrace. Roshanara's cricket team had some excellent national and international players—from Surjit Singh Majithia to Tiger Pataudi's father, Iftikhar Ali Khan Pataudi, to Prem Bhatia and Devraj Puri.

Often Tiger's mother, Begum Sajida Sultan, would be present and I can never forget her beauty and charm. Tiger himself was there too. He was a young lad then, about a month younger than me. He was accompanied by his liveried bearers, who threw balls for him to catch. Sometimes, if he was feeling amiable, he'd let me play too. It was a different Delhi, an unimaginable Delhi now—with empty streets, gentle soirees and lunches at new restaurants like the Volga.

If you drove from Civil Lines to Connaught Place, it would take you all of seven minutes.

In January 1948, the Mahatma was assassinated in the Birla House complex in New Delhi. I was too young to remember what the city and the nation might have felt at the loss of such a gigantic figure, but I do remember my father taking me to see the funeral. Those were the days before high security and inaccessible moments of mourning. We drove to Nigambodh Ghat, and my father parked his car a few hundred metres away from the giant pyre of wood. He lifted me out of the car and put me on the roof, so that I had a clear view. I remember the Mahatma's body being placed gently on the pyre, while his favourite bhajans were sung by the grieving crowd in attendance.

Eventually, when I was around ten years old, the time came to have me properly schooled. My father had no desire to let me stay at home and get spoiled by my mother, so he consulted Jagjit, who was not only over a decade older than I, but who had studied at Doon School. Like many old boys after his time, he thought little of his old alma mater and his categorical opinion was that Doon had gone to the dogs and that I must be sent elsewhere for a better schooling. And so it was that I was bundled off to Bishop Cotton School in Simla in 1951. My parents came to drop me to the Delhi railway station, from where I joined the school party to Simla.

Bishop Cotton School was founded on 28 July 1859 by Bishop George Edward Lynch Cotton—the first 'public school' in India. George Cotton was a scholar at Westminster School, and he graduated from Cambridge University in 1836. Cotton began teaching at Rugby School under the tutelage of Dr Thomas Arnold before moving on to be the headmaster of Marlborough College. It was the young Cotton who is spoken of as the 'model young master' in Thomas Hughes's famous book *Tom Brown's School Days*. He was the Bishop of Calcutta when he decided to set up a boys' school in the hills—in Simla—and thence came about Bishop Cotton School.

Beginnings

When I joined Bishop Cotton School in 1951, my class master was the unforgettable J.W. Jones, better known as 'Taffy' Jones. An elderly eccentric bachelor, teaching was Taffy's life. There could be no better teacher for youngsters in English, letter writing and handwriting. Taffy's handwriting was calligraphic. He was particularly kind to troublemakers; his worst fond rebuke being 'blessed pariahs'. Taffy never used the cane and was therefore regarded unfit to be a housemaster.

Taffy was, however, the school swimming coach and for him swimming meant the breaststroke. And if you didn't learn he sent you down the chute so that you needed to swim to save your life. He was always at hand to fish you out if you couldn't.

Taffy Jones lived by himself in his one-room apartment with his tomatoes, radishes and lettuces that he grew.

Even then, Bishop Cotton School had a fine air of dignity about it. It was—and still is—one of the oldest public educational institutions in India. The unique thing about Bishop Cotton in those days was that there was a chapel within the school premises, which students had to attend, seven days a week. At the time, with the characteristic impatience of the very young, we thought it was a bloody nuisance. But looking back, I can't help but marvel at what a beautiful tradition it was—one that continues, or so I am told, even today.

But despite the gracefulness of such a practice, Partition had not left Bishop Cotton untouched. There were, at the time, forty-two Muslim boys in the school. The school authorities were extremely concerned for their safety. If rioting were to break out, who would be responsible for their security? A plan was formulated accordingly by the school authorities to get these boys out so that they could go home.

Now, Bishop Cotton's main hall was known as Irwin Hall. This was a large room, reserved essentially for speeches, debates and prize-giving ceremonies. On Saturday evenings, we would all assemble in

Irwin Hall for a movie. The hall had three main exits—one in front, one at the back and one at the side that led off to the library and the dormitories. These forty-two boys were smuggled out of the side exit and the door was closed and locked behind them. It has never been opened since then, a perennial reminder of what had happened in 1947. In one of fate's little quirks, one of those forty-two boys, Humayun Khan, was to return as one of the most respected high commissioners of Pakistan in Delhi. In yet another quirk, the head boy in my time was a Parsi student, by the name of Jal Boga, who, after he left school, went across the border to settle in Pakistan.

I was never a student who excelled in my studies, preferring to enjoy life instead. That was a pattern that was to form for the rest of my life. The old British system of 'houses' persisted, with the entire student body divided into four houses. I knew a few of the boys who were already in school with me, from a house called Ibbetson House. As soon as I arrived, I was allotted Rivaz House—named after Charles Rivaz, the lieutenant governor of Punjab—whose motto was *Servamus* (which means 'we serve'). It would take me a while to be proud of my house motto and to try to live up to it. Now, each house, naturally, had its own traditions and positions as far as contests went.

Bishop Cotton tried to be as egalitarian as possible, insisting on full participation in every sport, including boxing, irrespective of whether you were good at it or terrible. Participation was more important than winning. It also produced a more rounded personality that public schools were meant for. Our main competitor in local contests was our sister school—also my wife's—the Lawrence School, Sanawar, just down the hill on the way to Kasauli.

Homesickness, loneliness and isolation were part of growing up in school. The way out was to involve myself in extracurricular activities—sports, which I enjoyed. I played cricket from my first year and represented the school Colts (junior cricket team) from my second year.

Representing the school against Sanawar was every schoolboy's dream. I enjoyed cricket from day one in school, and once I grew up and began representing the school, the cricket season was virtually heaven. Saturdays and Sundays were our weekly offs and we played cricket on those days. We looked forward to those special cricket lunches, which were invariably better than the normal schoolday lunches. But I think nothing sums up the essence of public school life more than the legend by Kipling, which hung in the gym at Sanawar: 'Send your son to Sanawar and make a man out of him!'

We had some excellent teachers in school. The headmaster was an Englishman by the name of F.H. Fisher, but the senior master, T.W. 'Tubby' Whitmarsh Knight, was a much more imposing personality. He was also our housemaster. We were familiar with him, but the junior boys in other houses were petrified of Tubby. One stare was enough to reduce some of the younger boys to tears. I remember one particular incident with Tubby, involving Marmite soup. Sometimes, for dinner, we were served Marmite soup, black and bloody bitter. I detested the damn thing and whenever I got a chance, I threw it under the table. One day, Tubby was on duty at dinnertime. He came and stood in front of yet another reluctant boy. 'Come along, drink up,' he commanded. The boy drank the soup obediently, his hands shaking in terror. Yes, old Tubby was quite the disciplinarian.

But there was, as there always is, another, darker side. Bullying was almost a tradition at school, and because I was a small fellow for my age, I was pushed around a lot. Caning was the punishment of choice. The masters at school believed in the old maxim of 'spare the rod and spoil the child', and if any boy transgressed, he was given six of the best. I remember one padre who held a Bible under his arm when he used the cane, thus ensuring that his arm didn't swing wildly, and the strikes administered were short and sharp. Today, there is immense concern about bullying and corporal punishment and its impacts on mental health, but in my time, it was a rough-and-ready way in which you learned to survive, to grow up and take care of yourself.

Take, for instance, our initiation into dormitory life. As kids, I remember our seniors wrapping us tightly in blankets and tossing us high, as high as the rafters sometimes. The blanket would inevitably fly off in another direction, and how you landed after that was all down to luck. In that sense, my early schooldays were, quite literally, the survival of the fittest. Then there was the question of hygiene. Now I had arrived in school from a very comfortable life at home. Bishop Cotton had a rather basic system of the community shower. There were two sets of showers, and each house used those showers every alternate day. That, too, took some time to get used do. After all, once you've been in a community shower, there's very little left to hide!

It didn't help—or perhaps it did, depending on your viewpoint—that we were not allowed to leave the school for the first nine months of our time there. There were, however, two breaks: one in June and one in September. During these breaks, you were allowed to go out into town. If your parents were around, you could even go and meet them.

As it happened, Simla was then the capital of Punjab. When I joined Bishop Cotton my father was elevated to the high court bench as a judge in 1953, which meant that my parents shifted base yet again—this time to Simla. While this could have meant that I became a day scholar, my father insisted that I continue staying on as a boarder in school. There was, he told me and my mother, no need to come home unnecessarily, except on weekends.

So, school was a world of restrictions and regulations, but it gave me a sense of regimen and discipline. It was at Bishop Cotton that

I learned that it is important to fight for what you believe in, and to own up to your mistakes. If you do something wrong, you put your hand up and say, *I did it*. I think that has stayed with me right through life. Telling the truth doesn't always come so easily to all of us. But the trouble with lying is that you can never stop, because somehow it makes things easier. Despite that, we all lie here and there, obviously, but in a sense, it made wholesale lying difficult for me, especially to your wife, a colleague or a trusted friend. In that sense, I think I have abided by Bishop Cotton's motto—*Overcome Evil with Good*—to the best of my abilities!

As I mentioned before, I discovered my love for cricket in school. My father rarely paid attention to my studies as long as I kept myself in the first half of the class rankings, and as long as my house reports were kind. Cricket has remained a passion for me throughout. After school, college and university, I played club cricket in Delhi, Chandigarh, Kathmandu and Bhopal till my postng to Srinagar virtually ended cricket. I did, however, have the privilege of playing a couple of times at the Sher-i-Kashmir Stadium in Srinagar, surely the most beautiful cricket ground in the world, more beautiful than Tunbridge Wells in Kent where Kapil Dev scored 175 after India was 17 for 5 against Zimbabwe that took him on to win the World Cup for India in 1983. Batting at the pavilion end with chinars all around one looked straight up to Shankaracharya, once referred to as Takht-i-Suleiman.

One of my more pleasurable cricket moments was batting with my son, Arjun, just out of school in a club game at the Bab-e-Ali Stadium in Bhopal, which had old-timers recalling that not since the Pataudis had they seen a father and son bat together on the same pitch. I think we scored 35 together, of which my contribution may have been 15, but Arjun scored a half-century that day and then went on to captain his college (St. Stephens's). Both Arjun and Priya were educated in the same college and made little of their grandfather, uncle (my older brother) and father having been educated in government colleges in Lahore, Ludhiana and Chandigarh.

In 1956, I sat for and passed my Senior Cambridge. School life, as I had known it for the last six years, was over. A new chapter was about to begin. A lot of people tell me that they enjoyed boarding school. I can't say that I did, but even then, it was a lot of fun and learning too. When I left, there was more than a twinge of sadness, and the nostalgia for those simple days kept me coming back to Bishop Cotton as an alumnus long after I had grown up.

Now that I was a young man, Father wanted me to come home. Here, he and my mother differed somewhat. She was keen that I go to St. Stephen's College in Delhi after school. It was a big name in those days—and it still is—and was the inevitable destination for all boys from good public schools. But in those days, if you came from a good family or a good school, then you could get in even with a third division. Father refused to hear of it. 'Why would you want to send him to St. Stephen's?' he demanded. Like the good Punjabi he was, he believed that Punjab University was superior in every way to Delhi University.

Looking back, there was a lot of method in the old man's way of thinking. His idea was to send me to boarding school to straighten me up, because he knew that I would be spoiled by my mother at home. But now that I was old enough to understand what 'home' truly meant, he felt it would a good time for me to come back.

I joined college in March 1957. I was sixteen years old and already life felt a little different. For one thing, there was a definite sense of freedom. Bishop Cotton, with its strict routines and schedules, was behind me now. But I had been so used to that style of life that it would take a while to adjust to this new sense of autonomy that one had. Yet, college was important because those were the years that gave me a sense of what reality was really like—those years grounded me as nothing else ever had.

It was also a pleasant surprise to find everyone speaking in Punjabi on campus. Again, school had fixed rules about that sort of thing. Given that the headmaster and several teachers had been British themselves, it was compulsory to speak in English all the time. Here, I found that we could speak in any tongue we liked! Chandigarh, then, is where Punjab, Punjabi and Punjabiyat all melded seamlessly into one for me. It was ingrained in me forever. Named Amarjit Singh, starting with the letter 'A' (in those days, remember, you had to choose the initial of your child's name out of the Guru Granth Sahib), I realized now that I was a Sikh. But what made me truly realize my Sikh identity was still in the future, in 1984. More on that later.

Chandigarh was very different from Simla. In those days, Chandigarh was a small little town, where everyone knew everyone else. The chief minister in those days was the founder of modern Punjab—Sardar Partap Singh Kairon. Jawaharlal Nehru, then the Prime Minister of India, had supported Kairon's vision to make Chandigarh what it was and what it would eventually become. These dreams were ably executed by the famous French architect Le Corbusier, who laid out the plans for the city.

We lived in the northernmost sector, Sector 4. One of the first sectors to be built was Sector 16, where most of the government housing was. In a charming idiosyncrasy, every sector that faced each other totalled thirteen—for instance, Sector 8 would face Sector 5, and Sector 9 would face Sector 4. Chandigarh was a quiet city, with little to no traffic, and we could bicycle from one part of the city to the other. Some of my friends had motorbikes or scooters, but my father—when my mother suggested that I too get one—refused point-blank. 'Why should he have a scooter? What's so special about him? He has a cycle, let him go around on that.'

I didn't mind at all. I enjoyed cycling to college and back, or with friends to catch a movie at Kiran Cinema. I took History and Economics as my majors in college. Punjab had a different system from Delhi University—where you did the intermediate first, then your BA or your graduation. We had some good teachers, at least in our history department. I must be honest: I enjoyed life far more than my studies! That said, though, I worked very hard for my graduation. I felt I had to do well, especially since I had taken honours. Today's generation might not know what 'taking' honours means—but essentially, even though your grades would be given on the basis of your main subject, you still had the load of three extra subjects. Most people, for that reason, left the honours part alone, but I was determined to get those honours. I worked really hard and I did do very well, getting myself a good second division.

My father was very happy with me, and asked me to finish my master's before sitting for the Union Public Service Commission (UPSC) examinations. Did I always know, you might wonder, that I wanted to sit for the UPSC examinations? For me, there was no 'knowing'. I simply had no choice in the matter. My father didn't believe in giving any lecture on any subject, but he was firm on this topic. For him, employment of any kind meant only one thing: government service. He would say so quite openly, '*Naukri sarkar di karo. Nahi toh jo marzi karo.* (Join government service, or do whatever you want.)'

So I knew I didn't have much of an option. I sat for my UPSC examinations for the first time in 1963, but as expected, did not make the cut. In 1964, I sat for the exam again and felt that I might make it this time. My father asked me how I had done. I said, '*Theek theek hua.* (It was okay.)' My father thought I wouldn't make the cut in the first round. He took it quite well, and for a time, I looked about myself for another option. Now, at that time a lot of my friends had gone to Calcutta, seeking jobs in corporate houses. I also wanted to go, rather than burying myself in some obscure dot on the map for civil service training. Seeing how determined I was to try my hand at this, my father acquiesced, and sent me off to live with my uncle in Calcutta in the winter of 1964.

It was the year that Pandit Jawaharlal Nehru died, after a long illness. I wish I could describe more elaborately what the atmosphere was like in the aftermath of his death, but—all I can say is—when Panditji died, India wept. A true legend had passed. I had never had the fortune of meeting him, but I remembered his charisma and how everyone would drop what they were doing and rush out into the streets whenever he came to town—just to catch a glimpse of greatness. Those are memories I can never forget, for they belong to an India that is now lost in the mists of time.

Calcutta in the early 1960s was, I think, at its absolute best, with leftovers of the Raj to be found everywhere. We were regular visitors to the city, because my mother often took us to visit her brother during winter. It was alive in every sense of the word, with a band at Ferpos (where you could have a meal and more for the princely sum of five rupees!) and other wonderful crooners at the city's popular restaurants. Pam Crane sang at El Dorado; there was a boy, Clive Hughes, who sang at Mocambo and at Trinca's, there were jam sessions for youngsters on Sundays. There were bands and bars also at the Metro Cinema and New Empire Cinema. The bands played before the show and during the interval. The best meals, of course, were found at Sky Room, and if you wanted to just sit down and have a cup of tea, you went to Flury's. Pretty young Anglo-Indian girls could be seen walking about Calcutta, in their colourful long skirts. Christmas brought the city even more vibrancy, with lights twinkling everywhere, parties by the dozen and races on New Year's Day.

I was twenty-three years old and this was the world I had always dreamed of. It made the prospect of getting myself a job and living there extremely inviting! My uncle, Shubh Sawhney of the Davis Cup fame, was working with the Birlas in Calcutta. He was very kind to me, taking me around to introduce me to the right people. I recall appearing for a lot of interviews, where I was always asked about my academic qualifications. My results from the UPSC examinations had yet to come out, and everywhere I went I was told to wait for the results before hoping for a firm prospect. To cut a long story short, as you might have guessed, I didn't get a job. The corporate life, it seemed, was not for me.

However, I qualified for the UPSC—but it wasn't the rank or cadre I expected. I had keenly wanted to qualify for the Indian Foreign Service (IFS), in the hope that it would give me a chance to see the world. Failing that, I wanted to qualify for the Indian Administrative Service (IAS). I had qualified for neither of those. Instead, I made it to the Indian Police Service and the Central Services—with high marks in the police service interview. Confused, I asked my father's advice on what I should choose. 'Take up the IPS,' he told me. 'It's an all-India service.' Plus, my brother was already working in the Income Tax Department, and as my father said, one child in the Central Services was more than enough!

Before I move on to telling you about my years in training, I must introduce you to my wife. Love also happened, for me, in Chandigarh, for that is where I met Paran for the first time in 1959. I remember every step of our courtship. Our fathers were both in the ICS, and our families—as it so happened—lived just a few houses away from each other. To my younger self, of course, her family's long and rich history made no sense, but as I grew older and developed a keener interest in these things, I discovered that the Jind family was really one to reckon with.

The erstwhile royal house of Jind belongs to the Phulkian family, the same family as the houses of Patiala and Nabha (a link to mine!). They trace their ancestry to one Baryam, who was granted the title of Chaudhuri by Emperor Babur in 1526. The state of Jind, however, was founded by Gajpat Singh, a great-grandson of Phul, in 1763. He built the foundations of the state, but fell into disfavour after he failed

Beginnings

to pay his land revenues. For this failing, he was imprisoned in Delhi until he could find a way to pay his debts. Eventually, favour was restored and he was awarded the title of Raja, by Emperor Shah Alam.

That's as far back as I can tell you about the beginnings of Paran's illustrious family. Maharaja Ranjit Singh, the Lion of Punjab and the founder and ruler of the formidable Sikh empire, had his *naankaa* (maternal home) in Jind, which is a noble link to have. His mother, Raj Kaur, was the daughter of Gajpat Singh, who had founded the Jind dynasty. But Paran's grandfather, Brigadier H.H. Farzand-i-Dilband, Rasikh-ul-Itiqad-i-Daulat-Inglishia, Raja-i-Rajgan Maharaja Sri Sir Ranbir Singh Rajendra Bahadur, Maharaja of Jind, comes much later down the line. He succeeded to the throne on the death of his grandfather in 1887. He was then still a minor and reigned under a Council of Regency until he came of age. A progressive ruler who was greatly interested in education, Ranbir Singh built schools and hospitals, established charities for widows and orphans and made primary education free throughout his state.

His personal life, on the other hand, was rather more colourful. A late riser, Ranbir Singh was fond of billiards and gambling, losing huge amounts every night. His penchant for fair and lovely young women also led him down the road to perdition quite a few times. The best-known case is that of Jaswant Kaur. She was originally Olive Monolescue, the beautiful daughter of Lizzie Coleman, married to Monolescue, a Romanian barber who owned a shop in Bombay. When Ranbir Singh came across Olive on holiday in Mussoorie, he was already deaf and reserved, with a deep love for dogs. More importantly, though, he already had two Sikh wives—Dhelma and Gurcharan Kaur. However, he wanted to marry Olive too.

He devised a scheme to get Olive to come to Sangrur, which involved the transaction of a healthy sum of Rs 50,000. Olive and Ranbir Singh were married in the princely apartments in his palace in Sangrur. Olive converted to Sikhism, and became known as Jaswant Kaur. Unsurprisingly, Lord Curzon—then the Viceroy of India—was outraged at this marriage, decreeing that Olive would never get the title of 'Maharani' of Jind. The Raj—then deeply devoted to outward shows of protocol and social hierarchy—refused to admit the royal couple to any of its major social occasions. Olive remained *persona non grata* for much of her time in Simla. Eventually, fed up, she divorced Ranbir Singh in 1928 and went to England, with her young daughter, Dorothy.

There are plenty of such colourful tales about old Ranbir Singh, but since the story is more about Paran and not her entire ancestry, I'll relieve you of the rest of it, by simply saying that Ranbir Singh's daughter, Princess Rajbir Kaur (also known as Ruby), was Paran's mother. Ruby married Balbir Singh Grewal, one of the last brown sahibs that I had the fortune to see while I was growing up. He was always immaculately dressed, 'propah' in every way, with an aura of aloof dignity. Only my mother-in-law's laidback ways could irk him, so that he would snap at her at times, 'The Jind family is mad!'

There was nobody who did not know Balbir Grewal. Just recently, I was talking to one of his old contemporaries, S.K. Misra. Misra was one of India's most illustrious bureaucrats from the Haryana cadre, principal secretary to all the Lals—Bansi Lal, Bhajan Lal and Devi Lal—before he ended up in the Government of India as Principal Secretary to Prime Minister Chandra Shekhar. Misra remembered my father-in-law: 'Mr Grewal was a senior officer we all looked up to for his fair-mindedness, but he could be obstinate and tight-fisted as well.' Miserliness possibly explains his loneliness in later years. Yet he left behind a large estate built largely on the wealth of the princess. Ruby, as she was named, was truly a gem. Money never bothered her. I often wondered whether she understood its worth. She lived in a world of long ago, where she still received a privy purse of Rs 750 a month. Warm and gracious to the end, she was truly one of the last of her kind.

Beginnings

When I first met Paran, she was fourteen years old, and I was eighteen. We were both waiting in line for tickets at Kiran Cinema. She was with her friends and I was with mine. One of my friends asked one of hers if she could get us a couple of tickets since they were ahead of us in the queue. There was something attractive about Paran, which struck me instantly. She was not beautiful in the conventional sense of the word, nor was she bashful. Both Paran and her sister were, in that sense, a lot more relaxed, which made talking with her much easier. Her father was away in those days, on deputation somewhere across India. And as youngsters often do, we found excuses to meet while she was home for the school holidays.

It helped that Chandigarh was a small town, where everyone knew everyone else. We naturally had friends in common, and that made it easy for us to meet nearly every evening. Sometimes, we went for walks together, chatting away about everything under the sun. I enjoyed her company greatly, but I knew that our time together would be short. She was much younger than I was then, and she needed to finish school. I was certainly looking around in those days. I had no idea what I was looking for, of course. Nobody who is eighteen years old knows definitely what he wants—and my father hadn't said a word to me about getting married or anything like that. About ten days after I had met her, she went away, back to school. I didn't even know whether she already had a boyfriend back in Sanawar. After all, it was a co-ed school. But those ten days were special, and in a way, sealed our future.

There is an inevitability about heartbreak in first love. When I hadn't heard from Paran for a year, I thought our story was over. I didn't see her for a couple of years after that. The mind often plays tricks on you with distance. At one stage, I gave up the nebulous idea that was floating about in my head and started going around with another girl. But fate is a funny lady—sometimes, there are plans that are greater than any that you can concoct. A bird not in hand, I like to say, is not as good as others in the bush! So I had found myself a new love till Paran found me again.

One of my friends who lived across the Grewal's told me that BSG (Balbir Grewal) was back and so was his beautiful daughter and she had been inquiring about me. I went to meet her shortly afterwards—and that, as they say, was that. During the years we had been apart, Paran had grown up into an attractive young woman, charming and easy to talk to and—to my delight—someone who loved sports as much as I did. The only sport she disliked was cricket. Those were the days of simple Test cricket, of course, and Paran found it immensely boring. 'All you do is sit there and clap,' she complained. 'What a bore it is!' But since she was going around with me, and since I was very much a regular player, it was somewhat compulsory for her to attend every game I played! Over time, she became reluctantly fond of the game, and today she knows as much about cricket as I do.

Between 1959 and 1966—a long, long time in those days—we were together, without any talk of being engaged or married. At its core, Chandigarh was a small town, and it wasn't long before every tongue in town was furiously wagging. Balbir Grewal was against the idea of our marriage. 'He's a policeman,' he told Paran. 'He'll never be able to afford you!' As far as my family was concerned, my mother may have had her reservations, but Father being Father, stepped in decisively to support me. After that, everybody had to accept the fact that Paran and I were serious about each other. Even today, people find it hard to believe that Paran and I could have been together for so long without the stamp of legality, especially in the early 1960s!

It's only now, looking back over the five decades that we have been married, that I see how deeply we have influenced each other and how greatly we complement each other. I also wonder how much of my renewed courtship of Paran was due to the fact that she was the haughty Balbir Grewal's daughter, and the fact that she had actually

Beginnings

just disappeared from my horizon for a couple of years before coming back into my life. Courtship then became a challenge supported all the while by my mother-in-law-to-be. After the decades we've been together, I can only say, whatever my subconscious motivations were, they have taken us to the happiest places. Paran was never very gregarious, but what I truly loved about her was that she never cared about who I was professionally. There are many wives and women who put much stock in how well their husbands are doing. Paran couldn't have given a damn about promotions, about where I was going or whether I was doing well.

In fact, while I was in the Vajpayee PMO (Prime Minister's Office), the rumour was that I would be ultimately promoted to governor of Jammu and Kashmir. When Paran heard of that, she insisted, time and again, that if the whispers turned out to be true, then I would have to make arrangements for another wife. 'I have no desire to be locked up in a Raj Bhavan,' she would declare. I knew she was joking, but there was an inherent kernel of truth in her words. Paran has never sought higher posts or greater publicity. At heart, she is as much a lover of life as I am. That has, over the years, been one of our greatest bonds.

But I digress.

I didn't marry Paran until I had completed my training. I started off my career by training at the police academy in Mount Abu. That was another new phase in life for me, possibly my best in the police service. Most probationers didn't like outdoor training, but I thoroughly enjoyed it and even represented the academy's hockey team. Hockey as a game was compulsory for all police officers. I joined along with a friend from school, a chap by the name of Arun Babbar. He'd been a year junior to me in school, but we had always been good friends. Arun had a swagger about him, which intimidated the other probationers. They kept telling me, '*Apne dost ko sambhalo.* (Control your friend.) He threatens us all.' But Arun liked to maintain that image.

We were new to Mount Abu and we quickly learned that it was a dry state, with no liquor. But you could, if you were resourceful, get it from three sources. Firstly, from the Gurkha Regiment, you could get some rum, if you knew the right people. Secondly, tourists coming up to Mount Abu were free to seek a permit and get six bottles of beer or a bottle of hard liquor. So sometimes, we sent our colleagues down to get hold of a random tourist and get him to get us some booze. The third method was the crudest of all, since it involved imbibing the local *tharra* (country liquor). In Rajasthan, the more sophisticated variety was called Kesar Kasturi, but it was neither kesar nor was it kasturi—it was bad, hard liquor.

One day, we were desperate and picked up a bottle of tharra for seven or eight rupees. Now, since I was one of the lucky guys in the academy who had a room of his own, next to the mess, my friends decided to have a drink in my room before going off to the mess to eat. It seemed a nicely convivial plan, and we sat about in my room, chatting and drinking tharra out of cups and saucers. When it was time to go to dinner, we'd reckoned without the effects of *tharra* on stomachs unaccustomed to it. One of our friends couldn't take the liquor so easily. He threw up richly in the mess, a dead giveaway. The next morning, the entire batch was lined up. The Anglo-Indian adjutant-cum-assistant commandant, by the name of Burge, swore at us angrily for what had happened the last night.

I went to Arun: 'This damn thing, I feel like going to Burge and telling him that we've made a mistake.'

Arun sighed, '*Tum saale pagal ho.* (You are mad.) This is not Bishop Cotton. Here, telling him that means dismissal.'

But I was truly disturbed. This might not have been Bishop Cotton, but my school had taught me far too much about sticking to your principles to forget them now. The next morning, we had class from nine o'clock in the morning until around lunchtime. I was always a backbencher since I wasn't averse to a little nap during the lectures. But that day, my mind genuinely couldn't concentrate. I kept thinking of what had happened over the last couple of days, especially with Burge. Eventually, I slipped out of class and went to the adjutant's room and knocked on the door. He was sitting at his desk and looked up as I put my head around the door. 'Come in, you bastard. Finally you've had the gumption to own up?'

'Yes, I have.'

'Where's that bloody friend of yours?'

'He's just coming.'

Five minutes later, my friend came in and apologized as well to Burge. His final words to me were: 'You shouldn't mix with people who can't hold their drink.'

Babbar and I went on to become Burge's favourites, but after our time in the academy together, our ways parted. Life was tragically cut short for Babbar. Allotted the Madhya Pradesh cadre, Babbar had the potential to be the brightest star among his batch, with his skills in anti-dacoity. He earned himself a gallantry award, and a stint in Mizoram (around the same time as my friend Ajit Doval) where he told me that he was in constant talks with Laldenga. He died before he could see the signing of the Mizo Peace Accord, felled by a heart attack much before his time, on the same day that Indira Gandhi was assassinated.

But that was much in the future. For now, Bishop Cotton's training had served me well. Mount Abu was also where Paran and I decided to finally go ahead with our decision to marry. But she was firm that I needed to seek her father's blessings for our marriage. I wrote a letter to her father, and also discussed it with my parents. My mother was deeply upset that I had decided to write that letter of my own accord, but this time, my father stepped in. 'If he wants to do this,' he told her, 'you must keep quiet.'

A LIFE IN THE SHADOWS

I have described the early years of my training in the Intelligence Bureau in *The Vajpayee Years*,[1] so I see no need to elaborate here. But there is one thing that I didn't mention there, which I feel I must mention now. I have often been asked how it is that I managed to compartmentalize an often stressful professional life with my home life, especially after our two children were born. I have to say that I wouldn't have been able to do that without Paran. Her indifference to what I did for a living made it necessary that I leave work behind at the office. Her support to me was wordless but deep. She would stay up for me, no matter how late I was. We always had dinner together, despite the hour. It was our time together after the day was done, and it was never done as long as we didn't sit down and talk about the kids, about friends, about mundane everyday things. As one gets older, one realizes that companionship is the foundation of life, and given that Paran and I were together for seven years before we embarked on fifty-five years of marriage, it's an entire lifetime together.

That is why Chandigarh, for me, is where it all began. It was a town where I came of age, in more ways than I can describe on paper.

Today, many of my friends (and me) have reached the age where we discuss mortality a bit more than normal. A lot of people say it's best to die in your sleep. There are others who say what's the fun in that? I've often argued about this with colleagues and friends. I know plenty who say they aren't afraid to die.

But I am afraid to die. You see, the problem with death is that nobody can tell you about it. There's no rehearsal and no mulligan.

I love life even now.

I hope I continue to do so, but I can't complain. God's been kind to Paran and me—it's been a good life.

Let me tell you about it.

---

1   A.S. Dulat with Aditya Sinha, *Kashmir: The Vajpayee Years,* Noida: HarperCollins, 2015.

2
Wilderness of Mirrors

JAMES JESUS ANGLETON, THE LEGENDARY CIA[1] SPYMASTER, thrived in what he called 'the wilderness of mirrors'. When I first heard the phrase, I couldn't help thinking that there was no better way to describe the world of espionage. It is a treacherous game. There is nothing pretty about intelligence gathering. You might decorate it with principles of nobility and patriotism, but in reality, these principles are a shroud for villainy and skulduggery.

Take Angleton's own story, for instance. In 1943, Angleton arrived in London, where he met Kim Philby, the then head of MI6's Iberian section. It was the start of a long friendship, in which Philby would become Angleton's prime instructor and in many ways, his mentor. It was Philby and his great betrayal of king and country that broke Angleton's heart, but it was also Philby and his devious ways that introduced the younger man to the darker side of espionage—a side paved with treachery and betrayal.

---

1   Central Intelligence Agency (CIA), principal foreign intelligence and counterintelligence agency of the US government.

In 1974, CIA director William Colby fired Angleton after *The New York Times* revealed that the counter-intelligence chief had overseen a massive deep-state programme to spy on American citizens involved in anti-war and black nationalist movements: a direct violation of the CIA's charter.[2] Coming as it did months after Watergate, the exposure of Angleton's operations set off a political avalanche of sorts. It was a crossroads in the history of American intelligence, when the CIA—its funding slashed for the first time since its inception—had to struggle with the implications of the legacy left by James Angleton, that master of mass surveillance and what some call the founding father of the American deep state. But that is a different story.

Let me come back to his favourite phrase: 'the wilderness of mirrors'. For Angleton, that phrase perfectly described the Soviet Union's espionage tactics, 'the myriad of stratagems, deceptions, artifices and all the other devices of disinformation which the Soviet bloc and its coordinated intelligence services use to confuse and split the West … an ever fluid landscape where fact and illusion merge'.[3] If there is a more perfect way to describe espionage and the shadowy world in which it takes place, I have yet to find it.

Another practice that the Russians resorted to at one time was the honeytrap for which particularly attractive young women referred to as 'swallows' were used. Such was the fear of the honeytrap

---

[2] Seymour M. Hersh, 'Huge C.I.A. Operation Reported in U.S. Against Antiwar Forces, Other Dissidents in Nixon Years', *The New York Times*, 22 December 1974, https://www.nytimes.com/1974/12/22/archives/huge-cia-operation-reported-in-u-s-against-antiwar-forces-other.html?_r=0

[3] Quoted from Jefferson Morley, 'The Wilderness of Mirrors', *The Intercept*, 1 January 2018. Available at: https://theintercept.com/2018/01/01/the-complex-legacy-of-cia-counterintelligence-chief-james-angleton/

that our officers posted to Moscow went through a special security briefing by the Bureau of Security in the Ministry of External Affairs. The honeytrap, of course, goes as far back as the legend of Samson and Delilah. But before a spook gets to that stage, there is a more humdrum beginning. Allow me to take you back to where it all started for me, as it does for most intelligence officers: at the desk.

Analysis is often underrated. I worked on the desk as an analyst for four years at the headquarters in New Delhi. I spent two years in North Block, sharing a room with the great M.K. Narayanan, and two more years under another master—K.N. Prasad. During my time on the job, I learned that in truth, deskwork is actually quite important. You get a lot of muck coming in from field reports, and often, those reports come in bulk. The idea is to winnow the wheat from the chaff, but of course, this requires some amount of understanding. Studying the kind of reports that come in prompt the curious mind to wonder—who are these reports coming from? Where are they coming from? What is the credibility of the source for your information? The same goes for the report that you present as a result of your analysis. This must be absolutely clear and lucid, based on your own understanding of the information you must have received.

A source report is the core of intelligence but at the desk, one never knows where it is coming from and nor should one know. That is what makes analysis fascinating.

My top boss (above my immediate boss, R.K. Khandelwal, whom Narayanan called 'Kandy') was an officer by the name of A.K. Dave who was very particular about draftsmanship. He insisted on rigorous instructions in writing, and was known to publicly pull up colleagues: 'What is this rubbish you've sent! This won't do justice to a sub-inspector!' So finicky was Dave that even the great Narayanan, who reported to Dave, used to get slightly irritable. I recall one holiday weekend we spent endlessly drafting and redrafting a report, simply because Dave sahib was not fully happy with the end results. But Dave's point was valid—draftsmanship is at the heart of a good, comprehensive report.

K.N. Prasad, on the other hand, was a different kettle of fish—a tough exterior with a decent interior, who was willing to teach the youngsters all that he knew. His method differed starkly from Dave's. If he didn't like a report you presented to him, he would make you sit down and he would sit with you, patiently correcting and rewriting. This process was a lot more informative, because it taught you where you may have gone wrong, and how you could rectify it in future. In that sense, Prasad sahib was a great teacher. Those were the days that the Intelligence Bureau would boast of classical learning that transformed policemen into intelligence officers and even men of letters.

So, in the four years that I was on the desk, I learned an incredible amount from some extremely experienced, knowledgeable officers. Analysing the answers to the questions coming in off the field hones your instincts in ways that the field itself can never do. This is something that I learned by watching M.K. Narayanan. He was a past master at distilling the information he got, and making the best use of that material. From him, I learned to tone down the natural excitement of a youngster, who is so thrilled at the reports coming in from the field that he blurts out everything immediately. When I was writing reports, I learned to keep them tight and compact. People reading them on the other end often had no time to read through pages and pages at a time. You had to be able to convey your message in a single page if you could.

When Narayanan received his files on certain subjects, I watched as he kept the reports to himself for a while, and mulled over them before making a presentation. He was a real artist, an acknowledged expert on communism (a hot topic in those days!), and even though my interactions with him were minimal back then, I knew I was in the presence of real greatness. In later years, I experienced that same feeling again—in the presence of the legendary R.N. Kao, for example.

Kao sahib is known today as one of modern India's greatest spooks, and it is with good reason. He was very different from Narayanan: a quieter, more withdrawn man. The popular myth is that no matter how hard you look, you will never find a photograph where Kao's face is clearly shown (till someone wrote his biography recently). In that sense, he was the quintessential spook, a man who truly lived his life in the shadows. But where Narayanan—a true analyst—took his time to mull over information, Kao was a man of action. He was a real operations man, one who lived and thought on pure instinct. Both men were, as I say, very different—yet in their own ways, they were Indian espionage's absolute best.

But that is a different story.

If M.K. Narayanan liked you, he liked everything about you. If M.K. Narayanan didn't like you, woe betide you.

I discovered that distinctive characteristic quite early in my career. In those days, he was the seniormost assistant director, waiting to be promoted. I, on the other hand, was the juniormost assistant director, ten years M.K. Narayanan's junior. MK would go on to play an incredibly important role in Indian intelligence, as everyone knows. In fact, I've talked quite a bit about MK throughout this book as well, because there were very few steps one could take in the intelligence field without MK's supervision or knowledge. Even in those days, he was already a legend, one of the top names that you could go to on the subject of communism. He spoke little, and as a desk officer, I watched how thick dossiers would be brought in before Narayanan. Despite the surfeit of information at his disposal, he would never leap to conclusions. He would take hours—sometimes days and weeks—to peruse a file, to mentally distil information and to produce the finest and most objective analysis.

From Narayanan, I learned that it is almost always best to wait before taking a decision, to mull over its every aspect. With information coming in from the field in particular, you don't often know its inherent biases and distortions until you have all the facets there are to be gathered on the subject. This means that you must wait, and there is often no telling as to how long and fruitful that wait might be, but intelligence is, essentially, a waiting game. There is nobody I have encountered who played that game better than Narayanan. He was everything that the much younger Dulat aspired to be as a senior intelligence officer. It was not to be expected that he would interact with young fellows my age, but he was observant—and he noticed always if I was disgruntled by my then boss, R.K. Khandelwal, who was a somewhat hard taskmaster.

'What's the matter?' he'd ask kindly. 'Another tiff with Kandy?'

As I grew older in age and career, I began to notice other things. MK was not always an easy man to fathom, and that is the greatest characteristic of a professional spook, but he was also someone who quite liked hero worship. He was well aware of his legendary reputation, even then, and he liked to be venerated. Indeed, it is said that none other than B.N. Mullick—best known as Prime Minister Nehru's intelligence chief, who wrote a three-volume book titled *My Years with Nerhru*—referred to MK as by far the greatest intelligence officer in Asia.

As I grew older, I realized that the awareness of your reputation is not really a failing, as much as it is a natural human tendency, but as someone who has stayed away from it myself, it was never a trait I personally understood. I have watched M.K. Narayanan always being the first to speak at the weekly Friday meetings, and watched the room fall silent in respect and awe when he spoke. He always had a finger in every pie, political or espionage. He knew what was going on at every given point in time, and he liked being depended upon to know everything—to be the man who was called first for any situation. It was a close similarity to J. Edgar Hoover because MK prided himself on having a file on every subject and every individual that he'd met in life. Few knew better how to navigate the corridors of power in Delhi.

This respect that others—especially the Gandhi family—had for him saw M.K. Narayanan always staying relevant in the espionage world. Rajiv Gandhi, in particular, had depended on Narayanan greatly for keeping abreast of the latest goings-on in the espionage world. It need not, I observed, have been a necessarily high-pressure situation either. For instance, Rajesh Pilot, in the days when he was interested in Kashmir, used to go to Narayanan to find out what was happening on the ground in Srinagar. When MK discovered that Wajahat Habibullah had been picked by Rajesh Pilot, then the minister for information and broadcasting, to keep him updated on Kashmir, MK decided to promptly attach me to Rajesh as well.

As one grows and gets into their shoes, one finds his or her own career path, and I can safely say I did the same, but I can equally safely say that watching the great M.K. Narayanan in action was an education.

To return to my own tale, the greatest irony of the early days of my career was that I didn't know a thing about counter-intelligence. It's ironical because subsequently, I spent a considerable portion of my career doing precisely that. But you see, in those days, we kids weren't supposed to know what counter-intelligence was. We were not to know that counter-intelligence involved looking for foreign spies within our own country. We were supposed to just concentrate on making all kinds of reports—from weekly reports, to reports that might go up to the highest levels of government. It was only later that I discovered that the field is a different ballgame.

I say this while taking into account the existence of technical intelligence (or as we call it, TECHINT). This essentially means the gathering of intelligence relating to the technical abilities of the enemy. TECHINT includes elements of imagery, measurement and signatures and signals intelligence. It's not an entirely new phenomenon, having been around since the Second World War. A basic example is that of the British, which followed a supply of heavy water to be used by the Nazis in building an atomic bomb, for several years, only to destroy it in transit from Norway to Germany. Technical and scientific intelligence operations proliferated during the Cold War and later, with inevitable upgrades coming to weapons and surveillance technology.

Despite the convenience of TECHINT, I have always been a proponent of the opposite end of the spectrum: HUMINT. You might have guessed the full form of this: human intelligence. This is the basic foundation of espionage, based on gathering information via techniques like surveillance and interrogation. Call me old-fashioned, but this is why I really enjoyed being out in the field. I am a laidback guy—and I like giving that impression—but I also enjoy talking to people. Nothing beats the good old spy or agent on the ground.

Engagement and dialogue is now what many people like to call the Dulat model, especially in Kashmir—but frankly, I see no better way to gather intelligence than by talking to people, all kinds of people. Today, counter-intelligence does not have the kind of importance that it used to have in the old days. Duane R. Clarridge, former senior operations officer for the CIA and author of *A Spy for All Seasons: My Life in the CIA*, acknowledged the IB's excellent skills in counter-intelligence in his book. Those skills, sadly, seem to have lost their edge these days. Counterterrorism has now rightly taken prime place, but it should not be at the expense of counter-intelligence. Cybercrime is another big threat where coping with China's capabilities is a huge challenge. The answer to China lies perhaps in diplomacy. We cannot appear neutral on Ukraine, for instance, and then be seen with NATO.

When I started out in the field, I was quick to learn that it can be an enjoyable place, because of a certain degree of autonomy that you enjoy as an officer. Yet, it can also be a lonely place—made lonelier still in times of crisis. Now, I have never suffered the traditional (somewhat stereotypical) loneliness of working undercover in a foreign country. But I can tell you of the loneliness of 1989–90. I had taken charge of the Bureau in Kashmir in 1988, and barely a few months later, militancy erupted, rendering Srinagar and its surroundings almost unliveable. It was my first test in the field, and I was out of my depth, alone in a situation that was rarely the same for a week at a stretch.

The optics for the Bureau was not the best either in 1989. The centenary of the Bureau's establishment was that year, and while on the one hand we celebrated (in a rather major way, too!) in Srinagar, on the other hand, things were going rapidly out of control in the state. Did we have ears to the ground despite this? Yes, to some extent—but it was not enough in the long run. We had no inner contacts within militant networks, though we had established rudimentary contacts with some of these boys. But those were nascent, still just about being consolidated.

It was not enough.

I have often felt that more than any other place, it has been Kashmir that taught me the real game of intelligence. In this game, as I was to discover, there are very few rules and the work is rarely gentlemanly or civilized. Nothing is above board in the world of spookdom. There was a young boy from a Punjabi family close to the Abdullahs, Praneet Sawhney, who knew certain useful things, since he was quite plugged into the local Kashmiri network. I went across and met with him to try to discover how much he could tell me. 'You're new here,' he told me, rather prophetically. 'You need to know that things here are not all right. *Yahan kuch gadbad hone wali hai.* (Things are not all right here. Trouble is brewing.)' He married shortly thereafter, but it was not long after that that he was shot dead in Srinagar. I had warned him against going back there, because of the danger to his life. 'Dad is there. He's alone,' he told me. 'I must go.' And so that was how his life ended. It was a very sad story, but for me, it was symbolic of the fact that in a place like Kashmir, there are rarely second chances if you don't learn to play the game fast.

There was only one feather in our cap at this point. We were on the hunt for our friend, Shabir Shah, the leader of the separatist People's League. Then all of thirty-seven years old, Shah had become a cult figure in the Valley, something of a people's hero. He had gone underground in April 1988, and it was whispered that he was planning to get himself across the border to Pakistan. We became determined to find Shah. It took us over a year to see results, but we managed to get word of his whereabouts in August 1989. In September, Shah was arrested on the Jammu–Srinagar highway near Ramban, along with Mohammad Nayeem Khan. The two had been apparently planning to cross the Line of Control near the Rajouri–Poonch sector, in order to enter Pakistan. It was undoubtedly a lucky break for the IB, struggling as it was to contain the rise of separatism in the state. In fact, when I rang up Farooq Abdullah to report the news of Shah's arrest, he was incredulous: 'Are you sure you've got the right man,' he demanded. When I assured him that it was, indeed, Shah who had been arrested, he was jubilant: '*Yeh toh kamaal ho gaya!* (It's wonderful!)'

But as the weeks passed, there was little time for jubilation. Militancy was increasing by the day in the Valley, and we were clueless about how to stem the tide. Eventually, inevitably, things got so bad on the ground that it simply wasn't safe to be in Kashmir unless it was absolutely necessary. There was word that two or three intelligence officers—who had sensibly left before the troubles broke out—had put in requests to be transferred out. Nobody wanted to be in Kashmir that winter. People were running away from Kashmir. Bombs exploding on the streets was a daily occurrence. In December 1989, the then Union home minister Mufti Mohammad Sayeed's daughter, Rubaiyya, was kidnapped—a crushing blow to the IB's already dented image.

Today, I talk of intelligence failures, but if I had to assign the blame, I would say honestly that it was my fault. I was the chief, new to the city and to a situation like this. It was stress like I had never known. Panic was running high in Srinagar. Most Central government employees had left the city. The fear was beginning to affect our officers too. One day, they got together and surrounded me, demanding that we talk. It was a rare, sunny day and, for some reason, I wanted the conversation to be outside, in the open.

'Come outside,' I told them, 'and we can talk.'

As soon as we were outside, a babel of pleas broke out.

'We can't stay here any more… Everyone is leaving, why can't we?'

'We can't leave,' I remember telling them. 'In our job, we cannot leave. I am here, and as long as I am here, you will have to be here too.'

These were simple words—I really had no other rationale to give them, because at one level I absolutely understood their panic too. Loneliness can drive you to do and say all kinds of things, and out in the field, whether you are undercover or not, situations develop fast and teach you lessons that no amount of time on the desk can.

One of the first and most brutal lessons—which became a guiding principle in my own methodology as a spook—that Kashmir taught me was that the gun is the most counterproductive means to an end. In January 1990 alone, the Intelligence Bureau lost four officers to the bullet within the space of three weeks. That helped crystallize my line of thought. We will all die by the gun, so why not talk? That was the most obvious question in my mind, as I watched the violence of the winter of 1989–90 come to a head. The idea is to get to the persons you're aiming to get—and engage with them. I have always felt that engagement is crucial, even if it must be kept secret. We spooks are sinners, after all—more than we are saints. We talk to our enemies more than we talk to our friends.

I look at it like this. Whether it is a politician or a prime minister, or even members of our bureaucracy, they are entitled to look at life differently. Spooks do provide politicians not only with crucial information but also a cover for accountability. A spook's way of looking at the same thing should be different, but yet we have had chiefs who have been too straitlaced. As a result, Delhi has seen things only in black and white. That doesn't work in difficult areas, like the Northeast, in Punjab or in Kashmir. Kashmir, in particular, is mostly grey and constantly in need of empathy, compassion and compromise. It took Delhi a very long time to understand Sheikh Abdullah, and even today we do not understand why Kashmiri leaders talk a different language in Kashmir and a different language in Delhi. None of this means that you need to stop engaging. To be a spook is to understand humanity in all its shades and nuances. For us, it has ever been the nature of the beast.

In the course of my career I have been relieved to discover that I am not the only one who has pushed for a greater emphasis on engagement and dialogue. My contemporary, Efraim Halevy, then director of Israel's intelligence agency, Mossad, told me at a meeting in Tel Aviv in 1999 that he believed firmly in the importance of dialogue. In his context, he understood, for instance, that Hamas, the Palestinian militant faction, could neither be got rid of nor subdued. Talking was the only way out. The reputed former director of Britain's MI5, Elizabeth Manningham-Buller, believed in much the same principle, advocating for a stronger engagement with al Qaeda, during her time in the service. And yet, this line of thinking has been considered soft by most of my colleagues in Indian intelligence. I have never quite understood it—because it is so contrary to my own line of thinking—but over time, I have come to discover the reasons behind why the other end of the spectrum exists.

In a word: Pakistan.

Pakistan lies at the heart of the paranoia, the mistrust, the lack of imagination and the absolute convention that governs much of the espionage game in Kashmir. Now, as far as convention goes, we're bound by the rules of the book, so it is obviously difficult to bypass it altogether. But the lack of imagination, I think, is what stands out ultimately, much like a sore thumb. In hard places like Kashmir, you need to be able to think outside the box (a phrase that I learned from Dr Manmohan Singh, who often used the same words). But the question here then becomes—does one need to be cautious beyond everything else, or does one take a risk or two? This is a debate that will never end, but my firm belief is that unless you *try* something, you won't get results. Certainly, you might—and you probably will—fail, but unlike in life, you don't get too many second chances in intelligence. The tricky part lies in your ability to walk that thin line between imagination and trust.

When it comes to intelligence officers, we all find it exceptionally hard to trust. We are terribly possessive about our sources, our information, our operations. But let's say that I am running an operation in Kashmir, and I want to get to someone. Now I don't have to be in love with him exactly, but trust does build over time. There is no such thing as instant chemistry in spookdom, and more particularly in a state as troubled as Kashmir. It took me years to get to know Farooq Abdullah, and even today I wouldn't dream of taking that relationship for granted. Even the best of our operators will be—and are—careful in hard zones. Yet when it comes to Pakistan, the hang-ups are immense, and the major stumbling block is always trust.

Running agents and double agents is par for the course in spy craft, so it is disappointing to acknowledge that when it comes to cooperating with American agents, for example, we have no such mistrust. Pakistan, in our minds, is our only adversary. That's not the correct approach. Every intelligence agency that operates on our soil is an adversary. Yet when it comes to Pakistan, we think twice—sometimes more—*Yeh Pakistan ke liye kaam karta hai.* (He is working for Pakistan.) My point is—*yeh Pakistan ke liye kaam karta hai* might be true, but doesn't that make him all the more important for us? Think of it this way. Let's go with the assumption that we remain hung up on Pakistan. Even with this hang-up in play, what would be the biggest feather in your cap, as an Indian intelligence agency? I would imagine it would be if you could get the Inter-Services Intelligence (ISI) station chief to work for you, or the defence attaché, or, indeed, any Pakistani here. Isn't that common sense? But somehow, we have an apprehension that a Pakistani is untrustworthy, that he will create trouble, that he is, simply speaking, a rascal.

Rascals, according to me, are the best agents. To believe otherwise shows a lack of confidence, a lack of imagination and a pervading sense of suspicion and mistrust. Counter-intelligence and its various facets—agents, double agents, moles—is a prime example of where you can use rascals best. When we talk of rascals and moles, though, I must make it clear that each of these guys can be and often are different, and not all of them have just one endgame. Moles, for example, have many uses. They are not meant to simply glean information and report back to their handlers. Their uses can be extensive if you apply a little imagination. There are moles within governments, and moles within intelligence agencies. As far as the latter is concerned, that gets a little tricky, because moles can work cleverly across each of the service cadres that these agencies might have. It was a mole, a plant, or a walk-in, who led to the assassination of Osama bin Laden at the hands of the CIA.

Take the R&AW, for instance. In 1983, the R&AW created its own service cadre, the Research and Analysis Service (RAS), to absorb talent from other Group A civil services, under the Central

Staffing Scheme. Each agency, of course, has its rascals as well as its moles but they exist, deep within the shadows, what Angleton called 'the wilderness of mirrors'. Anyone following this trail will come back to the central question of trust. Who do you trust and how far? When does a lack of trust hamper an operation or a gamble?

I can think of one particular story which, I believe, highlights how this plays out. One day, Shabir Shah told me that he wanted to go across the border to Kathmandu. He had a guy there, by the name of Mehmood Sagar. '*Maine Sagar sahib ko bulaya hai Kathmandu. Kuch baatein karni hain unse.*(I have called Sagar sahib to Kathmandu. It is time to discuss matters with him.)' We had a good relationship with Nepal in those days, so I told the chief that Shabir wanted to go. 'We'll have him escorted to the border,' I said. 'Let him go and let's see what he brings back to us.' I didn't tell the chief this, but I knew that the ISI would be waiting for Shabir on the other side of the border. The plan was that Shabir would travel to Nepal via Benares, by road. The entire plan was approved, but somehow, once Shabir had departed, the chief got a sudden case of cold feet. 'This is too much,' he told me. 'Call him back.'

I was taken aback. By this time, Shabir would be well on his way to the border. However, I pulled several strings and got Shabir to come back. He was—naturally—furious. Bypassing Delhi altogether, he went straight to Jammu in a sulk. I let him stew for a while, and then a week later, I went myself to Jammu and asked for his forgiveness.

'If you don't trust us,' Shabir told me, '*toh kaise kuch hoga? Aap hummey trust nahin karte, toh rishta kaise hoga.* (If you don't trust us, how can we have a relationship?) *Main toh sab kuch batata hu, par aap toh* trust *hi nahin karte.* I tell you everything, but you don't trust us.' This is similar to what young Mirwaiz Umar Farooq, the chairman of the Awami Action Committee, one of the two key factions of the All Parties' Hurriyat Conference in Jammu and

Kashmir, told me once. '*Aap kehte hain ham bahut jhooth bolte hain. Par jhooth bolna toh aap se seekha hai. Aap hume sach nahi bolte toh ham bhi aapko jhooth bolte hain.*(You accuse us Kashmiris of lying, but we have learnt it from you.)'

Strong words from both men, you might say. I would agree with you—but then, these are some of the results of a blatant lack of trust. In the end, all it really serves to do is hamper the process of intelligence gathering.

When I left the IB to join as chief of the R&AW in 1999, I was not—if I do say so myself!—an unpopular guy. But the transition from the IB to the R&AW was a difficult one. I was entirely unprepared to deal with a shift from domestic to international intelligence and I was an outsider in the R&AW. It was, in fact, the first time that an IB officer had been asked to take over as chief of the R&AW. Within the service, then, there was a certain level of suspicion and resentment—and to my mind, it's only natural. Some people, of course, were very kind to me, but by and large, it was an appointment that had made quite a few feel hostile towards me.

Indeed, at one point, I was quite angry myself. I had stuck on at the IB throughout; I hadn't sought a job anywhere else. There was a time when two or three people were brought into the IB from outside. This irked me enough to go to Arun Bhagat—then the director, Intelligence Bureau (DIB)—and demand an explanation. 'What's going on here?' I remember asking. 'I've served the IB for thirty years and here are guys only a year or so senior to me being brought in. What is *my* future here?' Arun pacified me as best as he could, but it was the truth as far as I was concerned. Then, Shyamal Dutta, my batchmate and a slot above me, was appointed DIB.

One day, Home Secretary V.P. Singh called me: 'Your batchmate is becoming DIB,' he told me. 'Would you like to go out of the Bureau? I can give you a chief's position in one of the paramilitary agencies.'

I refused. 'This has been my career for years. If I am destined to be No. 2, then so be it.'

I don't know if Shyamal would have enjoyed that, of course, since he went on to become DIB. Shyamal was also the one who got me the post of R&AW chief, and I've often said publicly that I owed that transition in my career to him. He first mentioned this to me in October 1998, when he said, 'Would you like to go to the R&AW?' and I said, 'As what?' He said, 'As chief, of course.' And I said, 'Why not?'

On 1 January1999, he took me to introduce me to the national security adviser (NSA) and principal secretary to the Prime Minister, Brajesh Mishra. Twelve days later, I was posted to the R&AW.

I have often privately wondered how it would have been had I stayed on at the Bureau. Our styles were so very different. Shyamal was more rigid and I was much easier in manner than he. Let me give you an example.

In those days, the IB had something of a durbar where officers came to present their concerns. As No. 2 in the IB, I was asked to attend one of these durbars. Shyamal's personal assistant was also present. I forget whose case came up for hearing, but I do recall telling Shyamal to do what the applicant was asking him to do.

'*Kar lo, sir, isme kya jaata hai aapka.* (Do it, sir, it's not a big deal.)'

'You're a dangerous fellow to have around,' Shyamal retorted.

'DIB sir, you should realize this is your durbar. If someone has come all the way here to talk to you, you need to take a more liberal, open view, rather than being rigid.'

'Since you're saying it now, I'll do it, but I don't think you're the right guy to have in the durbar!'

I digress by telling this story, but it was to make the point that I was an outsider to the world of international intelligence. There was nobody on par with my seniority at the R&AW either, and building a rapport with other officers in the agency was difficult, to say the least. As time went on, and I began to enjoy myself, I realized seventeen months was not enough for an intelligence chief. For instance, the MI6 chief gets five years and a knighthood thereafter. My contemporary in the CIA, George Tenet, served for seven years with two presidents—Bill Clinton and George W. Bush.

Gradually, I was also concerned about my successor because the R&AW had the nasty reputation of not knowing who was the chief until the last moment. I thought this was very unfair because as an outsider, you needed at least three weeks to prepare. I took my concerns to Brajesh Mishra, who surprised me by dawdling over the decision until I realized he wanted to bring in one of his IFS guys.

'Don't do it, sir,' I advised him.

'Tum keh rahe ho? Tum bhi toh outsider thhe. (You are saying this? Are you forgetting you were also an outsider.)'

'Isiliye keh raha hoon. (I am saying it because I have been through this situation.) It's not fair to the outsider and it's not fair to the organization. It's hard to adjust and there will possibly be resentment and hostility.'

It took six months for me to get the job properly at the R&AW, because the guy whom I succeeded wasn't willing to leave in a hurry, until he got a governorship for himself. In that time, I learned very little because nobody talked to me about anything that might have been important.

As I told you before, I quite like being perceived as a laidback kind of guy, but it is a fortunate aspect of my character that when I am pushed, the best comes out in me. I say this without conceit because that is exactly what happened in the early days at the R&AW: I was tested right away in my ways, from my knowledge of foreign policy to my leadership skills. I also was observing some uncomfortable truths by this time, given my experience. I put the blame on the founding fathers of our intelligence service, because to be honest, the clauses and conditions they had laid down created all kinds of potential for future obstacles.

For instance, I entered the R&AW at a time when there was a lot of dissatisfaction between the R&AW and its service cadre, the RAS. For me, the fact that I was not a purely R&AW guy helped me to stay dispassionate when I was dealing with problems like this. I was an IPS officer to start with, even with my experience at the IB, but I always felt that the best interests of the R&AW would be served by encouraging and supporting the RAS. I never discriminated between any service or cadre. I don't know how far I succeeded, but my aim was always to ensure that resentments and inherent prejudices got toned down within the agency. To my mind, it was the only way to prevent intelligence officers revolting or rebelling. It has happened in the past—in the quite recent past too—and it creates terrible rifts within what should be the backbone of security and intelligence forces in the country.

I had been in intelligence for thirty years by now, and I had noted not just inherent prejudices, rigidities and biases between services like the IB and R&AW, but also distinct biases against women and Muslims. About the latter I've spoken out publicly as well as internally, and have been supported by the likes of Gary (Girish Chandra) Saxena. One cannot hope to understand the concerns of Muslims in this country without Muslims in the services. The same goes for women. Look at the legends in Indian intelligence: from B.N. Mullick to M.K. Narayanan and from R.N. Kao to Ajit Doval, these are all men. This is not to say that there are no women in either the IB or the R&AW, but none of these women have managed to make it to the top. Why is that? That remains a question to be answered, and given that it's already 2023, that answer needs to come soon!

Yet another problem that I faced as I transitioned into the R&AW was in understanding subjects that I had no previous idea about. Whenever I had to go for a meeting, my staff officer would send me a note from the branch concerned, and ask whether I wanted to take the branch officer along with me. I refused to do this. I was conscious that the moment I compromised there, I would always need a crutch. It was important that I learned on the job and did my part. Otherwise what kind of chief would I be?

Very early on at the R&AW, I decided the best thing to do to try and understand the hierarchy I was confronted with was to meet with R.N. Kao himself. Kao sahib had long since retired, but I rang him up and introduced myself.

'I think I should come across and meet you,' I said.

'I think that's a very good idea!' he responded.

Mostly, during our chat, Kao sahib talked about how the organization was structured and established. He told me of the story of how he had gone across to England to meet with Sir Maurice Oldfield (former director of the Secret Intelligence Service, also known as the MI6) for advice on how to establish an organization similar to MI6 in India. The difference in the structure of the R&AW, of course, is that ours is a mixed sort of thing, with police officers, RAS officers and officers across security services. The MI6 or MI5, on the other hand, is a far more focused and specialized service.

Kao sahib told me: 'At the end of the day, you must have fifteen minutes to put your feet up and think about what has happened during the day and see if there are dots still left to be connected for the next day.' I never actually had fifteen minutes on any day, but the principle behind it made a lot of sense to me.

As part of my earliest assignments at the R&AW, I was asked to meet with my counterparts across the world. I decided that going to various places in the neighbourhood was the right place to start. In a region like South Asia, with neighbours as prickly as Pakistan and as inscrutable as China, it is best if you know who you are truly dealing with. And so, we return to my original questions—how much are you willing to visualize to get your answers? How much are you willing to imagine? Do you only go by the book and follow what is laid down? Or do you flip the page, and write your own script, if the occasion calls for it? I had to learn on the job and do it fast in this posting.

There were a couple of things for which I was mentally prepared. For one, I made up my mind that whatever happened, I was ready to defend my turf at the R&AW. For another, I decided that if anything untoward happened, I would face it myself. I would never take shelter behind anyone else. I remember one of my first Cabinet Committee on Security meetings. I was nervous because I didn't know what happened behind those doors. I called Shyamal for help.

'*Kya hota hai inn meetings mein?*(What happens in these meetings?)'

'*Bada simply, yeh hota hai ki chaar paanch minister honge, service chiefs honge, main hoonga aur tum hoge. Pehle main bolunga as DIB.* (Very simply, there will be four or five ministers, service chiefs, and us. First I will speak as DIB and then you will speak.) If anyone has any questions, they will then ask and if not, then that's the end of the meeting.'

It sounded simple enough to me, but I was definitely nervous. Every chief faces a hard time at some point or another. But my main crisis would come only later that year, a few months into my time as chief of the R&AW, when IC-814 was hijacked. Questions swirled about the nature and extent of the R&AW's knowledge of the event. It was a difficult time, that week. The main goof-up happened in Amritsar, where the flight was on the ground for a long time. We should have acted then and we didn't.

The fault lay squarely with Delhi. Later, of course, we blamed the Punjab Police and the director general of police (DG), Punjab. But the thing was that the DG (Punjab)—who happened to be a batchmate of mine—didn't want to take on that kind of responsibility without word from Delhi. Someone from Delhi should have given that word. Everyone in Delhi knew what was happening: from the Prime Minister to the home minister, from the NSA to the DIB, from the cabinet secretary to the chief of R&AW. So yes, it was a time of great weakness on Delhi's part, because once the plane took off again and departed Indian airspace, we lost control of the situation.

Yet another moment of awkwardness took place—just a few months, again, after I took over as chief—when the coup took place in Pakistan. I got a call from the Prime Minister at about quarter past eight in the morning, when I'm usually asleep.

'*Yeh Pakistan mein kya ho raha hai*? (What's happening in Pakistan?)' he demanded.

I was half asleep and had no idea so I quickly bought some time. '*Sir, main aapko aadhe ghante mein batata hoon*. (Sir, I will let you know in half an hour.)'

Now, the fact is that we were taken unawares. But then, a coup is no easy thing to anticipate. In any case, this particular coup occurred partly because of Nawaz Sharif's stupidity in first refusing to let Musharraf's plane land on Pakistani soil and later in insisting that Musharraf deplane in Karachi, instead of Islamabad. The follow-up that the Prime Minister wanted was to keep an eye on Nawaz Sharif as best as possible.

As chief of the R&AW, though, I have to say—quite proudly— that I managed to stay unconventional. I had worked in and on the subject of Kashmir for so many years that now, three decades later, I had no desire to give it up. In this regard, Brajesh Mishra was pleasantly surprised—because I insisted on carrying my knowledge and experience of Kashmir to the R&AW. After all, we were dealing with countries like Pakistan, Afghanistan and China and for all these countries, Kashmir was very important. I refused to let go of that. At a time when my mind was blank about how to deal with the posting at the R&AW, Kashmir would save me in many ways, allowing me to give nuanced perspectives on otherwise straightforward perspectives.

Not surprisingly, the IB didn't like this. Shyamal was upset with me. I was blunt with him: 'Look, if Kashmir is troubling you, I'm sorry. As long as I am in the R&AW, Kashmir will stay with me. But other than that, there aren't any problems that we can't sort out.'

In the event, there were none.

Shyamal and I got along rather well, but the relationships between the chiefs after us were never the same.

And so it was that I stayed in touch with Kashmir and Kashmiris, even during my time at the R&AW. Brajesh was pleased. I had the feeling he had underestimated me, and he approved of the advantage that my knowledge of Kashmir brought to geopolitics. He would often proudly tell those he was introducing me to, '*Yeh sab jaanta hai Kashmir mein.* (He knows Kashmir.)'

One day, when I was still with the Vajpayee PMO, a Kashmiri requested to meet me. He was what you would call a 'walk-in'. A 'walk-in' refers to someone who essentially walks in, off the street, to meet with an official, whose name he already knows as being useful to him. Normally, these guys aren't trusted at all. The general suspicion is that they might be plants. But if you take a risk on them, even if they are working for the other side, they generally provide you with good information. At around this time, a report landed on my desk. The report's implication was clear—this Kashmiri was a suspected Pakistani agent, a double agent. I read the report, and I understood fully the motive behind its sudden appearance on my desk: it was to discourage me from continuing any association with this guy.

But professionally, I looked at this differently. To my way of thinking, if this guy was actually a Pakistani agent, he was all the more interesting to me. I could use him for information on Pakistan that nobody else could or would give me. That has always been the advantage of a good double agent—if they are willing to work with you, it's always a plus. He would, in that case, be bound to bring me more than I expected him to bring, possibly minutes of ISI meetings. Certainly, some of that material could (and most likely would) be planted. Quite a bit of it could be lies. But there could also be something exciting in there. But again, convention forbids us to encourage this gamble too much.

As a result of this lack of trust, double agents working for Pakistan have never been trusted or used by India, often resulting in wasted opportunities. Take, for instance, the case of a prominent Kashmiri businessman, whose name I prefer to keep anonymous. I found him to be an interesting person, with great potential. The pity of it is that I met him towards the end of my own time at the PMO. But he did come to meet me after I left the PMO. He used to come home, in those days, full of stories. I thought he was a useful guy, so I recommended him to the IB. But nothing happened. Then I told him to meet a colleague in Srinagar, but that also didn't work out. All I heard was, '*Haraami hai.*(He is a scoundrel.)' Nobody considered the possibility that rascality serves its own purposes.

Then, there is the example of Shabir Shah, with whom I had a lot of personal rapport. In my book *The Vajpayee Years*, I called Shabir a 'hell of a let-down'. I look at it like this. Shabir had an opportunity. He was being treated as a prima donna. He was given maximum importance, because we felt he was important at the time. We built him up, but maybe *we* were the let-downs. It's not a one-way street, after all. If I were to meet Shabir today, I would want to know what he feels in retrospect. Does he feel he made a mistake by not going the whole hog?

The same thing happened with this lot of boys that were picked up by the National Investigation Agency (NIA) in money laundering cases. I used to call them the 'Dirty Dozen'. But nothing was done with them either. More importantly, when combined, all of this lets the process of intelligence gathering down.

None of this means that you end up beating convention, or going against it altogether. It just means that you must learn to do new things, to get better results. In my case, I learned that it was important to talk to people, to let trust evolve. In doing this there must be reciprocity, even if you run the risk of being unconventional. I'll give you another example, because in my business, the examples are plentiful. Before N.N. Vohra was appointed interlocutor in Kashmir, K.C. Pant was given the job. At the time, the Government of India felt that a more important, more public face was required for such a mission. So when Pant sahib was leaving for Kashmir, he called me, to ask me to arrange meetings for him.

'I'll try to arrange meetings, sir,' I replied. 'But meetings are not so easily arranged.'

Still, I did what I could. Towards the end of his visit, Pant sahib asked me, 'I'm told you know Shabir?'

'Yes, I do.'

'I want to meet him.'

So I went to Shabir and informed him that Pant sahib wanted to meet him. Had I not developed a personal rapport of some kind with Shabir, such a thing would have been unthinkable. But since I knew him well enough to take a chance on this, I could go to his house and ask him to meet an official from Delhi. The results were as I had hoped.

'Okay,' said Shabir. '*Main mil lunga, par aapko yahan laana padega, mere ghar.* (I will meet him, but he will have to come here.)'

I knew this was a difficult call, but I went back to Pant sahib with the news that Shabir was agreeable to a meeting.

'Great,' said Pant sahib. 'How do we do that?'

'Well, sir,' I said, 'we do it by you getting into the car with me. I will take you to his place and you can meet him there.'

Pant sahib was a little taken aback at the idea of a senior minister going all the way to Shabir Shah's house for a meeting, but we went anyway. It was a successful meeting, but there was, as there always is, a price to be paid. Once the meeting was over, Pant sahib told me: '*Bhai tumhare kehne pe main Shabir ke ghar chala gaya nahin toh main jaata nahin. Aur ab tumhe usko Dilli laana padega, mere ghar.* (I went there because of you. Now you have to ensure that Shabir comes to Delhi and to my home.)'

'Sir,' I said, '*yeh bhi koshish karte hain.* (I will try.)'

And so, I did. I brought Shabir Shah to Delhi, and to Pant sahib's house.

I recall yet another incident, in Russia, when I had visited Moscow in 1999 to meet my KGB counterpart, Vyacheslav Ivanovich Trubnikov. It was an excellent visit, the only caveat being that I wished I had insured my liver before I got there! The Russians love their liquor, as was attested by Trubnikov who arrived to meet me at ten in the morning, waving a bottle of vodka. 'Come on,' he said merrily, 'let's drink to your visit here!'

My discussions with Trubnikov were pleasant, but they were also an eye-opener into the many ways in which intelligence often provides the platform on which diplomacy can make its first public strides. During one of our chats, Trubnikov asked me: 'How do you react to the idea of Russia–China–India cooperation?'

'It's a great idea, Chief,' I replied. 'But what makes you think that the Chinese would want to cooperate with us?'

'You leave that to me. But just think of what the Pakistanis would think if we were all having tea together!'

The idea was innovative enough for me to mention it in China, when I visited Beijing in 2000. In their trademark style, my Chinese counterparts nodded wisely. 'Very interesting. We'll examine it.'

Soon after that, of course, the diplomatic trilateral dialogue between Russia, India and China did begin. Indeed, the big plus point of my visit to China in May 2000 was that Brajesh Mishra was invited by his Chinese counterpart to visit China in November that same year. I was informed by Brajesh that he would be taking me along on the trip as well. I was surprised. 'Why don't you take the China expert along?'

'*Nahin*. It's you or nobody. Either you come or I don't want anyone from the R&AW.'

With that statement, I could hardly refuse, especially when Brajesh threw in the tempting bait of talking about my successor. Little did I know that this entire conversation had an agenda too, as did so many of Brajesh's conversations: he wanted me to join the PMO.

But the real prize of my trip to Russia was a meeting with Vladimir Putin, then the premier of Russia. It was a brief, formal meeting, which took place in a bland anteroom just off Putin's office in the Red Square. I had the impression that Putin was a careful man, who preferred to watch, far more than he spoke. He said all the right things, of course, but that meeting was to cause me slight embarrassment a year later, when Trubnikov came to visit, still in his capacity as chief of the KGB. Upon his arrival, he sought me out and jovially insisted on meeting the Prime Minister. This was awkward—because it was a well-known fact that Atal Bihari Vajpayee didn't really meet with intelligence chiefs. But Trubnikov wouldn't hear of it. He had introduced me to Putin, he said, and now, I must reciprocate.

With some trepidation, I went to Brajesh and explained the situation. It speaks volumes of Brajesh's equanimity that he merely said, '*Milwa dete hain*. (We will arrange a meeting.) The Prime Minister can offer him a cup of tea.' It speaks equal volumes about Vajpayee that, given his notorious disinclination to sit down and have tea with intelligence chiefs, either current or former, he did actually give Trubnikov some of his time. The Russian went away a happy man: all he had wanted was to report back to the Kremlin that he had managed to meet the Indian Prime Minister in person.

So, you see, trust and reciprocity are at the heart of an imaginative or innovative approach, particularly when it comes to human nature. As a species, we find it hard to trust easily. In spookdom, it's even more difficult. In many ways, it is a transactional, almost cold, business. What is the motivation for anyone to talk to you or cooperate with you? The answer to that lies in the depths of human nature. It comes in the shape of greed—which makes the person you're angling for accept the promise or potential of monetary gain. It comes in the shape of vulnerability—a beloved family member might be desperately ill, and to help that family member, you reach out for help. Help will always be given—but it will come at a price. *I have done this for you—now you tell me, what can you do for me?* A kind of one-upmanship perennially exists between an officer and an agent. *Who is fooling whom*, we wonder.

I've often thought about trust and why it matters to us so much. We put so much emphasis on a lack of trust, without thinking that if there is to be trust, it must evolve. No relationship starts outright with trust. In 1991, when I was first put on the job of talking to the separatists, it didn't start with trust either. Instead, it started with the news that here was a sahib who was ready to talk, travelling far and wide. I was in Delhi at the time, and pretty soon, people—separatists, the common Kashmiri—began coming down to the capital to meet me. Some of them were genuine. Many of them were fake.

I developed a habit of saying directly: '*Baat karni hai, toh sachhi baat karo.* (If you want to speak, speak the truth.)' The point was to let them know that if they were coming to see me on behalf of someone else, they would be wasting their time. There was, of course, the other side of the coin. Not all of the boys who came to see me were eager and approachable. There were also those like Yasin Malik, who was arrogant and desirous of making a point. He didn't particularly like me and, because I sensed his dislike, I never invited him home. I met him in a safe house, as per protocol. One day, as I entered the room in which we were to meet, I recall that he leaned back in his chair, swinging his boots up on to the table. It was a clearly aggressive message, but I chose not to react to it.

Occasionally you do meet with behaviour of this kind, but once I got to know these Kashmiris—the *ordinary* Kashmiri as much as the political Kashmiri—I would call them home. Now, the IB has safe houses for this kind of thing. Each colony in Srinagar, let us say, has a safe house. But I chose to eschew that for the relative unconventionality of my own house. My logic was admittedly very different from my colleagues'. To my way of thinking, this was a difficult time, with little to no contact with the Kashmiris. If you called them home, however, the tables turned. I was hauled up for doing this, of course. But by the time the talks with the Hurriyat, for instance, really got under way, I was already out of the agency. So in that sense I couldn't really be blamed. This was the time that Ajit Doval, who was at the time special director IB, also wanted to meet the separatists. I informed the DIB whose reaction was, 'Certainly not at your residence'. Ajit, however, came along and met the Hurriyat leadership at my residence.

But these fellows were in and out of my house on a regular basis, sometimes even coming unannounced, if they were in trouble or if they needed something. Once, there were two guys on opposite sides of the Hurriyat spectrum who showed up at the same time and were, understandably, rather miffed at seeing each other. One of them asked me, in an aggrieved fashion: '*Iske saamne mujhe kyun bulaya?* (Why have you called me in front of him?)' I said: '*Maine nahin bulaya, tum khud aaye. Aur usko bhi maine nahin bulaya, woh bhi khud aaye. Toh ab aap aapas mein sambhalo.* (I didn't call you; you came yourself. And I didn't invite him either, he too came on his own. Now you manage.)'

So you see, unconventionality is a good thing, particularly if it is helpful. The boys who came to see me got—over time, of course—the impression that here was someone who was ready to talk to them openly. It helped to build trust. I carried on that practice for myself, even when I returned from Kashmir in March 1990. The situation then was so bad that I was advised, even though I was no longer in Kashmir, that I should have security for myself. I refused. After all, as I told the official who suggested that I agree to protection, anyone who wanted to kill me could easily do it, irrespective of a police watch on my house. I have never had any personal security in all my dealings in Kashmir, until the kidnapping of Rubaiyya Sayeed. That is when everything changed suddenly and irrevocably. We were all vulnerable. I would leave Srinagar in about three months, but even so, during those three months, the only security that I got was a bulletproof car. Nothing else.

Good surveillance, then, is at the heart of espionage. It is an art in itself. After all, you're looking for a needle in a haystack, and sometimes, that needle might not even be there. If you want to keep someone under watch, it must be sophisticated and very subtle, and it definitely cannot be over a long period of time. It's a tough job and in intelligence, we try not to do too much of it. In my opinion, the Brits do a better job of it than we do. I recall former Delhi police commissioner, Yudhvir Singh Dadwal, telling me about his experience in London. When he returned, I asked him if he'd enjoyed himself. 'Enjoyed? When I saw how things work at Scotland Yard and how they keep track of every movement of yours, all my enjoyment was finished,' Dadwal retorted.

My point is this—I've spent a lot of time working in counter-intelligence, and I've seen the way that our boys sometimes stand out. You might be sitting in a fancy car, but you're smoking a beedi. It's small details like this that can give you away if you're working in surveillance! I've always been a proponent of not just blending in well, but of men and women working together. If you come across a man and a woman sitting together in a park, for instance, the last thing you might suspect is that they are watching you. That's where the Brits are excellent, and where we need to be more sophisticated.

There was a debate on this subject once, when I was in the IB under Narasimha Rao's government. The Ministry of External Affairs (MEA) was complaining then—as it often does—that the ISI was harassing our men in Islamabad. The MEA line was that we should reciprocate, with their man in New Delhi. The Prime Minister asked for the IB views on this. I was one of the officers asked to share their thoughts. I was perfectly forthright, stating that from the perspective of a purely professional IB officer, aggressive surveillance was counterproductive. In our lingo, we call it 'bumper to bumper' surveillance. The meaning is clear—for instance, if you are a R&AW man in Pakistan, every time you go out, you will notice yourself being tailed closely by an ISI car. To my mind, if we started doing that, the process of intelligence gathering would go out of the window.

Surveillance—as a tool of espionage—must remain secret. If we have our eyes on a target, what we try to do is to 'house' him. What does that mean, you might wonder. It means that you follow him only up to a certain address. That address could belong to his mother, his wife, his mistress or his children. The point is that the address doesn't matter as much as the house itself, which gives you a platform to start additional inquiries—who lives there, for how long have they lived there, and the like. Too much of this, though, and any operation you might be running stands the risk of being badly bungled.

Something like this happened in my last days in the Vajpayee PMO, in 2003. It had to do with an ex-military officer named Rabinder Singh. He had done a couple of postings abroad—in Damascus and The Hague—and then he had returned to New Delhi. After he returned, suspicion developed about this fellow. He was, it was said, asking too many questions. At some stage, these questions became probing enough for the R&AW to go on alert. There was an idea that he might be passing vital information to the Americans.

Perhaps he was, perhaps he wasn't—we'll never know, but to cut a long story short, one day, Singh was stopped and his briefcase was searched. Alarmed, he fled the country, taking refuge in Nepal. There has, to my knowledge, never been a full audit of how much damage he did while he was here. He had been kept under surveillance for too long, instead of being immediately lifted and interrogated.

In 2019, John le Carré published his final novel, *Agent Running in the Field*.[4] The plot is set against the backdrop of Brexit, but at the heart of the thrilling cat-and-mouse game and tip of the hat to technology in twenty-first-century espionage, lie age-old questions. How do you approach your target? What do you think might appeal to him? What are his weaknesses, his motivations? What makes him get out of bed every day? And yet, agent-running requires an amoral heart, a heart of stone. It's not for the squeamish.

I've often been told by many of these boys in Kashmir of how they are handed over from one person to another without getting the desired results. When you're dealing with sources and targets in the field, memory is a vital thing. Nowadays, you switch on your recorders and your wires discreetly, but in those days, there wasn't any such convenience. I used to carry a notebook around with me at all times. Some of the people I spoke to were more open than others, and from their conversations with me I would make notes on the spot. When it came to more guarded sources, I would keep the notebook in another room. During the course of the conversation, I would slip out of the room on the pretext of going to the bathroom, and make a quick note before I went back in. One can't remember everything, of course, but the important things are another matter. In many ways, this is also a kind of engagement, a participation in someone else's story and life so that you can extract the results you'd

---

4 Viking Books, 2019.

like. It also led to the habit—which still persists—of jotting down notes in notebooks. After all, not everything is achieved by force!

In 1994, the IB broke four militants out of militancy. For its time, it was a sensational coup by the Bureau, but it was driven by engagement. It is this principle that is at the heart of Jonathan Powell's *Talking to Terrorists: How to End Armed Conflict*.[5] In it, Powell quotes Hugh Gaitskell, the former leader of Britain's Labour Party. What Gaitskell meant, Powell explains, is that governments everywhere, of all political shades, repeat ad nauseum that they will never talk to terrorist groups. Of course, they almost always end up doing just that, engaging with the public faces of terrorist outfits. It was this same idea that lay behind our engagement with militant groups in 1994, but what is interesting to me is not the relationship between governments and militants. My task, as a former spy chief, has been to engage not just with the heads of these outfits but with the men who work, at a much lower level, in these organizations. Interrogation is crucial here, especially when all other forms of intelligence fail. As a tactic, it has played an important role in gleaning information in both Punjab and Kashmir, in the worst days of militancy in both states.

Before I go any further, I must point out that, in this context, it is important for intelligence officers to remember that they are not policemen. In the history of modern Indian espionage, this has been a problem, in the R&AW and particularly in the IB. I first heard this from Indira Gandhi, when she was addressing one of our police conferences. 'You people need to remember that you are intelligence officers,' she said firmly. Rajiv went a step further on the issue. He never let intelligence officials forget that they were *not* police officers and nor could they behave like police officers.

---

5 Penguin RandomHouse, 2014.

That being said, interrogation, as I was saying, is an important weapon in intelligence. Now, I know there will be questions about methods of interrogation. What I can tell you is that the difference between a state like Punjab and a state like Kashmir is that a Sikh would tell you the truth straightaway, but a Kashmiri would twist and turn the story before he got to the kernel of truth. The use of third degree (to put it politely) is often mentioned in the context of interrogation, and indeed, the Americans are known to have used it to chilling effect, Guantanamo Bay being a case in point. However, the best interrogators, in my opinion, are those who don't need to use force. Why do I say this? Because in my years in service, I have observed that the playing field between these men and their bosses is rarely a level one. That alone gives you, as the interrogator, an advantage. So all you have to do is capitalize on patience, and play the waiting game.

According to me, grabbing a suspect and stringing him up is hardly the best way to get information. Yet, there are people who believe that interrogation must provide results. True or false, that is not the idea behind interrogation. The idea is certainly to get to the truth, if you can, but waiting for the truth is a long but patient game, which can take days, if not weeks. The truth is not a sitting duck, waiting to be procured by thrusting a tape recorder into your suspect's face. For instance, in 1994, the easiest comparison that we used in our dialogues with these boys was quite simple—what kind of lives do you live? What kind of lives do your bosses live? What is your long-term motivation? Come on, you guys aren't killers. You're not in this to kill people. Why don't you become politicians? Come overground, start talking, start engaging.

These were tactics designed to rankle, to make these boys think about the consequences of what they were doing. After all, the public faces of separatist parties in Kashmir had a far cushier time, with access to money and freedom and ease of travel. The lower rungs were perennially in hiding. And so, when the IB succeeded in breaking these militants away from it all, what lay behind the coup was dialogue. It didn't happen overnight. We had to build trust. We had to keep talking and talking—until they became almost one of us. There is a school of thought that does ask—what is the need to do that? *Usko goli kyun nahin maari?* (Why not shoot the fellow?) Sure, you could do that too—but you have to be able to identify who is an asset and who is a liability.

There are some, of course, who have been in this field far more publicly than I have. Martti Ahtisaari, the former president of Finland, won the Nobel Peace Prize in 2008 for his great efforts, across decades and continents, to resolve international conflicts. Born in Viborg in 1937, Ahtisaari was a witness to the annexation of his home town by the Soviet Union in the Winter War of 1939–40. The trauma of his family motivated the man in his commitment to peace. Following many years in the Finnish Foreign Service, Ahtisaari was appointed UN Commissioner for Namibia. He was a major contributor to Namibia's achievement of independence in 1990, and was an arbitrator in the peace talks in Kosovo in 1999 and again in 2005–07. In 2005, even as he dealt with Kosovo, Ahtisaari helped to bring the long-running conflict in the Aceh province of Indonesia to an end. It was a lifetime dedicated to engagement, to talks, to dialogue, to precisely what I have tried to do as an intelligence officer in Kashmir, and in my time at the Vajpayee PMO.

With both Vajpayee and his national security adviser, Brajesh Mishra, I pushed and pushed for talks with the Hurriyat. In October 2003, my urgings were finally heard. At a meeting, Atalji finally said, quietly, '*Baat toh karni padegi.* (We will have to talk.)' Jaswant Singh, then minister for external affairs, was sitting next to him, and was visibly startled. 'Atalji, *Kiske saath baat karni padegi?* (Talk with whom, Atalji?), he asked.

'*Hurriyat ke saath* (With the Hurriyat),' Vajpayee replied.

Dazed, Jaswant tried again: '*Atalji, aap baat karenge?* (Will you talk to them?)'

But the old man was too clever for Jaswant. '*Nahin, nahin,*' he said calmly, '*Advaniji karenge.*(No, Advani-ji will.)'

And that was the start of the talks with the Hurriyat by the National Democratic Alliance (NDA) government in 2003.

Today's more muscular policy hampers the process of engaging with separatists or, indeed, with the possibility of using militants as potential agents. This is not to say that a muscular policy has never been used against militants before. There was a time, as I recall, when it was being implemented, albeit differently, in Punjab and Kashmir. I mention Punjab because there was a time when Kanwar Pal Singh Gill was DGP. This tall, somewhat formidable 1957 batch IPS officer of the Assam cadre played a central role in eliminating Khalistani terrorism from Punjab, in the shattering aftermath of Operation Blue Star. Indeed, Gill's first huge success was Operation Black Thunder, which liberated the Golden Temple from militants, with none of the devastation caused by Operation Blue Star. It was here that Gill demonstrated his rare but true knack for counterterrorism, combining force with psychological operations and dynamic leadership.

In his memoir, *Bullet for Bullet*, Gill's predecessor, Julio Ribeiro would write: 'He had spent many sleepless nights and had been working almost without any rest... His energy was tremendous, his presence imposing...' For the *Hindustan Times*, senior journalist Harinder Baweja would recall: 'He ordered water and electricity to be cut off and finally forced the terrorists to surrender in the full glare of television cameras. The sight of "khadkus" walking out with their arms up broke the proverbial back of the Punjab militancy ... a few evenings later, when I met him again, for a one-on-one chat, he said, "The turban must always be held high".⁶ This maxim was to be tested time and again throughout his career, for Gill's methods differed greatly from those of Ribeiro, who would acknowledge: 'He really enjoyed it, even enjoyed being harsh at times though on that score I would often differ. I certainly differed from him on the core issue of how this "nationalistic" form of terrorism could be put to rest...'⁷

Between 1991 and 1995, the combination of political instability and rising militancy within Punjab led Gill to collaborate with the Indian Army to eliminate a succession of terrorists. He gave a free hand to the Punjab Police under his command as well. Naturally, then, even as he gained the eponym of 'Super Cop', the excesses of the police in the state came into question, with a sharp rise in the number of tortures and custodial deaths. But Gill always maintained that force was necessary. In an essay for the South Asia Portal in 2001, he would write: 'The "liberal" mind has always remained ambivalent when confronted by the fact that the State, among other things, is a coercive instrument, and that it must, from time to time, exercise its option of the use of force—albeit of judicious, narrowly defined and very specifically targeted use of force—if it is not to be overwhelmed by the greater violence of the enemies of freedom,

---

6   Harinder Baweja, 'The Cop I Knew: Obituary', *Hindustan Times*, 27 May 2017. Available at: https://www.hindustantimes.com/opinion/the-cop-who-could-recite-shakespeare-wield-torture-implements-the-kps-gill-i-knew/story-IL9C7yZ3LsU5s3WYGi8oaJ.html

7   Julio Ribeiro, 'KPS will always be remembered as the terminator of Khalistani Terror', *The Times of India*, 27 May 2017. Available at: http://timesofindia.indiatimes.com/articleshow/58865522.cms?utm_source=contentofinterest&utm_medium=text&utm_campaign=cppst

democracy and lawful governance.'[8] Gill's case is definitely an exception, but I wouldn't accept his story to be the norm. As Martti Ahtisaari put it, force never wipes out insurgency—a statement which, in the current Indian context, is given weight by our ongoing battle against Naxalism. We have fought that battle for years, but it is not over—and is not likely to be any time soon.

If you asked me, as a former intelligence officer, whether a muscular policy, or one more heavily dependent on the use of force, was counterproductive to the process of intelligence gathering, I would say: not always. In Gill's time, for instance, we were still getting intelligence. Are we getting it today, in the aftermath of the abrogation of Article 370 and the current government's Naya Kashmir policy? To repudiate the thought entirely would be unfair, since I don't have first-hand knowledge of what our guys are doing on the ground today; but without prejudice, what I *can* say is that we're not doing much, simply because we don't know what to do.

Look at the political side of things: you released Farooq Abdullah, for whatever reasons you may have had. To my mind, Delhi had him in mind for a particular purpose—but what has happened since then? Why has he not been made use of? After all, he is still willing to cooperate. In the middle of his release recently, the Enforcement Directorate had hauled Farooq up, and he spent an entire day in Srinagar sorting it out. I met him shortly thereafter, and I asked, 'Is anyone talking to you about anything?' He replied: 'Who would be talking to me about what? They've called me a thief and a crook. What's there left to talk about?'

When a muscular policy spills over the boundary between force and sheer harassment, that is when people—politicians or not—start choosing self-preservation. It's a natural human tendency. Today,

---

8 K.P.S. Gill, *Endgame in Punjab, 1988–1993,* South Asia Portal, 2001. Available at: https://www.satp.org/satporgtp/publication/faultlines/volume1/Fault1-kpstext.htm

in Kashmir, there is alienation and hatred. The boys I speak to on occasion tell me that nobody wants *Azadi*, but nobody wants Pakistan either. They are currently dying in the name of Allah. So, what is happening in the face of this new muscular policy is the radicalization of Kashmir. I would call that a failure of our policies in Kashmir.

Muscularity in our foreign policy leads to much the same thing, quite often. Take Bhutan, for instance. While I was chief of the R&AW, I had an interesting three-day visit to Thimphu in 1999. India has prided itself historically on its special political relationship with this Himalayan kingdom. The unique political dynamics have resulted in a unique intelligence dynamics too, yet a conversation with the old King Jigme Singye Wangchuck told me otherwise.

'We have sustained this monarchy for long enough,' he told me frankly. 'The mood is changing now. Democracy is coming sooner, rather than later. But you guys are making things a little difficult for us. The Chinese are breathing down our necks. We consider ourselves very much a part of India, but by pushing us too much, you guys don't make it easy for us. We are having problems with the Chinese. Those problems will only increase.' And so it has proved—with the military standoff between the Indian armed forces and the People's Liberation Army (PLA) in 2017, over Doklam, an area spread over less than a 100 square kilometres, comprising a plateau and a valley at the trijunction between India, China and Bhutan.

Doklam is strategically located close to the Siliguri Corridor, connecting mainland India with its northeast. Not surprisingly, then, the corridor (known also as 'Chicken's Neck') is a vulnerable point for India. Controlling it would give the Chinese a commanding vantage point over the Chumbi valley and the Siliguri Corridor.

India stepped in on behalf of Bhutan, which had already protested to China that 'the construction of the road inside Bhutanese territory is a direct violation of the agreements and affects the process of demarcating the boundary between our two countries'.[9] Three years later, in 2020, despite clashes in the Galwan Valley of Ladakh between Indian forces and the PLA, new satellite images emerged, showing that in addition to setting up a village more than two kilometres within Bhutanese territory on the eastern periphery of the contested Doklam plateau, China had also built a road in the same area, some nine kilometres inside Bhutanese territory.[10] The old king was a sharp man, and looking back, his remarks have been prophetic.

At the moment, then, what I observe is that there are more questions than answers when it comes to the process of spooking. When it comes to Pakistan, in particular, there is a strange kind of suspicion, bordering on hostility, that hampers even the conventional process of gathering actionable intelligence. Actionable intelligence varies between red-hot information and a vague kind of hunch that something may go wrong. A hunch can be dismissed on the simple grounds of being a hunch. The latter is what happened during the Kargil war. You see, so much of the kind of intelligence that we gather with regard to Pakistan, in particular, is entangled with domestic and foreign policy that it is hard to know where to begin and where to end, particularly when events occur that leave you with more questions than answers.

Richard Helms, the former CIA chief, once said that 'it's not enough to ring the bell. You have to make sure the other guy hears it.' Take, for instance, the case of the attack on Parliament in 2001. I've talked about the incident itself in great detail in *The Vajpayee*

---

9   Quoted from Josy Joseph, 'What is the Doklam Issue All About?' *The Hindu*, 28 January 2018. Available at: https://www.thehindu.com/news/national/what-is-the-doklam-issue-all-about/article22536937.ece

10 See Vishnu Som, 'Exclusive: Satellite Images Hint at Renewed China Threat in Doklam', NDTV, 22 November 2020. Available at: https://www.ndtv.com/india-news/exclusive-satellite-images-hint-at-renewed-china-threat-in-doklam-2328660

Years, but what I didn't dare ask publicly then was a single question that has stayed with me all these years.

That question is: Was the attack on Parliament born of Musharraf's frustration at the fallout of what happened in Agra? After all, the summit at Agra in July 2001 was a foreign policy milestone for its day, and both India and Pakistan looked at it with real hope, until it came to a dead end. But as with most foreign policy milestones, this was also a carefully engineered operation. Again, the Agra summit has been discussed in *The Vajpayee Years,* and I won't go into it in much detail here, but what is not mentioned outright there is that the summit, from our side, was a cleverly run operation.

While on the face of it the architects of Agra were L.K. Advani and the Pakistani high commissioner Ashraf Jehangir Qazi, Agra was actually an operation conducted purely by Brajesh Mishra and aided by George Fernandes. Nobody was more frustrated by its failure than Brajesh. In times of stress, even the best of diplomats, like Abdul Sattar (who knew Delhi better than anybody else), miscalculated Agra's potential. Musharraf, of course, blamed Vivek Katju. He told one of our officers in Dubai, 'The villain (in Agra) was not really Advani, but that Joint Secretary [Katju] of yours.' That is why I ask the question, as tough and difficult as it is, whether the attack on Parliament was one engineered out of frustration by Musharraf.

Then there is the tragic case of 26/11, when terrorism at its most vicious rocked Mumbai. The main villain of these terror attacks was David Headley, as we all know. Obviously, he was a double or a triple agent—working with both the ISI and the CIA, and quite possibly, with the Drug Enforcement Agency—and he had been coming and going from India, with a fair amount of impunity. Now, the intelligence which came from the Americans in September 2008 was obviously gleaned from Headley himself. It's a fair presumption. Did the Americans then know when the attacks were going to take place? That is also a fair presumption, though it's still doubtful whether they gave us this information deliberately or if plans were delayed. After September, there was silence from the Americans. By November, the Indians forgot about it entirely. The R&AW maintains to this day that they had provided the requisite intelligence. Of course they did—but following the radio silence from the Americans, nothing was done. In so doing, we laid the foundations for a disastrous intelligence failure.

The story of 26/11 is not what I am going to get into here, since it is one that has been richly told before. What I do want to tell you is of a little trip I took to Mumbai in December that same year. It was a couple of weeks after the attacks. We stayed at the Yacht Club, where we usually stayed unless I was on an official trip. The Yacht Club adjoins the Taj. I took a stroll around the hotel, to assess the atmosphere. It was pretty grim; the shock of death and disaster still haunted the city. But people were fairly willing to talk, and from those that I spoke to (without, of course, revealing who I was), I gathered various interpretations. These boys seemed to have come in from two directions: from the front and from the side entrance in a two-pronged attack. The people I spoke to insisted that some of those boys had been seen on the premises regularly. As a result, on that fateful day, nobody had bothered to give them a second glance.

The other thing that I found curious was that, when I examined the building itself, there was a block in the heritage building that had been badly burned while one block was absolutely clean. This struck me as strange. Quite possibly, one (maybe two) of these boys had been inside the Taj all along. This part of the operation, then, would have been an inside job. I suspect that the management was of this opinion too, because immediately after this attack, an X-ray machine was installed outside the Taj, to scan the baggage of visitors arriving to stay at the hotel.

The operation itself was Lashkar through and through, and was certainly based out of Karachi, even though I say the real villain was

David Headley, who was picked up soon after the attacks by the Americans. He was already too dangerous to be left floating around. But questions on just how much the Americans told—or didn't tell—us; on the role of Pakistan; on the whereabouts of these boys in the days leading up to the attacks remain. More importantly, questions around our intelligence ties with Pakistan continue to linger. It is one of the major obstacles that hinder smooth cooperation on issues of terrorism, counterterrorism and intelligence gathering.

It is precisely with the aim of trying to answer some of these questions, and to try to seek a way forward, that I began advocating a Track-II dialogue between intelligence agencies. For a long time we have not had a formal agency to agency relationship with Pakistan, and I find that absurd, given how crucial Pakistan is in all our strategic calculations. That is why when Peter Jones, from the University of Ottowa, asked Asad Durrani and me to conduct a spook to spook dialogue, we agreed immediately. I've often been asked, by senior foreign service officers, what this Track-II business is all about. What do you expect to achieve, they want to know. I tell them all the same thing: 'I go for a jaunt, meet friends and have a good time.'

This is true, but it's actually a lot more meaningful than that. When we first began the dialogues, we were looking at all our retired intelligence chiefs. Our friend, Ajit Doval (then a former DIB) was roped in. We thought we would get Shyamal Dutta (of the IB but also a former governor of Nagaland) but he backed out; Vikram Sood, the former R&AW chief, was also busy. But the dialogues continued successfully for a couple of years before they fizzled out.

Dialogue and engagement, those two vital principles that I continue to strongly advocate, seem to have been left by the wayside more and more now. With Narendra Modi's government introducing a more muscular state policy in Kashmir, post the abrogation of Article 370 in 2019, talks with the Hurriyat seem to be a distant dream. This is where I find another problem with how Indian intelligence functions today. The estimation of risk is quite a large concern. Everyone estimates differently, of course, but in my case, I estimate it by going out on a limb as far as possible.

There could be certain outcomes, but if you don't take a chance at all, how do you get anywhere? Let's take present-day Kashmir. Why is it that we have stopped interacting with separatists? The reason is the paranoia of Pakistan. My question remains: So *what of Pakistan?* We have been working for years to turn these guys around, and in return, these guys will certainly provide you with intelligence, apart from helping in the mainstreaming of Kashmir.

So why stop now?

The two issues that always arose during the government's engagement with the separatists were that the clock could not be turned back, and there could be no discussion outside the ambit of the Indian Constitution. The Hurriyat was well aware of this when they began talks in 2003–04. When asked this question at Srinagar airport, Prime Minister Vajpayee had deflected the issue by invoking Insaniyat, Jamhooriyat, Kashmiriyat. The Hurriyat as it existed is dead, all that remains is Mirwaiz Umar Farooq who was always different from the others and should now be more than ready to enter the mainstream.

Not engaging, therefore, makes no sense because our main aim, ever since 1947, has been to mainstream Kashmir. That is not possible without engagement. Over the last five years I have noticed a steady decline in that process. The introduction of a more muscular policy has led to militants being shot dead straightaway. There are no more stories of surrender, of arrests and rehabilitation or of people being turned around. During the Cold War, for the Americans the ultimate prize was a Russian defector. In the same way, for us in Kashmir the top priority was to turn around a terrorist. Think of the goldmine of information he could provide. Today's muscular policy neither gives confidence nor encourages anyone out of sync with Delhi to engage in dialogue. It assumes that there is never a level playing field between the militant and his intelligence handler.

This is not to say, of course, that this is a policy that had suddenly come into effect with the current Bharatiya Janata Party (BJP) government. I would definitely say that in my years in intelligence, I noticed the existence of the seeds of this policy. There were always some people within the establishment who believe in *maaro saalon ko goli se* (shoot the bastards). Those who are anti-India play into that narrative. To give a rather important example, there are plenty of people who felt this privately about Syed Ali Shah Geelani, Pakistan's last man standing in Kashmir. But these ideas were never a full-blown strategy, because the green light for that would have to come from the top. I can never imagine, for instance, an Atal Bihari Vajpayee or a Manmohan Singh implementing this policy. But now, it's a different ball game, and one sometimes gets the impression that the IB is out of it.

The root of it lies in the interest of those at the top in all aspects of intelligence. There have been prime ministers who have been supportive of the need for intelligence, and there have been those who didn't have time for it at all. Some prime ministers have enjoyed full, detailed notes on certain subjects, while others haven't minded brief outlines. For example, Narasimha Rao was a very intelligent man, but he had contempt for this species of what he called 'chuglikhor' (mischief makers). On the other hand, Rajiv Gandhi was fascinated by intelligence, and the results it could produce for foreign policy as well. He enjoyed meeting with Narayanan, whom he greatly respected. In fact, their late night meetings—complete with chocolates and coffee—were something of a legend within the espionage establishment.

Rajiv always wanted to know what the embassies and the foreigners in Delhi were doing on a daily basis, and to that end, surveillance deeply interested him. Arun Singh and Arun Nehru once even joined the surveillance teams of the IB to see how things ran on the ground, during Rajiv's time in office. That was the level of interest that the young Prime Minister had in the workings of spookdom. But even someone as enthusiastic as Rajiv had to be schooled in the principles of espionage. Narayanan once told me of how the Prime Minister, excited at the information he had received, pressed him for the source of Narayanan's intelligence. But he responded: 'Prime Minister, my job is to provide you intelligence, but you have no right to ask me who my source is.'

That is why I feel that, for both national and international leaders, it's an advantage to be in direct and constant contact with spooks. After all, deniability is the great benefit of conversations with us. The kind of information we have to offer will always stay secret. Secrecy is, after all, the very currency of espionage. Satyabrata Pal—the then high commissioner in Pakistan and a wonderful human being, the likes of whom I meet very rarely—once told me something curious that Musharraf had said. According to Pal, Musharraf told him: 'What spooks are up to, we don't know. I don't know what the ISI does and I'm sure you don't know what your spooks are up to.'

That is, quite simply, the maxim we live by. For us, it is important to not only play those games, but to recruit those who can play the same games with the best of them. Hashim Qureshi, former terrorist and hijacker of the Indian Airlines aircraft Ganga, flying from Srinagar airport to the Jammu-Satwari airport, in 1971, who had a fair experience of intelligence agencies, told me of how a former CIA official had once advised him that a 25 per cent success meant a good agent. This brings me to a story about George Tenet, my CIA counterpart. His first question during his morning meetings was invariably, 'Have you recruited anyone new since last night?' He knew that there was no point in going about pretending that this was not actually the basic principle of our business.

Another advantage we offer—and in saying this I know I will be challenged by many contemporaries—is that spooks understand the depths of human nature much better than diplomats do. Intelligence can be an important tool for the handling of difficult geopolitical dynamics as well. I don't mean in the court of diplomacy, of course—far be it from me to step on the toes of our venerable diplomats! But certainly, the kind of information that we gather can aid the process of coming to better conclusions in geopolitical affairs.

The Americans are beginning to believe—particularly of late—that India was committed to supporting the United States against China. Do what you will with that diplomatically, but I think that's wishful thinking. Even though our relations with the US have improved since Vajpayee's time and more so since the India–United States Civil Nuclear Agreement or the nuclear deal, signed on 18 July 2005 by Prime Minister Manmohan Singh and US President George W. Bush, our overall foreign policy hasn't changed too much from the basic foundation of non-alignment. Russia, for example, remains a crucial instrument in diplomatic and trade assessments, even during these current days of war. If you know what's going on behind the scenes with these leaders, it can only serve to shore up diplomatic efforts.

In my years in intelligence, I have witnessed recognition of this fact by both national and international leaders. In 2000, I received a call from our man in Colombo. The imposing, attractive Chandrika Bandaranaike Kumaratunga was President of Sri Lanka then. *The lady wants to see you,* I was told. Mrs Kumaratunga had, by this time, quite a reputation. After all, running a country plagued by ethnic strife, terrorism, electricity and water shortages and an economic slowdown was no joke. Not to mention the fact that at the time she was one of the world's most wanted leaders, on the hit-list of most terrorist outfits. In October 1999, she had called for an early presidential election, but at her final election rally at the Colombo

Town Hall an assassination attempt (allegedly by the separatist Tamil Tigers) caused her to permanently lose vision in her right eye.

Even though she defeated Ranil Wickremesinghe to run for another term in 2001, the profiles on her, as most profiles on public and political leaders do, varied from portraying her as corrupt and inefficient, to feisty and wholly committed to public duty. I had never met her, nor had I expected to meet her in my current career. Slightly taken aback, I went to Brajesh Mishra and reported that the President of Sri Lanka was asking to meet me.

'*Jao, milo*', ('Go and meet,') he said.

So off I went.

When I arrived in Colombo, I went straight to the Indian embassy, to let the then ambassador (Shivshankar Menon) know that I was there. He was, if that's possible, even more startled than I had been, and not a little suspicious. 'But you must know why you've come,' he demanded. 'I have no idea why I'm here,' I said. 'All I know is that the lady has summoned me.' After reassuring Menon that I would return to brief him about the meeting, I went to meet with Mrs Kumaratunga at her residence.

Horagolla Walauwa was then the family seat of the Bandaranaike family. Built at the turn of the twentieth century, it is a sprawling, colonnaded property, set amidst acres of lush greenery. I was ushered into a massive drawing room and made to wait. I was offered tea, but I refused politely. Fifteen minutes later, I was offered coffee, and I refused that too. A full half hour passed before the President entered the room. Later, Shivshankar Menon would tell me that that was her style. In fact, her tardiness was somewhat notorious. She had once kept the Indian President, Shankar Dayal Sharma, waiting an entire 40 minutes—and that too on a day when her official calendar had been absolutely free of prior engagements.

When she did eventually come in, I was struck by her poise and calmness. She was carrying a rolled map under one arm, and she unrolled it on the table in front of me. It was a close-up of a map of the southern region of Sri Lanka, where the Liberation Tigers of Tamil Eelam (LTTE) were prominent. 'Tell me,' she said without any preamble, 'where is Prabhakaran?' If I had been taken aback by Chandrika Kumaratunga's summons, I was absolutely gobsmacked now.

'Madam,' I said, 'I wish we knew.'

'Of course you know,' she said assertively.

'No, we don't,' I insisted. 'But since we know this is of paramount importance to you, we can get some information.'

I can't really go into details of the background to this story, but the suspicion was that India had links with the LTTE. Primarily, from where I stood, Mrs Kumaratunga was actually conveying a message to New Delhi, via me—it wasn't so much about finding the elusive Prabhakaran, but an implicit warning: *You guys are responsible for what is happening in Sri Lanka and you know where he is.*

We had a pleasant conversation, but something that she said towards the end of it alerted me to the fact that this confident woman was actually a lot more aware than she seemed to be. 'We'll take care of you while you're here,' she told me. 'But let me tell you, I don't trust X. Be careful what you say to Y and to Z.' For obvious reasons, I cannot take their names publicly, but it struck me as fascinating that here was a president—a very embattled one at that—who knew perfectly well who was working against her within her own system.

Chandrika Kumaratunga's six-year term ended in 2005, but she was one of the few foreign leaders who, in my time, have preferred to keep direct links with heads of intelligence agencies. Yet another leader to do so has been Bangladesh's Prime Minister, Sheikh Hasina, who liked to get her intelligence briefings directly from the head of the R&AW. Inheritor of a troubled legacy, Hasina served as Prime Minister from 1996 to 2001, after defeating her arch-rival, Khaleda

Zia. The 'other lady', as we called her, was always in the shadows, waiting for a chance.

In 1990, the two had formed an unlikely (and ill-fated) alliance to overthrow the military dictator, Hussain Muhammad Ershad. However, their mutual mistrust and dislike—which led to their nickname the 'Battling Begums'—led to a political crisis that prompted the military to step in. It wasn't for long, though. Known for her fiery speeches and her equally fiery ambition, Hasina has also lived to tell the tale after several assassination attempts on her. Her critics call her authoritarian, but her supporters say she is the true leader of Bangladesh. The ISI is whispered to be active in Bangladesh, and they can't be very happy with Hasina. But for the present, she remains our best bet.

How long she lives to tell the tale is a story waiting to be told—but my point is that here was yet another leader who understood the importance of intelligence and of intelligence agencies.

I am sure over the years not too much has changed. The R&AW is perhaps more highly regarded by the powers that be now than in the past.

As I said at the opening of this chapter, spookdom is a treacherous game. In that sense, the more things have changed, the more they have stayed the same. At the heart of it, there is crookery, double-dealing and cold transactions, even if and when it is all done with a smile. If you are looking for Mother Teresa, you won't find her in the CIA. It is always left to intelligence services to do the dirty work, flirt in the grey areas.

It is not easy to estimate risks. Every intelligence chief faces a defining crisis, like we did when IC-814 was hijacked. At times, you could get red-hot intelligence suggesting that there could be an attack—9/11 and 26/11 are prime examples—and sometimes you realize that there is something not right somewhere—like when Kargil happened. Intelligence is most important in difficult times. The

CIA and the KGB never stopped talking throughout the Cold War. Kennedy's letters to Khrushchev, it is believed, may have saved the world from a catastrophe.

Yet, the shadow games of today are not the same ones that I learned when I started out decades ago. When we were first being tutored, nobody mentioned the word 'actionable'. Today, intelligence gathering is faster-paced, more result-oriented. Every piece of intelligence you gather must be actionable. Everything must be red-hot. But we shouldn't ever forget that so much of intelligence comes from open sources and open areas. Given that, it's hard to act on everything you glean, harder still given the levels of propaganda that are swirling about. Intelligence is defenceless against bad propaganda. Its successes are never known. It is known only by its failures. Today, India's intelligence operations seem to be at a crossroads, particularly in conflict zones like Kashmir.

John le Carre once said: 'If you're looking for the psyche of a country, its secret service is not an unreasonable place to look.' In 2022, truer words have never been spoken. This brings us to the question: which is the best intelligence service. I would say we are pretty good, better than the ISI with which we are constantly compared as professionals. As much has been conceded even by my friend, the former ISI chief, General Asad Durrani. Every spy service, of course, tends to mythologize itself.

There is an old Eagles' song, *Hotel California*, which has this lyric: '*You can check out anytime you like; but you can never leave*'. I think that's perfect—you never really stop being a spook. Once you've been inside the secret tent, you never really leave it. It is our own Hotel California. Even today, because I prefer to listen rather than talk, I have had friends say to me: 'You are difficult to follow; too deep.' Guess that's where the term deep state emerges from. My wife still complains of my 'cover stories'!

3
Nepal

IT WAS 1976.

I was in Chandigarh, six years into my time at the IB, when a call came through from Frank Dewars, the joint secretary in charge of the Bureau of Security at the MEA. Dewars was, even then, something of an institution. He knew the ins and outs of the entire business, and looking back, he managed his part pretty well. He asked me to come to Delhi. Posts were open in Washington, Moscow, London and Kathmandu, and I was to be interviewed for one of these, along with five other colleagues.

I was delighted—and even more thrilled to learn that Islamabad was opening up. Diplomatic relations with Pakistan had been pretty rough in the 1970s, and now that things were looking a little more promising, the Bureau needed someone to be posted there as well. I was hoping to get one of these plum postings—if not Islamabad, then certainly either London or Washington. The interview went well (I think!) and in the end, I was definitely asked whether I would like to go to Islamabad.

'I would love to!' I said enthusiastically.

Alas, that enthusiasm didn't last. Dewars, himself a skilled intelligence officer, wasn't too keen that a young officer with an intelligence background be sent out to Pakistan at this delicate moment. And so, Kathmandu was where I was to end up.

I have no regrets about that posting. I was quite excited about it, in fact, and I read up on everything, from the foreign policy to the climate, to understand whatever I could about Nepal. It was my first foreign posting, and we thoroughly enjoyed our time there. The kids were young—Priya, our daughter, was barely four years old and our son, Arjun, eight. They were also excited at the prospect of a foreign posting, but when we arrived in Kathmandu, they said: 'This is not a foreign country; it is a village!' Even if it was a village, it was the most delightful countryside.

In those days, Kathmandu was a different world, unrecognizable from the city you might see today. The Nepalese were a lovely people, laidback and full of fun. I was designated first secretary (administration). This sounds loaded, but in truth, it meant very little work, since it entailed looking after the security of the embassy and liaising with the Nepal Police. Occasionally, when the head of chancery went on leave, I would deputize for him, but the IFS guys were notoriously finicky about their turf so, as you can imagine, that didn't last long either!

Paran and I were in Nepal for three and a half years, from September 1976 to March 1980. For India, it was a difficult time. The Emergency, which had been declared on 25 June 1975, was in full swing. I have no qualms in saying that that period of India's life didn't touch me personally, and so I was able to put it behind me and look ahead to the future. I recognize the privilege I have in saying this, of course—because in terms of India's history, the Emergency was a dark milestone.

From the pinnacle to which Indira Gandhi had ascended by 1972, there was perhaps no other way to go but down. Her trajectory until then, after all, had been nothing short of spectacular. She had won a difficult election by a landslide; pursued a war effort that had successfully vanquished a hostile neighbour and birthed a free nation and engineered a sequence of victories in the state assembly elections that stamped the presence of the Congress across the Indian political landscape. For those reasons alone, it was a supremely interesting time to be posted to Kathmandu. India had just proved its dominance in South Asia under Indira Gandhi, with the Bangladesh war in 1971 and the annexation of Sikkim—a Himalayan kingdom in itself—in 1975.

But luck has an annoying habit of running out.

Bad monsoons over successive years crippled agriculture, reducing Prime Minister Gandhi's grand ambitions of 'Gareebi Hatao' (eradicate poverty) to a caricature that she couldn't control. Her more reliable advisers—like her principal secretary P.N. Haksar—were pushed out of the inner circle, leaving the Prime Minister dependent on the likes of Arun Nehru and other ill-informed sycophants. As opposition to her rule began to coalesce—led by the doughty figure of Jayaprakash Narayan—Indira Gandhi began to push back by cracking the mould of democratic checks and balances herself. The rest, of course, is history and it has been told by others more well versed than I. But I was a young fellow then, and I was looking at a career trajectory that had already given me a ticket out of the country to comparative safety. And yet, even though I was not in the country at the time, I couldn't remain blind to what was happening in India. I joke often, saying all I did in Kathmandu was watch India and play cricket, the latter of which I did a lot of during my free time. Cricket made me a lot of friends. Cricket, after all, is life.

Frankly, though, observing India at the time, and from that distance, only proved the point that this was an unstable period in

Indian politics and history. On 16 April 1976, a highly controversial family planning initiative—for which, among other things, Sanjay Gandhi is remembered with anger—was announced, involving the vasectomy of thousands of men and the tubal ligation of women, either for payment or under coercive conditions. In that same month, Sanjay ordered the Turkman Gate demolitions, which ended in unnecessary bloodshed and considerable violence.

In 1977, general elections were held in India, between 16 and 20 March, to elect members of the sixth Lok Sabha. The elections took place during the Emergency. But on 23 March 1977, a day after the election results were declared, Indira Gandhi got B.D. Jatti, the acting President, to revoke the internal Emergency. The results themselves were astonishing, a heavy defeat for the Indian National Congress, with Indira Gandhi losing her seat in the family bastion at Rae Bareli and Morarji Desai becoming the fourth (and the oldest at 81!) Prime Minister of India. I remember noticing that the senior members of the Indian embassy in Kathmandu were thrilled with the results. The general feeling seemed to be that Indira Gandhi deserved the drubbing that Morarji Desai and the Janata Party had handed her! I also noticed that diplomats tend to air their views more freely when abroad.

Among the local residents of Kathmandu also there seemed to be a sense of relief that Indira Gandhi had been checked, even if it was temporary. India and Nepal could now move on to building on an already rich foundation of partnership and shared history. This was important, I think, because of the perception that had been—to a large extent fuelled by New Delhi—that the palace was an outdated institution. Now, the mid- to late 1970s were a time of some unease for Nepal. King Birendra, then thirty years old, was the reigning ruler, a monarch with traditional links not only to the heavens but also to Harvard, which he had attended after a stint at the University of Tokyo. Under his reign, Nepal was a constitutional monarchy, but the

Constitution recognized the King as the sole source of governmental authority. Importantly, political parties were banned too—and had been since 1960. But even as Birendra—with the help of his Prime Minister, Dr Tulsi Giri—tackled important policy issues, politics in India was threatening to create some turbulence to this plan.

The Emergency brought home the importance of press freedom, and the strict controls of those members of the Nepalese Opposition who had been operating in India and had been considered too close to Indira Gandhi's political opponents drove home the image of India in a new light. Prime Minister Indira Gandhi had been quite rightly proud of her formidable strategic reputation in the aftermath of Bangladesh and Sikkim, but in Nepal there were concerns, with King Birendra stating that, 'The prosperity or security of a nation no longer depends upon living within the umbrella of a powerful nation' while addressing the Non-Aligned Nations Summit Conference on 17 August 1976 in Colombo, Sri Lanka, albeit without specifically mentioning India.

It was a line that struck me as important, for it resonated with my own personal belief that India should have always treated Nepal as a special protectorate, much as it had Bhutan. Yet, in the diplomacy that I saw playing out in those years in Kathmandu, I saw the Nepalese desire to turn to India as a 'big brother', while India was, for its part, a big bully. I observed some local resentment about how hard India was pushing its smaller neighbour to conform to its own views. To some extent I think it boils down to India's own colonial history, particularly during the time of integration and accession, when the attitude towards princely states and privy purses was scornful to say the least. Indira Gandhi's government abolished the privy purse in 1971—after years of its continued existence as a political hot potato—but a perception that New Delhi viewed the palace in Nepal, too, as an antiquated institution seemed to have travelled across the border.

The irony here—and this is where I feel our diplomacy of the time failed—was that Kathmandu was a small place with small embassies. I don't think any embassy in the country was more important for the Nepalese than ours, and yet we found it difficult to gain entry into the palace. This was a big failure from where I stood then and where I stand now. Since time immemorial, intelligence has always supported bigger players; it has always played games to win political agendas. But in Nepal, our first target as an intelligence agency should have always been the palace. Even if, from an intelligence perspective, you want the monarchy toppled, you must have access to the key power players. We should always have had free access to the palace, instead of landing up in a situation where ambassadors and senior diplomats alike were restricted from accessing King Birendra.

This is where I feel diplomacy, despite having some of our best diplomats as ambassadors in Kathmandu, failed in those years in Nepal. So perhaps did intelligence. India was always trying to tutor the Nepalese on how to run their own country, and it was deeply resented within the palace and by the palace. On the other hand, the Ranas—then out of power—were still crucial political players on the chessboard of Nepalese politics and still the elite of Nepalese society. Among the Ranas, there were some born generals too. But we gave them no leeway.

Some of the Rana boys were in school in my time. One of them, Prabal, and his charming wife, Shanti, we met frequently in Kathmandu. Belonging to the Nepalese foreign service, he was posted as ambassador to London before he came back and retired as foreign secretary. There were some seniors too like General Samrajya and Sharda Shamsher (Dr Karan Singh's father-in-law) who were particularly kind to us during our stay in Kathmandu. We were at Genral Sharda's bedside when he passed away.

The lifestyle of some of the Ranas was quite like that of some of our old maharajas. Most of them also drank heavily. In the Punjab we refer to a large drink as a 'Patiala peg'. The Nepalese peg was twice as large! The Americans always had a glass full of cognac at parties for one of the generals who had a healthy capacity for alcohol.

Sagar Rana—author of *Singha Durbar*,[1] a comprehensive history of the Ranas, who was rather balanced for his tribe—politically stood steadfastly with the Nepali Congress. Sagar became a good friend, both on and off the cricket field.

It was an already changing society, even then, and we began to make mistakes. For instance, our support to the Madhesis—which began around my time in Nepal—was something that I didn't agree with. It was—and still is—a raw nerve in Nepal. If such a thing had to be done, it needed to have been done much more discreetly and subtly. I had spent some time in the IB myself by then and for me this little venture of ours was far too much out in the open. To have made mistakes as crude as this in a country that has always shown its inclination to be helped and protected by India is unforgivable.

Take, for instance, the question of rival intelligence agencies and rival interests in Nepal. In those days, there were no proper roads in Nepal. But you could ask a minister: 'Why don't you have roads constructed?' The response, no matter whom you spoke to, was unfailingly on the lines of, '*Toh aap banwa lijiye na*. (Why don't you get it done?)' We never took them up on that hint, and we missed a huge opportunity here when the Chinese stepped in to build Nepal's first major ring road around the capital city. In so doing, Beijing burnished its credentials on the Nepalese periphery of attention. Money was a big factor in Nepal in my time. The kingdom, despite Birendra's best attempts, was always in need of money for development and infrastructure. I think much more could have and should have been done by India.

---

1 Sagar S.J.B. Rana, *Singha Durbar: Rise and Fall of the Rana Regime of Nepal*, New Delhi: Rupa Publications, 2017.

Nepal

I feel that we should have been more sensitive to Pakistan. In comparison to us, the Pakistanis had a three-member embassy, a small little place. But even that used to trouble us—what is that Pakistani doing, we used to wonder. I disliked that notion even then. Let me tell you a little story that might illustrate my point better. Pakistan had an ambassador in the kingdom and a third secretary in the embassy, a chap called Nayyar Zaman. We met here and there, at some social events and became quite friendly, to the point that Zaman and his wife, Nazakat, began visiting Paran and me at home. They were a fun couple: he was something of a badmaash, and she was the placid, motherly counterfoil to his personality. However, when Nayyar began dropping in regularly, I went to Ambassador N.B. Menon and explained the situation.

Menon said: 'I've been watching this. There's no harm. It's always good to have a window open there. It's fine. Go ahead if you're confident.' Yet Nayyar Zaman was more worried in case his ambassador found out. One day, I told him that I had told my ambassador that we met socially. He said: '*Aap logon ki aur baat hai. Jab aapke ghar aunga, toh garage khol dena, meri gaadi yaahan nahin dikhni chahiye.* (You guys are different. But when I come to your house, please open your garage so that my car can be parked inside and not seen outside your house.)'

It's the best story I can think of to illustrate the point that we were—mutually—so deeply suspicious of each other's intentions in Nepal. But at this point, Pakistan was not doing much in the country. Later, of course, Kathmandu would develop into a busy ISI station of sorts. It would also become the unfortunate starting point of the hijack of IC-814 in 1999, when a Pakistan embassy official was present at the airport when the plane was taking off—and when I was chief of the R&AW. Had we been more vigilant in 1976–80 and even in the years after that, the hijacking might have been prevented.

So, these mistakes that we made inevitably reflected in our relations with the palace. In my three and a half years in Kathmandu, the king never visited the embassy except once. He was always invited to the big occasions, but he never attended. It is deeply unfortunate because it would be decades before the life of the monarchy would be cut so brutally short, but in my day, the palace still ran Nepal. For the Nepalese, even despite pockets of protest, the king was still the king. Why were we trying to create an impression that was counter to the narrative that already existed?

I think it was to sort out that end that in July 1977, Atal Bihari Vajpayee, then a young foreign minister with rich potential, came to Kathmandu. He spoke at the Nepal Bharat Maitreyi Sangh. He was at his oratorical best that day, a masterly speech to a packed hall. The women in the audience came out, wiping their eyes, for he had moved them so much with his words. I took away my first impressions of a much younger Vajpayee: a beautifully assured speaker, and a man with the kind of cool intelligence that would serve the country so well decades later. What a Prime Minister he would have been then!

Later that year, in December, Vajpayee would come to Nepal once again, this time with Prime Minister Morarji Desai. As first secretary, I was in charge of their security arrangements. They were put up in a special guest house in Kathmandu—whose name I forget—a couple of rooms apart. Every morning, I would be up and waiting early to escort the Prime Minister to his car. Morarji was particularly punctual and liked everything and everyone to proceed on time. One morning, he entered the lift and a minute later, Vajpayee dashed in.

'*Videshmantriji*,' the Prime Minister remarked, '*aap hamesha late hote hain.* (Foreign minister, you are always late.)'

Vajpayee's sangfroid was unruffled, '*Pradhanmantriji*,' he riposted, '*Ham kya karein! Aap hamesha time se pehle aa jate hain!* (Prime Minister, what can I do! You are always ahead of time!)'

Nepal

The visit went very well, with both Morarji and Vajpayee taking pains to reassure their Nepalese counterparts of India's continued friendship and insistence on declaring Nepal to be a 'zone of peace'. I had no reason to be present in the room during the talks, of course, but I had other concerns at the time. Right around the time of Desai's visit to Nepal, there had been a run of violent attacks on Indian diplomats in many capitals around the world, masterminded by the extremist Ananda Marga organization. Members of the organization, both in India and abroad, had hoped that Morarji would free their guru and former railway accounting clerk, Prabhat Ranjan Sarkar, who had been put behind bars on murder charges by Indira Gandhi. But Morarji's government had no desire to cater to the Ananda Marga, which had an incredibly unsavoury reputation, despite its leader being revered as 'bliss personified'.

Sarkar's followers—'monks' and 'nuns' who were perennially clothed in saffron robes and often carried daggers hooked into their belts—were furious at the government's indifference, alleging that he had been poisoned, tortured and otherwise mistreated during his time in jail. It didn't help matters that Sarkar had chosen to go on a fast, due to which his weight was rapidly dropping. With Desai's visit and the preceding trajectory of violence on diplomats and embassies, there was a definite security concern about the Prime Minister. Now, remember as you read this, that these were the days before Indira Gandhi's assassination. In those days, there was no Special Protection Group (SPG). Security was handled solely by the IB, and usually a joint director at the IB would travel with the Prime Minister, just in case.

Still, given my designation at the embassy, I couldn't afford to be lax, and so I took my concerns to K.J. Baral, the inspector general of Nepal Police. Baral was a good guy, someone whom I'd certainly call a friend of India. He had been trained in Mount Abu, with the 1956

IPS batch, some of whom were friends of his. However, Baral was rather more laidback about most concerns than I would have liked. '*Arey, kya, Dulat? Kya Marga? Yeh Nepal hai! Yahan ek hi Marga chalta hai!* (What Marga are you talking about? This is Nepal. We have only one Marga here.)' In the event, of course, the visit went off perfectly well, and I received a congratulatory letter from K.P. Medhekar, the joint director, IB, who had come out to Kathmandu with Morarji.

I sometimes wonder what would India have been had Sanjay Gandhi lived? What would Indira have been had her youngest son survived the airplane crash that killed him, much too young, in 1980? It's hard to say. But one thing is for sure, something died in Indira Gandhi on the day that her son lost his life. The Indira Gandhi of the 1980s was a different person. Sanjay was no longer on the scene, and neither was Haksar. Those losses left her weakened in confidence and perception. Those around her encouraged her to be autocratic, and therein lay her downfall. As I watched this happen, while I sat in Nepal, I found it to be an enduring lesson: autocracy, in any form, never works.

It was a momentous lesson, witnessed in an equally momentous time in Nepal. Between 1979 and 1980, even as the political landscape in India changed and changed again, politics in Nepal was equally uncertain. Between April and May 1979, students across the Himalayan kingdom rose up in protest, insisting that the monarchy concede to holding a referendum on the possibility of a multiparty system in the country. So widespread was the unrest that thirty-seven of Nepal's seventy-five districts were affected by violence. At one point, the students managed to march right up to the gates of the palace—a deeply disturbing moment for anyone who believed in the monarchy (and indeed, for the monarch himself!). King Birendra was forced to negotiate with the dissenters, forming a five-member commission, headed by the Chief Justice of the Supreme Court, to present a report on how to deal with the student movement.

The Royal Commission suggested giving in to the students' demands on abolishing the education policy of 1972, on scrapping entrance examinations for universities and for the right to establish independent unions. On 23 May 1979, King Birendra publicly announced that a referendum with universal adult suffrage and secret voting would be held, so that the people of Nepal could choose between a multiparty system and the retention of a non-party panchayat regime. That referendum was held on 2 May 1980. It was a landmark moment for the nation, yet I think it was a kind of rehearsal for bigger things to come. I had already left Nepal at this point, but I thought of it as a fitting milestone for this happy, easy-going country where I had enjoyed a short, yet full time.

I had made quite a few friends by now, including an American consul in Madras (a CIA guy) who was visiting Kathmandu at the time. India was holding the general elections of 1980 at the time, and he asked me, 'What do you think will happen?'

'I have no doubt that Mrs Gandhi will come back quite comfortably.'

The American was astounded. 'No, let's have a bet.' He insisted. We bet on a bottle of whisky—me backing Indira Gandhi and he backing Jagjivan Ram. In the end, of course, he sent me that bottle of whisky, which I must say I quite enjoyed!

I was also in touch with K.P. Medhekar, who kept persistently asking when I was coming back. He wanted me to serve with him, I recall. There was a visit scheduled to India by the Pakistan cricket team in 1980.

'Come back,' Medhekar told me, 'I want you to look after the security of the Pakistan cricket team.' I was thrilled, needless to say, but it didn't happen in the end because I couldn't return in time.

Yes, they had been three and a half wonderful years in this lovely Himalayan kingdom. But as I boarded my flight back to Delhi in the spring of 1980, I wondered to myself how long the monarchy would survive in Nepal.

The beginning of the end, typical of Nepal and its monarchy, came amidst bloodshed. On the hot evening of 1 June 2001, an angry, lovesick and drunk Crown Prince Dipendra massacred almost the entire royal family before shooting himself. Because, as the story goes, his parents, more notably his mother, Queen Aishwarya, were opposed to his marrying the girl of his choice, the beautiful Devyani Rana, daughter of the aristocratic Pashupati Shamsher Jang Bahadur Rana.[2] A report filed by a commission and eyewitness accounts blamed the massacre on Dipendra, but as Barkha Dutt and some other mediapersons reported, the Nepal street never bought the official version.[3] Many blamed Gyanendra and his notorious son, Paras, known for drunken brawls and hit-and-run vehicular assaults, of having engineered the killings to take over the throne. This suspicion was heightened by Gyanendra's absence from the royal get-together and the fact that Paras and his mother survived.

Gyanendra, once Delhi's favourite, was to earn himself the reputation of a thief before he became king. He ruled for seven years but was neither liked nor trusted. Macbeth-like, he was constantly haunted by the events of 1 June 2001. When his rule finally ended on 11 June 2008, after the Constituent Assembly abolished monarchy, Gyanendra for the first time referred to the gruesome destruction

---

2 'Nepal inquiry blames crown prince for royal massacre', *The Guardian*, 14 June 2001, https//www.theguardian.com/world/2001/jun/14/nepal

3 'Massacre of the royal family of Nepal', https://www.ndtv.com/video/shows/reality-bites/massacre-of-the-royal-family-of-nepal-aired-june-2001-2 73721

of his relatives before driving away with his wife into history.[4] Nepal's 240-year-old monarchy was dead. The palace was to become a museum.

Devyani, who virtually went into hiding, was later to marry Arjun Singh's grandson on 23 February 2007 at the Scindia Villa in New Delhi. Her mother, Usharaje, was Madhavrao Scindia's sister.

Nepal remains politically unsettled to this day. The massacre was a huge tragedy whose immediate fallout may have been the closer proximity between China and Nepal.

To my mind, Nepal was more complicated than Kashmir. If Kashmir was more of an obsession, Nepal has remained in some ways obsessively endearing. Both Nepal and Kashmir taught me a great deal about the complexities of life.

---

4 'Deposed Nepal king surrenders crown', *The Guardian*, 11 June 2008, https://www.theguardian.com/world/2008/jun/11/nepal; see also 'Nepal's last king endorses ending of monarchy', *India Today*, 11 June 2008, https://www.indiatoday.in/latest-headlines/story/nepals-last-king-endorses-ending-of-monarchy-26199-2008-06-11

4
A Handful of Greats

In the spring of 1980, when I returned from Nepal, I was appointed to counter-intelligence. During this period, I did duty as security liaison officer with visiting dignitaries from time to time. The designation may sound rather boring, but it was part of the natural trajectory of my career at the IB and formed yet another facet of our training across different spectrums of security. During my time here, I had the privilege of working closely with a number of visiting dignitaries and heads of state.

Looking back, it was a rather fun part of my career, since many of these grand men and women were, underneath the official veneer of their positions of power, rather charmingly human. Yet this is not just about the powerful people I met at this time. It's also about some of the legends we have had on Indian soil too. I have, after all, worked with the likes of the great M.K. Narayanan, and I have had the fortune of claiming friendship with Rajesh Pilot. These are the kind of people you encounter but once in a lifetime, and if you lose them too early—as we lost Rajesh—it is a void that is never quite filled.

Ashwini Kumar

Punjab produced many fine police officers but an institution, a legend and an inspiration for me while joining the service was Ashwini Kumar. Born in Jalandhar on 27 December 1920, Ashwini Kumar joined the Indian Police (IP) in 1942. His father, Dr Vishwanath, was a renowned physician in pre-Partition Lahore.

Ashwini Kumar remains one of our most highly decorated police officers. He got the President's Gallantry Award twice, was awarded the Padma Bhushan in 1972, and adjudged Policeman of the Millennium in Sydney in 2000 for his contribution to Olympics security. He retired in December 1978 as director general of the Border Security Force (BSF). The BSF mess in Nizamuddin, New Delhi, bears his name.

He attracted Prime Minister Jawaharlal Nehru's attention and came into the limelight when he liquidated the notorious Bhupat Gang in Saurashtra, where he had been handpicked and sent from Punjab in 1951. Ashwini Kumar also hunted down Chief Minister Partap Singh Kairon's killer, Sucha Singh, after a dramatic chase in Nepal, having in the bargain to spend a night in the police lock-up in Kathmandu for intruding into Nepalese territory without informing them.

Such were his leadership qualities that in his native Punjab the men in the force were prepared to give their life for him. 'No' and 'never' were not part of his vocabulary.

Despite his tough exterior, Ashwini Kumar was an extremely sensitive man with a heart of gold. He was a connoisseur of all the good things—music, art, literature, poetry and sports. An outstanding sportsman himself, he made a great sports administrator as president of the Indian Hockey Federation and vice-president of the International Olympic Committee, apart from many other sports bodies he headed. His first love was, of course, hockey. He even nicknamed his firstborn, Rohini, 'Hockey'.

In his later days, when he felt things were going wrong, he would recite his most favourite line in Urdu—'*Kahaan gaye woh kaafiley jinpe hamein naaz tha*'. He could forgive but never easily forget, and readily burst into his favourite Urdu and Persian poetry. The Harballabh festival of classical music in the winter in Jalandhar was close to his heart.

After retirement, Ashwini Kumar devoted most of his time to his family. His charming wife, Renu, was always by his side and bore the brunt of his ire. Chhoti (Yamini), his younger daughter and the love of his life, troubled Kumar sahib because he saw too much of his rebellious self in her. He was only at peace when she finally decided to marry.

In his later years, Ashwini Kumar was not in the best of health having fractured his hip in the Winter Olympics in Vancouver in 2010, which immobilized him. But his will to live was strong enough to enable him to dance even in a wheelchair at Chhoti's wedding.

Kumar sahib treated us like family and expected us at his home in Delhi's New Friends Colony at least once a fortnight for a drink. If we missed out, he would call to inquire what was wrong. Listening to his anecdotes over a drink was an education. His words of wisdom were unforgettable, more so because he spoke mostly in chaste Punjabi. He knew Punjab like the back of his hand, often telling me about my ancestors much more than I knew.

Yasser Arafat

Even as the Palestine Liberation Organisation (PLO) and its leader, Yasser Arafat, were being globally vilified as 'terrorists', India, which had always taken a principled stand in those days on the Palestine issue, allowed the PLO to open an office in New Delhi in 1974. Soon after, delegations representing both the PLO and its main constituent, Al Fatah, began visiting India regularly, building strong political links with the Congress and the Left parties. In the spring of 1980, Yasser

A Handful of Greats

Arafat, then the chairman of the PLO, was invited to India by Prime Minister Indira Gandhi on what the Government of India called a 'friendly official visit'. As the security liaison officer, I was assigned to look after Arafat.

From the outset you could tell that this was going to be a visit like no other. An official instruction had come in from the PMO—*Yeh delegation aa rahi hai, inke liye sab kuch karna padega.* (This delegation is coming. We need to provide special treatment to them.) Considering the bureaucratic nightmare that the sorting out of their passports was (someone was from Syria, someone else was from Jordan!), I thought the PMO had issued a generous instruction, but only when I went to pick up Arafat at the airport did I realize just how generous! A PLO delegate was already there waiting to receive the chairman, but the flight that was coming in with the delegation on board didn't seem to have much security with them.

'I say, aren't you worried about your chairman's security?' I demanded.

'Worried? What do you mean?'

'I mean, he could be hijacked in mid-air!'

'By whom?' The PLO fellow looked genuinely amused. 'We're the ones who do all the hijacking!'

Funny as that repartee was, when the plane landed I discovered the meaning behind it. Arafat strode off the plane, a small, slight man, wearing a maroon and white keffiyeh, khaki shirt and black trousers, with a revolver in his holster. He was his own security officer. Now, India permits no foreign heads of state or their security entourages to carry arms. We take pride in looking after their security arrangements, and if arms are needed, Indian arms are provided. But though we (me!) were taken aback, Indira Gandhi was quite clear. An exception was to be made on this occasion.

The visit went off supremely well. Yasser Arafat was a simple, sincere man, and his fondness for Indira—she called him her 'rakhi brother'—was well known. He was here for a mere two days, during which I learned that he was not given to idle chatter. He also had no airs and graces, nor any ideas above his station in life. In fact, when he first strode off that plane, he greeted me with the typical Arab hug. I was, right from the start, one of his entourage. I was a part of all the photographs the PLO delegation took during their brief time in New Delhi, and I sometimes wish that I had had the sense to keep some of them!

Abu Ammar, 'immortal father', as he was referred to by his people, Arafat was awarded the Nobel Peace Prize along with Shimon Peres and Yitzhak Rabin in December 1994. Rabin was subsequently killed and so was Arafat. Interestingly, when the Jordanians pushed Arafat out of the country in the late 1960s, it was Brigadier Zia-ul-Haq—who went on to become General and then President of Pakistan—at the time military adviser to the Jordanian army, who came into conflict with Arafat. Zia was commanding a Jordanian brigade which attacked the PLO. After that Arafat shifted to Lebanon where he remained till 1982 when the Israelis invaded the country. Once again, Arafat had to leave but the Israelis got no respite because instead of Arafat's Fatah, they had to thereafter deal with Hezbollah.

I wish I had had the occasion to meet Yasser Arafat again. He was clearly an interesting man, with erudite, important opinions and no pretensions. As the story goes, he was ultimately poisoned to death. Arafat's official medical records state that in 2004 he died of a stroke. But in 2012, amid continuing claims that he had been murdered (Palestinians, obviously, accuse the Israelis of this), his body was exhumed. A Swiss forensic report, obtained in 2013 by Al Jazeera, would show that Arafat had been poisoned by radioactive polonium.[1]

---

1   Al Jazeera Investigative Unit, 'Swiss Forensic Report on Arafat's Death', 6 November 2013. Available at: https://www.aljazeera.com/news/2013/11/6/swiss-forensic-report-on-arafats-death

A Handful of Greats

Scientists from the Vaudois University Hospital Centre (CHUV) in Lausanne, Switzerland, tested samples of Arafat's bones and the soil samples around his corpse, and concluded that the results 'moderately support the proposition that the death was the consequence of poisoning with polonium-210'.[2] A more definitive conclusion has never been reached, and Israeli foreign ministry spokespersons were quick to dismiss the test results as 'more soap opera than science'.[3] What the truth is, the world will never know, but undoubtedly, Yasser Arafat was the most spied upon leader in modern times.

In the Indian context, he reminds me a bit of Bhim Singh, the founder of Jammu's Panthers Party, who had incidentally himself spent quite a bit of time in the PLO camps. Sadly, albeit due to less dramatic circumstances, Bhim Singh is also no longer with us today.

Charles, Prince of Wales

Now, this was a lovely visit, not least because Charles was, then, a young man, just growing into his shoes as the Prince of Wales. He was here for about two weeks in the winter of 1980. His schedule was packed, criss-crossing India from Delhi to Amritsar, Amritsar to Bharatpur, Bharatpur to Agra, Agra to Jaipur, Jaipur to Bombay, Bombay to Bangalore, Bangalore to Madras, Madras to Calcutta. When I heard the schedule, hectic as it was, it sounded very much like a delightful holiday! I didn't quite expect it to keep me on my toes as much as it did. For one, his two and a half day schedule in the capital was crammed with official engagements—from a presidential banquet to official receptions and visits to educational institutions.

---

2 Ibid.
3 Yolande Knell, 'Yasser Arafat "may have been poisoned with polonium"', 6 November 2013. Available at: https://www.bbc.com/news/world-middle-east-24838061

His agenda for each day was packed to the minute, even as he clocked mile after mile in the royal jet. But the visit started slightly badly for the young prince. In New Delhi, Prime Minister Indira Gandhi invited him over to her residence for a quiet family lunch. The British high commissioner, John Thompson, and I dropped him off and waited dutifully until we were summoned to collect His Royal Highness. But it wasn't the confident prince who came out. Charles exited the Prime Minister's residence looking like he'd been caned!

On seeing the Prince of Wales's expression, Thompson asked: 'How did the lunch go, Your Highness?'

'Don't ask,' Charles said, getting into the car with an air of relief. 'That lady can freeze you. You know, I've met leaders all over the world, but this woman doesn't speak a word!'

Clearly, Indira Gandhi had thought here was a boy who didn't need pandering to! It was an unfortunate example of an occasion where the Prime Minister had turned on her notorious coldness, instead of her famous charm.

We left Delhi for Amritsar the next day, with the entourage divided across two aircraft: an Indian plane carrying the diplomatic paraphernalia, and the royal jet, in which I was ensconced alongside the prince. It was a short flight but not without its alarming moments. Charles seemed happy to be away from the public eye, free to just be himself for a moment. Unfortunately, in moments like these his natural exuberance also came bubbling to the surface, and I had to step in quickly to see that nothing untoward happened.

On the flight to Amritsar, for instance, he decided to take the controls himself. I was profoundly alarmed and had to speak quietly but firmly to his security officer, a man by the name of John McLean, 'This is not on. Maybe he does know how to fly an aircraft, but in his position, we wouldn't like him to be flying around here. If something were to go wrong, I will be in deep trouble. So rather than me approaching him, please let him know that this isn't on.' Luckily, the prince was an accommodating young man, but it often put me in the position of being embarrassingly firm with rather important people.

In Jaipur, for instance, I had to speak quietly with the Rajmata herself. This was a private visit, since Gayatri Devi had invited Charles to stay on the premises of Rambagh, in a beautiful little cottage that adjoined the main palace. It seemed only fitting because Jaipur and the Crown have long had a historic connection. More personally, Maharaja Sawai Man Singh II (fondly called 'Jai' by Gayatri Devi) and Prince Charles's father, Prince Philip, had long been polo-playing buddies. The rest of us were staying at the hotel, but Gayatri Devi came to see me before whisking the Prince off.

'The Prince of Wales is my guest,' she said imperiously.

'Madam,' I said politely, 'he may be your guest, but his security is my responsibility.'

She smiled. 'Mr Dulat, I won't take him anywhere without your approval.'

'Not only will you not take him anywhere,' I retorted, 'but I will go with him everywhere he goes. I'm making an exception for him to stay in this cottage because this is your private property, but if he goes anywhere else, I will be with him.'

The Prince of Wales really enjoyed his stay with Gayatri Devi, reserving his single rest day in an otherwise packed itinerary for her company. The Rajmata entertained him in style, with buckets of champagne, a polo match for the polo-loving prince and a visit to Moti Doongri, the hill around which the city of Jaipur flourishes. That evening, there was a special dance programme for the prince's entertainment, and he joined in with gusto, dancing with the pretty Rajput belles.

As Charles's visit across India continued, I began to see that he was truly enjoying himself, though he certainly had the proverbial British stiff upper lip. In Bharatpur, for instance, he wanted to wake up at five in the morning, just in order to go birdwatching! For someone like me, who prized my sleep, I can't say I was thrilled, but it was quite a fun morning, nonetheless.

In Bombay, he visited Rajkamal Studios where he was garlanded by the actress Padmini Kolhapure who also gave him a peck on the cheek. The incident made big news in both India and the UK.

Everywhere he went, my room was always adjoining his, but I can't say that we had much conversation in the early days of his travels. There was not much one could say to an English royal, beyond 'Good morning, Your Highness' and 'Good night, Your Highness!' But it was in Chennai (then, of course, it was known as Madras) that things changed a little for the better. At the outset, the Prince insisted on going for a jog down the beach at Fisherman's Cove at six in the morning. Now, His Highness is a good number of years younger than I am, and I can tell you, jogging on the sand is not one of my more pleasant memories!

Charles also wanted to go for a swim, and that caught me off guard. I hadn't been expecting His Highness to be quite so active, and I hadn't brought any swimming costumes with me, so I had to borrow from his own security entourage in order to keep an eye on him! Then, there came an evening towards the close of the prince's visit to Madras when his schedule had to be changed slightly because it was pouring. He didn't have such an important engagement that he simply *had* to go out and so the delegation chose to stay back in Raj Bhavan instead.

The Prince of Wales asked for his dinner to be served in his room, and the rest of us would have to come down for dinner to the dining hall. I just happened to inquire from the chefs about the menu. I was told that the food would be entirely continental.

'Are you guys okay with it?' I inquired from the delegation.

'Well, we would have preferred a curry,' was the response.

Now, I have no doubt that they would have politely eaten what was actually on the table, but the implicit suggestion here was that I try to see what could be done to improve matters for His Highness. So I went off to the kitchen to inquire if the chefs could throw some Indian food together.

It was already late, and the staff naturally looked put out. '*Sahib, ab toh late ho gaya hai. Ab kya karein*? (Sir, it is too late to change the menu now. What do we do?)'

We were all nonplussed for a moment, before the charming wife of Sadiq Ali—then the governor of Tamil Nadu—appeared in the doorway.

'What is happening,' she asked in a demanding tone.

The staff and I informed her obediently that the prince and his entourage wanted Indian food for dinner.

'Well,' she said, with considerable aplomb, 'if you want Indian food, give us a bit of time. We'll have to order it from outside.'

A delicious meal was duly ordered and the word that went to His Highness was that I had done everything I could to make the evening a memorable one, at least in the culinary sense of the word! Our working relationship took a distinct turn for the better after that evening. Now, every morning, when I met him outside his bedroom door there would be a bluff joke, 'Good morning, Mr Dulat, I do hope I wasn't snoring *too* much last night!'

The gradual thaw in Charles's behaviour allowed him to become slightly more open about his concerns and apprehensions for the rest of the visit. We were due to visit Calcutta next and Charles was a little anxious about the kind of welcome he would receive from the current communist government. He kept asking me what it would be like to visit the city, clearly nervous about facing any demonstrations and protests. For my part, I didn't see anything that he should worry about and true to my instinct, when we arrived in Calcutta, and were driving through Park Street to Raj Bhavan, we saw huge banners strung up, welcoming Charles to the city.

'Look, Your Highness, what a welcome you're getting!' I told him.

'Oh that,' Charles responded despondently. 'Dulat, you sit in front, wearing your dark glasses. I get the feeling that they're waving at you, not at me!'

I laughed and disclaimed, because the welcome was genuinely a spanking good one. Charles sighed. 'But that's just Lord Swraj Paul. What about the rest?'

But in reality, it *was* a good visit. The Bengalis enjoy their pomp and show as much as anyone. They were, after all, the last of the brown sahibs after the Raj, and no matter where they stood on the political spectrum, the Prince of Wales was still the Prince of Wales. In fact, on the way to the Dunlop factory the cars were besieged by crowds. Charles was delighted, taking it to be a clear sign of his popularity. Yet again, he got swept away by the moment, and he chose this precise instant to roll down his window. Quick as a flash, a hundred hands stretched into the car.

'Sir, put that up immediately,' I exclaimed, alarmed. 'These boys will enter the car in no time!'

Yes, that was a lovely visit, full of fun and excitement. Charles was due to go to Kathmandu after his time in India, and naturally, I was not involved in that leg of his travels. But before he left, the prince gave me a pair of cufflinks, and asked me frankly for my opinion on how the visit had gone.

'I think it was fantastic,' I told him honestly. 'You were worried about Calcutta and look how well that went.'

'It's a tribute to Britain, not to me,' he said modestly.

Charles's security officer John McLean was still in India, having stayed back while the prince went off to Nepal. He and I travelled back to Delhi together. John had a flight back to London soon, but there was something very lonely about the man, which I couldn't quite put my finger on. To this day, I don't know what it was, but whatever it was it prompted me to ask him to come over to my house for a meal before he left.

'Oh surely that's not fair,' John protested. 'You've been away from home for twelve days. I'd feel like an intruder!' Naturally, I refused to listen to a word. I took him home with me for drinks, and then Paran and I took him out for a hot meal at Moti Mahal. When John got back to England, he wrote me a letter of thanks.

'Next time you're in London, come and stay with us at Buckingham Palace!'

Who could've imagined that the young prince would be the oldest to ascend the British throne forty-two years later, as King Charles III!

Margaret Thatcher

Margaret Thatcher came out to India twice and coincidentally I was on duty with her both times—in 1981 and 1983. She was to come again to attend Indira Gandhi's funeral in 1984, but I was then posted in Bhopal. On the occasion of her first visit I asked her security officer, Gordon Cawthorne, whether he might have known Charles's security officer, John McLean.

'Those aren't security officers,' he snapped contemptuously. 'Those are courtiers!'

That first visit was a bit stiff on both sides. It was a much-hyped visit, with the popular media hook being that it was going to be a meeting between two 'iron ladies'. Naturally, each lady was then on her mettle and the visit was not quite as successful as either side would have liked.

Indira Gandhi could be exceedingly charming, but she could also freeze the blood in your veins, as the Prince of Wales had unfortunately found out. There was an incident in Bombay that might give you an insight into how badly it went between the ladies. Prime Minister Thatcher was due to address the Bombay Chamber of Commerce at around two in the afternoon. We were staying at a hotel, and the distance from the Chamber of Commerce meant about a half an hour ride. Indira Gandhi was in town that very same day too, and she, too, was travelling across the city. Now, naturally, all traffic was held up across the city for the Prime Minister. This meant a solid delay for the British Prime Minister. Not one to tolerate lateness of any kind, Thatcher began to get visibly restless after a while of waiting at the hotel.

'What is the problem? Why can't we leave?' she snapped. 'I'm getting late.'

Cawthorne came to ask me what the delay was.

I explained that Prime Minister Gandhi was in town and so the hold-up was temporary but necessary. Ten minutes later, we hadn't moved and Margaret Thatcher was furious.

'So what if the Prime Minister is travelling? Who does this lady think she is?'

'You know,' I told Gordon Cawthorne quietly, 'in our country, no matter who the VIP is, our own Prime Minister gets precedence when it comes to security, so you'll have to bear with us.'

With omens like this, it could hardly be said that the visit would be a success, but thankfully, the second visit went off much better. When I picked Margaret Thatcher up at the airport, I took her straight to the Prime Minister's office, because Indira Gandhi was waiting to meet her. An entire press corps was assembled, waiting to hear what the two Prime Ministers would say. After a pause, Indira Gandhi strode out. 'I want to make it clear,' she told the media, 'this visit has to be a success. I want it to be a success, so please take note of it.' I thought it was exceptional for her to come straight out and say that.

There was a retreat for the leaders attending the Commonwealth Heads of Government Meeting (CHOGM) during this visit, which is when we went to Goa. Like I said, Indira Gandhi knew how to charm, if she wanted to. At the dinner at Fort Aguada, after the guests had arrived, she came down in a lungi and a colourful top.

A Handful of Greats

Everyone was instantly charmed, not to mention disarmed. Goa was a lovely visit, simply because Mrs G was determined to make it so. It was about six months or so after the Irish Republican Army (IRA) had bombed a hotel in Brighton where Prime Minister Thatcher was staying for a party conference. Despite her security concerns and the threat to her from the IRA, she never gave up on peace.

So this visit had accompanying security concerns for the British Prime Minister. In Goa, therefore, all the huts where we were staying (and the hill behind the property) had been secured by the BSF. Just before dinner ended that evening, Cawthorne asked me, 'Are you spending the night with me?'

I was considerably startled. 'The night... with *you*?'

'Yes, yes, I will be spending the night, sitting outside Mrs Thatcher's hut.'

'Whatever for?' I asked, even more mystified.

'You don't know the kind of threat she faces.'

'There's more than enough security here.'

'There may be enough for you guys, but not for my Prime Minister. If you don't want to sit with me, that's fine, but I will sit here.'

'I have no need to sit here,' I said. 'I think the security situation is well taken care of.'

I escorted them all back to their beach huts, of course, but as we reached, Thatcher turned to Cawthorne. 'Gordon, are you serious about spending the night here?'

'Yes, ma'am. Of course, I am.'

'Then,' said the Prime Minister, 'wait a minute. It's cold out here. Let me get you one of Denis's sweaters.'

I thought to myself, *hamaare yahan toh aise koi nahin karega*. (Nothing like this would happen in our set-up.) I was supremely impressed.

Something similar—on a more minor scale—happened at the banquet at Hyderabad House. Here, Queen Elizabeth was also present, having come to India for CHOGM. Understandably, this meant a considerable crush of traffic outside Hyderabad House. The official car had me and the driver in the front seat, with Prime Minister Thatcher and her husband at the back. As the car pulled into traffic, we noticed Gordon Cawthorne jogging alongside. After a point, Thatcher leaned forward. 'Gordon is trotting alongside the car,' she said. 'Is there any way we can accommodate him inside?'

Normally, my answer should have been no. But in this case I said, 'Sure, madam, we'll accommodate him in the car.' I opened my door, but she said quickly, 'No, no, you can't be uncomfortable. He'll sit with us at the back.'

I hadn't ever seen anything quite like it. The Prime Minister of Britain was willing to squeeze three into a back seat, rather than inconveniencing her security officer.

Maanani padti hai, goron mein bhi kuch khoobiyan hain! (One has to admit, there is something about the British.)

Lee Kuan Yew

It is hard—even now—to figure out much about Lee Kuan Yew the man. That alone should tell you what an enigma he was. That he commanded power, I have no doubt. It was in the way he held himself, in the way he really didn't even need to issue an instruction or a command. He just expected things to be done—and somehow or other, they were. His security entourage was more like family, comprising three young boys in their mid-twenties who clearly both adored and feared him. I could see straightaway that for them he was not just akin to God, but he was God himself.

For myself, I was hard put to recognize just what was so charismatic about Lee Kuan Yew, but eventually I realized that these three boys, at least, were treated like family by Lee's wife! These boys were in total awe of Lee, who never exchanged more than the necessary word with them. But his wife, Choo, treated them like family and one could gauge that Lee was totally dependent on his wife. While he ran the country, Choo looked after the home, apart from being a top lawyer of Singapore. When she passed away, the inspiration and joy went out of Lee's life.

His visit to India during CHOGM was a brief one, but it was not without its own quirks. On the day he arrived, for instance, there was to be a cultural show (at around six in the evening, if I'm not mistaken), followed by a banquet at Hyderabad House.

That evening, all was in readiness, until one of Lee's boys came to me. 'Our Prime Minister will not be attending.'

I was aghast. 'How can he not come? Our own Prime Minister is coming!' I went off to find him to try to explain matters, but he was quite matter of fact.

'I've excused myself from this evening and I've spoken to your Prime Minister too.'

Now, why had he excused himself?

Because the timing of the cultural show coincided with Lee Kuan Yew's schedule, which stated that at six in the evening he would be jogging. The man was an absolute health fiend. You couldn't smoke in his presence and if he had anything remotely to do with exercising on his schedule, then he wouldn't and couldn't be budged from it. Accepting this (I couldn't do much else!) as an idiosyncrasy that I would have to live with during Lee Kuan Yew's time in India, I began to wonder where he was thinking of jogging. The Singapore delegation was staying at the Ashoka Hotel and there wasn't exactly room to jog around the premises! But one of his boys kindly explained matters to me. The founding father of Singapore would be jogging around behind the tennis courts.

'One of us is going to jog with him,' the boys announced. 'Would you like to jog too?'

I refused hastily and was rather relieved when Lee Kuan Yew decided to go off to Kathmandu for a day while he was here. At least it meant freedom from watching the Singaporean leader jogging or exercising!

In the evening, I went to the airport to pick him up, rejoicing in the fact that it had rained quite heavily during the day. It would be too late and the ground would be too slippery for him to do anything tonight.

Alas, I was still naïve!

When Lee Kuan Yew landed, he asked, 'I hear it's rained heavily?'

'Yes sir.'

'So you advise against jogging?'

'Well, sir.' I was beginning to see where this was going, but I held my ground feebly. 'The ground *would* be quite slippery.'

'Right.' He mused for a moment, then he brightened. 'Well, then, I think I'll swim instead!'

And so it was that instead of an early night, which I had been hoping fervently for, I ended up sitting in a deckchair by the pool of the Ashoka Hotel, waiting patiently while the Prime Minister of Singapore completed twenty laps.

The retreat during this particular official trip was at the Rashtrapati Bhavan, over lunch. Usually, we go out of Delhi—as we did during Prime Minister Thatcher's visit—but I forget what caused us to stay in the capital during Lee Kuan Yew's trip. It being a retreat, I thought the lunch would continue until about three or four in the afternoon, but I was a little taken aback by the lack of arrangements made for the attendant security contingent.

I asked the secretary to the President, '*Itne saare security log hain, inke khane ka kya bandobast hai?* (There are so many security people. Is there any arrangement for their food?)'

'*Kuch nahin*,' was the brisk response. 'They have to fend for themselves.'

Fend for ourselves we did, but in the bargain the lunch at the Rashtrapati Bhavan ended so much earlier than we had expected that we missed the official convoy. So while we got back at the Rashtrapati Bhavan dead on time, on arrival, we discovered that Lee Kuan Yew had already left the Rashtrapati Bhavan. The boys were frantic with fear, and quite rightly so, because they felt they should have been on duty.

They begged me to intervene in the matter. 'This isn't something we'll be forgiven for.' The sheer panic made me realize just how respected and feared Lee Kuan Yew was in Singapore. I went off to Lee Kuan Yew and apologized honestly for our mistake.

'It's all right,' he said quietly, but I could see that it wasn't all right at all.

Our interactions were brief, not to mention eccentric in many ways, but once you met Lee Kuan Yew, you couldn't ever forget him! Lee was certainly one of those leaders who shaped history. What I could figure out during the trip was his adroitness and close rapport with President Jayawardene, whom he repeatedly spoke highly of.

As Lee said: 'If you are just realistic, you become pedestrian, plebeian, you will fail. Therefore, you must be able to soar above the reality and say, "this is also possible".' That is how during his rule, Singapore became one of the most prosperous countries.

Rajesh Pilot

My friendship with Rajesh was one I hold dear to this day.

The first time I met him was at a meeting he had convened in Srinagar, with the chief minister, to discuss Kashmir. But our real friendship began a few years later, in the summer of 1988, soon after I was posted to Srinagar. My daughter had finished Class X while we were still in Bhopal, and we were having some difficulties in finding a good school for her in Srinagar. That problem resolved itself when we got her admission in Sanawar, Paran's old school, in the same year when Omar Abdullah was the head boy.

Founder's Day was in October, and as it neared, Farooq Abdullah called me. 'Aren't you going to your daughter's school for Founder's Day?' he asked. I laughed. 'Sir, to do that, I have to take leave!' In his inimitable way, Farooq said, '*Chodo na, mere saath aao.* (Let it be. Come with me.) Tell Delhi that you're watching the chief minister. Come with me in my chopper.'

That, of course, wasn't something I could do, but as it turned out, the guest of honour at Sanawar that year was Rajesh Pilot. He returned to Srinagar with all of us, and Paran and I were sitting in the same row as he was. Rajesh recognized me in that style so typical of him.

'What are you doing here,' he asked, before engaging both of us in courteous conversation. My initial impressions of him were of a fresh young man, extremely polite and with an open manner, free from any pretences. I liked him instantly and as fate would have it, I was to continue my friendship with him. That year, 1988, was when militancy broke out in Kashmir, beginning the modern troubles for the state. Rajesh was Rajiv's man on the subject of Kashmir, and he often returned to the Valley to meet the citizens of Kashmir, Farooq and other political players in the state. He also called me every time he came to the state. This meant that we were meeting quite regularly, because as I have often said, things were pretty bad in Kashmir between 1988 and 1989.

When I returned to Delhi in 1990, Rajesh was then minister for information and broadcasting. His interest in Kashmir continued, though (not surprisingly, I think, because Kashmir is not a state that you can take your eyes off once you start getting interested). By 1991, he was meeting the Jammu Kashmir Liberation Front (JKLF) boys quite regularly as well. To his house in Delhi I was often invited to chat with him. He stood on no ceremony with me or anyone else. The telephone would ring and it would be Rajesh's cheerful voice down the line: '*007, kya kar rahe ho? Aa jao, chai peetey hain!* (007, what are you doing? Come, let's have tea!)'

I would go to his house, and find Ashok Jaitly, Wajahat Habibullah and Hindal Tyabji all waiting to talk about the same thing: Kashmir. Rajesh's main concern was always the same: *What should we do about Kashmir?* Our opinion was unanimous: *You're a minister. If you meet with these boys, it's a big deal for Delhi and Kashmir. So talk to them. Keep the dialogue open.*

Rajesh's interest in Kashmir was a strong bond of commonality between us. Even when he became minister of state for home affairs and when he had plenty of other things on his radar, he continued working in Kashmir's best interests, personally and politically. His friendship with Farooq, for example, continued to deepen over the months. They got along very well, and were great buddies. But with Rajesh's rise through the rungs of political power in Delhi, our friendship grew too. I was gaining some importance in Kashmir at the time, and since Rajesh was dealing with home affairs, it gave him more official reasons to call me regularly.

By this time, he had shed any inhibitions that he might have had when it came to talking to me frankly about many subjects. For instance, he had rather pithy observations to make about Narasimha Rao. 'Our Prime Minister,' he used to say musingly, 'is very smart...' Nor was he a great fan of S.B. Chavan. 'You know what the Prime Minister tells me when I go to see him? He calls me *Home Minister*, but when I get back to office, the home minister, no fan of mine, actually speaks a totally different language with me!'

It was a remark typical of Rajesh, who (as much as he respected Sonia Gandhi) loved to challenge entrenched authority. Once out of frustration, he said to me, '*Yehi hamesha chalayenge?* (Will they rule forever?)'

I would laugh, '*Sir, jab tak Madam hain, unki hi chalegi.* (Sir, as long as Madam is around, hers will be the last word.)'

This entrenched authority was often what both of us came up against in our careers. Many years later, after I had joined the R&AW, I got a call from Rajesh, again asking me to come by for a cup of tea.

'Tell me about the Naxalite problem,' he demanded.

Naxalism isn't my specialty but I told him what I knew. It excited his interest enough for him to insist that I accompany him to meet with Sonia Gandhi to tell her what I had told him.

'Sir, normally, I would have had no hesitation in accompanying you,' I said. 'But I've just joined the R&AW, and this may not go down too well. So please excuse me.'

Going back to the late 1980s, these were also days of growing militancy and unrest in Punjab, and Rajesh was bothered by this as well. Between Kashmir and Punjab, it was a bit of a full plate for him. It didn't help that General Krishna Rao (Retd) was governor in Kashmir in those days, and he disliked Rajesh, considering him to be a meddling youngster. Not, of course, that that deterred Rajesh—yet another quality I really liked about him. But sometimes, even his optimism dumbfounded me. One day, for instance, Rajesh suggested to me: '*Kashmir ka masla theek nahin ho raha. Gill ko bhejte hain Kashmir.* (Kashmir is not settling down. Let's send Gill to Kashmir.)'

Now, I had—and still do—great regard for the great K.P.S. Gill. He was capable of great strength and strategic foresight, but I really didn't think he would be ideal for Kashmir. So naturally, I was somewhat taken aback. 'Sir,' I said, 'as... what?'

Rajesh explained that he had offered to send K.P.S. Gill as governor to Kashmir to try and solve the problem. Gill sahib had refused the offer, but had qualified it by saying that he should be sent as DG.

'What do you think?' Rajesh inquired.

'Sir, I have the highest regard for Gill sahib, but there is a lot of difference between Kashmir and Punjab. Kashmir requires more tactful handling.'

In the event, of course, Krishna Rao stepped in and sabotaged Rajesh's plans by immediately appointing M.N. Sabharwal as DG in Kashmir.

After I left service, Rajesh and I continued to be friends. Our family was always treated like one of their own by the entire Pilot family, from Rajesh to his wife, Rama, and his daughter, Sarika. Paran and I were always invited—he would insist—to his birthday parties. It was always the kind of event that you simply could not and did not miss. But I noticed always that whenever we went for these informal, happy occasions, there were no politicians present. Rajesh was never a pretentious man, nor did he enjoy always networking with politicians. At his birthdays, for instance, his real and dear friends were present.

When Rajesh's daughter got married, Paran and I were invited for both the cocktail and the wedding itself. We went for the first event, and there was a small crowd, all drinking and dancing merrily. The wedding was a couple of days later and as expected, there was a larger crowd in attendance, but even here, I didn't see those whom I was expecting to see. The reception was surprisingly devoid of politicians. When I asked Rajesh why Madam was not there, he said this was his daughter's wedding and politicians were best kept out of it.

I lost a dear friend when Rajesh died. I heard the news of his tragic passing in 2000, when I was chief of the R&AW. We were on our way back from China, and had decided to spend a night in Bangkok on the way. It was our man in Bangkok who told me the news. As soon as I returned I went straight to Rajesh's house to condole, and found young Sachin—freshly returned from Wharton—there.

'*Politics kab join karoge?* (When are you joining politics,)' I asked him, in the course of the inevitable small talk that one has to do on such occasions.

'Uncle,' Sachin replied, 'never. I never want to get into politics.'

'It's in your genes,' I remember telling him. 'How can you not?'

How could he not, indeed.

Life and fate have a funny way of intertwining. Today, Sachin is in active politics, and Rajesh is no longer with us.

Madhavrao Scindia

My friendship with Madhavrao Scindia was a coincidence. A common friend, Jasbir Singh Tiwana, whom I knew from Chandigarh and who had been a classmate of Madhavrao in Scindia School, suggested that I meet the 'Maharaj' once I got to Bhopal. A couple of months later, Madhavrao himself got in touch. He was visiting Bhopal, he said, and would like to meet me. When I went to meet him, he said jokingly, 'I am told you are one of us!' meaning, I presumed, a public school boy. Then onwards, we were good friends. Madhavrao never stood on any kind of ceremony. It was a paradox of his character that he always treated you as an equal and a friend, yet at the same time, you never forgot nor did he let you forget, that he was 'Maharaj'.

But for all that he was at heart a decent, courteous man, whom India lost far too soon.

Soon after our meeting in Bhopal, I was to meet Madhavrao in Bhilai where he accompanied Rajiv Gandhi whilst he was still general secretary of the Congress, but to whom he appeared to be particularly close. Madhavrao's star then was clearly in the ascendant, and as fate would have it, he was to become the minister for railways with Rajiv Gandhi in 1984.

We were to meet frequently after that. I never missed an opportunity because unlike most politicians, there was a lovable

Maharaja Ranbir Singh of Jind, my wife's grandfather. The photo was interestingly discovered at the Royal Bombay Yacht Club.

My father as a student in England in the 1920s.

My older brother with father on his return from England in 1935 at the age of seven, when Barnaby became Jagjit Singh.

My father with my grandfather, Sardar Bahadur Gurdial Singh Dulat, in the 1930s.

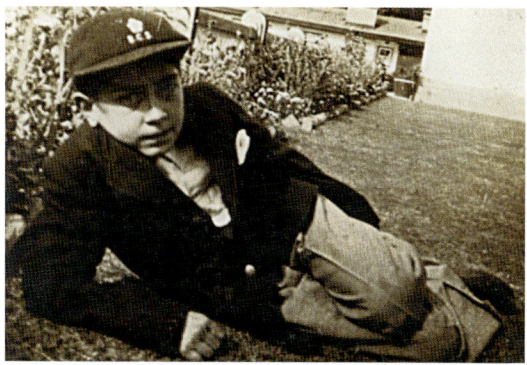

The year I joined school at the age of ten.

The famous Uncle Shubh, national tennis champion who represented India at Wimbledon and the Davis Cup, broadcasting on BBC during a Davis Cup tie in London in 1949.

My parents in Nabha soon after their wedding in 1939.

My in-laws, Balbir Grewal and Princess Ruby Rajbir Kaur, in the early 1950s.

My father and mother with Dr Rajendra Prasad at the Roshanara Club in 1950.

A rare photograph of mine in my father's arms in Dharamsala in 1945.

And my son, Arjun, in mine in Bhopal in 1971.

With Paran in Chandigarh in 1962, when love began to bloom.

With my sister, Poma.

As an IPS probationer under training at Mount Abu, 1966.

With close friends in the coffee shop outside the Lal Bahadur Shastri National Academy of Administration in 1965, all but one of whom have passed away. (Left to right) Ashok Sharan, myself, Swatantra Kumar Alok, Trinath Mishra, Arun Babbar, Satish Mishra (with back to camera).

The whole team in Bhopal with our skipper, Prakash Shah of the Foreign Service, on the extreme right and Daljeet Saxena with his hand on his hat in front of me. Prakash represented Bombay University under Ajit Wadekar and Daljeet played for Delhi as well as North Zone.

Waiting to bat for the Central Secretariat cricket team in the All India Civil Services tournament in Bhopal, 1971.

Early days in Kathmandu, when the kids were young, in 1977.

Escorting the Prince of Wales (now King Charles) to meet Mother Teresa in Kolkata in November 1980.

Paran and I with Doctor Sahib (Farooq Abdullah) at our 25th anniversary, our 50th anniversary, and the 'Last Supper' when he visited us on 19 October 2022. In the last photo are what he described as three of his favourite 'Kashmir hands', (left to right) Mrs and Mr K.M. Singh, Doctor Sahib, O.P. Bhutani, me and Paran.

Being seen off from the IB by my friend Shyamal Dutta in January 1999, and then handing over charge at the R&AW to my successor, Vikram Sood, in December 2000.

With Giani Zail Singh at Arjun's wedding reception in 1994.

M.K. Narayanan (left) with Aftab Ali and O.P. Bhutani at lunch in Gupkar Road, Srinagar, in the summer of 1989.

Ajit Doval (right) with Subhash Tandan and I at lunch in our home in New Delhi in the early 2000s.

Madhavrao Scindia (left) with Arjun and I at Priya's wedding in 1998.

The legendary Ashwini Kumar at our 50th wedding anniversary.

With Rajesh Pilot at Arjun's wedding reception in 1994.

Being toasted by my counterpart, I.V. Trubnikov, on my arrival in Moscow in the winter of 1999.

In Beijing, whilst accompanying Brajesh Mishra on his visit in the winter of 2000.

With CIA chief George Tenet and his wife, Stephanie, at the Taj Mahal in Agra, in May 2000.

Welcoming Prime Minister Atal Bihari Vajpayee in the R&AW in 2000.

Vajpayee with the moderate Hurriyat leadership in 2004. This photo is also on the cover of my book, *Kashmir: The Vajpayee Years*.

With former king of Bhutan, Jigme Singye Wangchuk, in 1999.

A letter from the king after I demitted office, showing Bhutan's close links with the R&AW.

The most unforgettable character in Kashmir, Agha Ashraf Ali, father of the celebrated Kashmiri-American poet Agha Shahid Ali, at his library in his residence, Sufiya Nishan, in 2014.

informality about Madhavrao even though the Scindias were private people. Maharaj did introduce me to his beautiful, charming daughter, Chitrangada, married to Dr Karan Singh's older son, Vikramaditya, whom we got to know fairly well. Chitra is almost a replica of her father.

I made it a point to visit Madhavrao whenever he was in Delhi. Once on a visit to Srinagar, he called me and we spent a pleasant afternoon together. Meanwhile, he had defeated Atal Bihari Vajpayee in Gwalior in the 1984 parliamentary elections, in the course of which I visited Gwalior twice to meet Maharaj and wish him the best, still not believing that Atalji could be defeated. The Congress then won all forty seats in Madhya Pradesh, a big feather in Arjun Singh's cap.

Madhavrao was not a dull, hypocritical politician but a man of many parts. Socially, he was to be found at all the right places with a cigar and a glass of cognac, always in attractive company. Cricket was a common passion we both had, and also played against each other at least twice in the annual MPs versus Civil Servants match at the Feroz Shah Kotla grounds. Madhavrao's batting was sedate but he always played with a straight bat, in keeping with his character, which got him to be chairman of the Board of Control for Cricket in India (BCCI). Another friend I made at this annual fixture was Sheila Dikshit's colourful husband, fondly referred to as Dickie ever since his student days at Hindu College, who was more of a bowler but the two of us had great fun batting together. Sadly he too was to die young, of a heart attack on the overnight Lucknow Mail to Delhi.

When Priya, our daughter, was getting married, Madhavrao arrived early, but he waited politely for the baraat for over an hour, before quietly leaving.

Tragically for India, and the Congress party, both Rajesh and Madhavrao met with untimely deaths in different accidents. For me, they were both prime ministers in the making, though retrospectively,

Maharaj may have pipped Rajesh to the post because of his greater proximity to the Gandhi family. Ironical, isn't it, that Jyotiraditya should have left Rahul and the Congress for the BJP. Who knows where Sachin will end up.

Of this, I have no doubt: both men had the quality and the substance, and India would have been the richer with their continued existence in life and politics.

These are little vignettes, then, of some of the people I have had the privilege of interacting and working with over the course of my career. With some, I have had the fortune of claiming friendship. With all of them, there are memories which I can never forget.

5
Travels with a President

I SOMETIMES WONDER WHAT WOULD HAVE HAPPENED IF I HADN'T missed the Lucknow Mail.

It was 1982, a couple of years after I had returned from Nepal. With my initial stint in counter-intelligence over, the Bureau was now asking me to go to Lucknow, where there was an urgent requirement for an intelligence officer. My tickets were booked on the Lucknow Mail for the night of 31 July 1982.

But I never caught that train.

On the morning of 31 July, I was at the branch office in R.K. Puram to say goodbye to my colleagues and to sign off from the office when I received word that my father had collapsed. By the time I got home, he was gone. The next couple of weeks were a blur, but the Bureau was very kind to me in my time of grief. Some days later, I received a polite call, asking if I had had time to give any thought to Lucknow. It was out of the question. My mother was all alone for the first time in her life. She wasn't doing so well in the aftermath of my father's passing, and I couldn't think of leaving her alone just then. So, I requested and took a two-week-long leave.

It was an odd feeling to return to work at the end of that time off, because even though I was posted back to counter-intelligence, I knew instinctively that I was professionally at some kind of a loose end. Little did I know that I would be—quite literally—saved by the bell. Yet another telephone call, from my boss at the Bureau. Someone (and that is usually a someone who is a Deputy Inspector General [DIG], which I was then) was needed to travel abroad with Giani Zail Singh. I had caught his eye, precisely because I was at a loose end, and because I had the added advantage of speaking fluent Punjabi.

In the early 1980s, Giani Zail Singh was very much in the news. Born Jarnail Singh on 5 May 1916, to a simple family in Sandhwan in the princely state of Faridkot, he grew up trained in the ways of religion and spirituality, well versed in everything from the Sikh holy scriptures to Hindu mythology. It was, in fact, after completing a course at the Shahid Sikh Missionary College in Amritsar that the young man earned himself the title of 'Giani', conferred upon individuals proficient in religious studies. But those were the days of the freedom movement, defined by intense ideological and political churn. Revolution was in the air when Giani was growing up. The execution of Bhagat Singh propelled him into politics, where he lost no time in making some fairly revolutionary moves himself. For instance, he established a unit of the Indian National Congress in Faridkot in 1938, an act which landed him promptly behind bars for five years.

During his time in prison, Giani Jarnail Singh changed his name to 'Zail Singh'. As soon as he was released from jail, he set up the Praja Mandal in Faridkot, which was a staunch ally of the Congress. The 1950s saw Giani's real rise in politics, as he became a central player in the PEPSU government. His work brought him to the attention of Jawaharlal Nehru, who got him elected to the Rajya Sabha. Giani's loyalty to the Nehru–Gandhi family was legendary. He emulated Nehru's mannerism of wearing a rose in the buttonhole of his *achkan*, and there was always a supply of fresh roses in stock in the fridge at the Rashtrapati Bhavan when he became President.

The faithfulness continued after Nehru, to his daughter, Indira. Giani never failed to support her, even when Indira Gandhi was voted out of power after the Emergency in 1977. Later, when she returned to power, Indira Gandhi acknowledged Giani's loyalty to her, by naming him minister of home affairs, a post which he held until 1982, when he became the Congress (I) party's presidential candidate.

Giani won that election by an overwhelming margin, though not without his share of criticism. Those were the days when Punjab was facing increasing unrest. The rumour was that Prime Minister Gandhi had named Giani as President only to mollify the Sikh extremists in Punjab. Giani staunchly and publicly refuted those rumours. Indeed, he is reported to have said: 'If my leader had said that I should pick up a broom and be a sweeper, I would have done it. She chose me to be President.'[1]

Here, I think it is Tarlochan Singh who was actually Giani's saviour in many respects. I have never seen a better press secretary, more capable of handling even the worst of criticisms. For instance, when Indira Gandhi informed Giani that he would be taking over as President of India, she threw a dinner for him at Hyderabad House. Tarlochan Singh knew perfectly well what the media would

---

1 Quoted from Priyanka Sood and Gunjeet K. Sra, '10 Stories that changed in our lifetime', *India Today*, 19 December 2008. Available at: https://www.indiatoday.in/magazine/nation/story/20081229-10-stories-that-changed-in-our-lifetime-738583-2008-12-19. Also see Aastha Singh, 'Giani Zail Singh: The Indira Gandhi loyalist who remains India's only Sikh President', The Print, 25 December 2018. Available at: https://theprint.in/theprint-profile/giani-zail-singh-the-indira-gandhi-loyalist-who-remains-indias-only-sikh-president/168649/#google_vignette

say about this. Since he was accompanying Giani that evening, he suggested that they use the ten minutes they had to go and quickly drop in on Khushwant Singh, that famous journalist, writer and Rajya Sabha member. A visit to the eminent journalist would serve the President's long-term interest. They went off to Sujan Singh Park, where Khushwant lived, and needless to say, Khushwant was delighted to see the first Sikh President of India at his house. There was a short interlude of conversation, which charmed Khushwant so much that he was always a Giani bhakt of sorts.

Tarlochan was also the man who suggested that the Indian diplomat and hugely influential journalist Prem Bhatia accompany Giani on his world tour. Prem had done this before in his lifetime, with Jawaharlal Nehru, and during Giani's tour he was editor of *The Tribune*. To my mind, these were great examples of how well Tarlochan could use public relations to smooth over awkward situations.

But I digress, as usual.

Shortly after his appointment as President, Giani developed a rather severe heart problem. His cardiologist advised him to travel to Houston, in the United States, for treatment. Now I had met Giani before, but that was under very different circumstances and that had been about a decade ago. In itself, that's a lovely little anecdote which I must tell you.

It all began with—yes, you guessed it—a telephone call.

'The chief minister wants to meet you.'

I was a little startled by the request at first, but in all honesty, I thought Giani Zail Singh's office had mistaken me for my boss, Subhash Tandan. Tandan sahib later became commissioner of police and was a gem of a human being, but it was part of his job profile to liaise with chief ministers, such as Giani. So, I politely told the voice at the other end of the line that Tandan sahib was out of the country on business. He would be back the next week.

Travels with a President

'*Nahin, nahin,*' I was told. '*Woh abhi milna chahte hain, aur aapse hi milna chahte hain* (No, no. He wants to meet now, and he wants to meet you.)'

I was by now considerably surprised, but one could hardly refuse the chief minister. A day or two later, I was summoned to the Union Territory Guest House at the extremely odd hour of one o'clock in the afternoon. I arrived at the appointed hour and a few minutes later, Giani entered the room, bearing his tiffin box.

'*Aao*,' he said hospitably, '*mere naal roti khao.* (Come, join me for lunch.)'

So, the two of us had lunch companionably, chatting away in fluent Punjabi, the language that Giani was always most comfortable in. But I had no idea where this meandering conversation was going until Giani suddenly came to the point. 'What is your news about what is happening within the Congress party?'

Now, to put this story in a little context, this was the early 1970s in Chandigarh, a period in which dissension was rife within the Congress party in Punjab as India approached—very slowly—the grim days of the Emergency. Giani's natural concern then was not the dissension within the state Congress itself, which he was confident of managing, but rather the possibility that it might be reported to Delhi. If that happened, he could be hauled up by the Prime Minister in Delhi and be asked to explain what was happening.

I knew all of these dynamics and I knew who was creating mischief. '*Sir, yeh Mahinder Singh Gill jo hain*—he is the one who talks against you. That's where the hub of dissidence lies,' I said. In a manner that I was to learn was typical of Giani, he immediately challenged me on my opinion of someone he considered a true friend.

'How can this be?' he demanded. 'He's my dearest friend, like my brother. If I have to die at his hands, then I deserve to die.'

This rather dramatic conversation was the last I had with Chief Minister Giani Zail Singh.

The Emergency followed shortly thereafter. As a young officer in the Bureau, I recall that at the time one tended to side with the government. That's what we were trained for. Perhaps, there was no other option—because we didn't know that the Vajpayees, Advanis and George Fernandeses of our time were being sent to jail. At least, there was no word of it on the quiet streets of Chandigarh. In an earlier chapter in this book I've talked about being transferred at about this time, in 1976, to Kathmandu. My transfer ensured that I didn't cross paths with either Giani or the repressive impact of the Emergency, but when I returned to Delhi, I found a different Indira Gandhi. She was surrounded by a sycophantic coterie, who was giving her all the wrong kinds of advice. That's what led to tragedy after tragedy.

For his part, Giani was always devoted to Indira Gandhi, and it was only the events of 1984 that deeply hurt him and his identity as a Sikh. Today, he's been sidelined in public and popular memory. It's a pity we don't pay much attention to a man who was essentially a kind, warm and quirky human being. He was never a difficult man to approach, and when I began working with him in 1982, we lost little time in establishing a very good relationship. The President had his own sense of fun.

'You seem to have rubbed Giani the wrong way,' I.S. Bindra told me. Bindra was joint secretary in the home ministry whom I had known earlier during his days as commissioner, Patiala, while I was in Chandigarh. He was to become a good friend later.

I was mystified. 'What do you mean?'

'He keeps insisting that you're an Akali!'

I have to tell you it took me a while to get over that one!

The President could also be slyly provocative. On many of our earlier trips he thought nothing of introducing me as being from the IB—'*Isse bachke rehna* (Beware of him),' he would say humorously. 'He is from the IB!'—until I pleaded with him to stop. Watching

Giani carry out his duties as President was a great learning experience for me. The President was a kindly, simple soul, possessed of great charm and equal amounts of candour. Working with him was also not without its occasional awkward moments. The only problem, for instance, with an otherwise excellent orator was that he spoke only in Punjabi.

There was a bit of an embarrassing moment in Athens, Greece. We were trying to find a young interpreter who could work with both Greek and Punjabi. It wasn't easy, but we finally managed to find a young girl, fresh out of university, who was Punjabi and could speak Greek. She was given a copy of the President's prepared remarks for the evening. Now, Giani liked to speak extempore. He rarely, if ever, consulted his notes. However, nobody thought of telling this young girl to be prepared for this eventuality. So once his speech started, this girl—who had no idea of the presidential idiosyncrasies—was completely unaware that Giani had deviated from the prepared speech. She was in deep trouble about five minutes into the speech. Ultimately, Giani snatched the paper from her hands. 'Madam,' he snapped, '*aise nahin chalega. Aapko Punjabi nahin aati.* (This won't do; you don't know Punjabi.)' To his mind, if you were not familiar with the idioms of his language, then why were you there in the first place? It was not, of course, the girl's fault, and I felt sorry for her.

Translators are always difficult to come by. Tarlochan Singh told me later that Giani's tendency to speak extempore was a trait that kept everyone around him on their toes. The President liked to speak without preparation, preferring it to any kind of scripted speech, because he was a naturally good orator. Singh remembered that in a conversation with the Sultan of Bahrain, the Sultan referred to him as 'Emir ul-Hind', to which Giani responded with *ayaats* of the Quran. He quoted quite a few, startling the Sultan into whispering to his interpreter, 'Is the Emir ul-Hind a Muslim?'

Giani's ability, despite his simple exterior, to win the day with his undoubted charm was a profoundly beneficial trait. The President was open and warm and extremely hospitable. In 1986, Subhas Chandra Bose's daughter, Anita Pfaff, was staying with Giani at the Rashtrapati Bhavan. He brought her with him for the Republic Day parade, much to the astonishment of the spectators. For Giani, this was hospitality, and a gesture of warmth.

At every official reception, he always stressed on the fact that India stood ready to be friends with every country he visited. The gist of it would be: '*Ham aapke desh aaye hain, aapka dil jeetne.* (We have come to your country and the sole purpose of our visit is to win your hearts.)' It was his trademark line, and he would repeat this in country after country. He was a man of deep faith, and everywhere we went, he would always inquire where the nearest gurdwara was. If there was none to be found, he would encourage the local Sikh community to set up one, something he did in Bahrain as well.

Like Giani, his family was equally simple—warm, kind folk with no airs and graces about who they were. The President's elder brother, for instance, was coming along with us to Houston, and there was not one moment where I could say that he considered himself to be 'The President's Brother'. He was a simple man, from their native village in Punjab. He never pretended to be anything other than what he was—a man from the *pind*, always dressed in a lungi, which in Punjab we call *tehmat*. Everybody soon recognized Sardar Jagir Singh from a mile away because he was so conspicuous. When all is said and done, he just wanted to be there to look after his brother. I deeply appreciated the sentiment, for that simplicity of heart is something I respect.

There was another streak to Giani's personality: one of almost uncomfortable candour. In November 1986, we were visiting Poland. In Warsaw, we had found a Sikh interpreter to help Giani with his speeches and conversations, but Giani was never fond of being told what to say and how to say it. One evening, we were walking down the cobbled streets of the city: the President, someone from the host country, an interpreter from the embassy, and I was a step behind. When he was in the mood, Giani could be quite provocative. We were, at the time, passing a church, and the President joked with the local guy, 'How do you people say that you don't believe in God? Isn't that a church in front of us? There are people coming out of there. They don't believe in God?'

The man looked embarrassed.

The Sikh interpreter tried to intervene but only got as far as 'Please, sir', when the President brushed him aside.

This question may have seemed embarrassing to everyone else, but it didn't deter Giani from demanding answers from state leaders across the world. It was curious that it was always the same question. Perhaps the President was looking for different answers! In 1986, when the President of the Soviet Union, Mikhail Gorbachev, visited India, Giani asked him the same question as well: 'How do you say you people don't believe in God? That's why you're in the mess that you are!'

With Giani's trip to Houston being confirmed, I travelled out to the United States for a recce. The official entourage would be quite small, since this was a private visit. All told, there was the private secretary to the President, a very nice fellow by the name of A.C. Bandyopadhyay; I.S. Bindra, whom Giani had brought with him to the Rashtrapati Bhavan; a couple of ADCs to the President and me. Giani's elder brother, his two daughters and one son-in-law made up the rest of this group that travelled overseas to Houston. The plan was really quite simple: to admit Giani into hospital and let the capable doctors there take care of him.

But the journey to the United States turned out to be a lot more fraught than I expected. Giani had stopped overnight in Geneva, in order to break what was undoubtedly a long, hard journey. I had reached Geneva ahead of the presidential entourage and was awaiting Giani's arrival. Long after we had retired for the night, I was woken by a sudden commotion outside my room. There was shouting in the corridor and footsteps were scurrying past my room. Alarmed, I jumped out of bed and went to see what was happening. As I came out into the corridor, I bumped into Bindra.

'*Ki ho gaya?* (What's happened?)' I asked.

'Gianiji's not feeling well,' Bindra replied nonchalantly. 'It's probably just acidity or nausea.'

Relieved, I went back to my room, but some instinct kept nagging at me. Something was not quite right. Acting on my hunch, I went to see one of the three senior cardiologists who were travelling with Giani, a man by the name of Dr P.N. Chuttani.

'Sir,' I said bluntly, 'I need to know what's going on. I don't buy these rumours that the President had acidity at five in the morning, and that you can't sort out something as simple as acidity.'

'It's nothing to worry about,' Chuttani said dismissively, 'Not to worry.'

This just made me more determined to get to the bottom of things.

'Doctor sahib, I am going to ring up Delhi and say the President is not well unless you tell me honestly what it is.'

Succumbing to my insistence, Dr Chuttani told me that Giani had actually suffered a heart attack. He asked me to go back to my room for the time being and revert after three hours.

By now, it was morning. I went back to my room and called up the then DIB, T.V. Rajeshwar, to let him know that the President of India had suffered a heart attack. He said: 'Okay, thanks a lot for telling me. Who else knows?' I told him that my source had been Dr Chuttani himself.

'Right then, I'm going off to tell Mrs Gandhi, but nobody else must know.'

I agreed but, in my mind, I was wondering whom he thought I could tell. I was hardly going to speed dial my wife with the news! At around 11 a.m., the doctors checked up on Giani and gave him a clean chit of health, stating that he was fit enough to travel. It was probably best that he was getting to Houston, given the circumstances. The stint in hospital, though, turned out to be a long one, given the heart attack. My job—along with that of the ADCs, the secretaries and of Bindra himself—was to keep a vigilant eye on the President.

On the first day alone we visited him about three times; then we made it a routine to visit the hospital room twice a day. I would go in every day at around ten in the morning and spend a couple of hours until lunch. Then I would leave to eat, rest, and return at five in the evening for my next shift. My brief was to ensure that the President faced no administrative glitches or security breaches during his stay in hospital. The rest of the time was my own and given that we were all staying at the Sheraton as part of the presidential entourage, it was, if I say so myself, quite a good holiday!

The cardiologist and surgeon in charge of Giani's case was a man by the name of Denton Cooley, one of the top surgeons of the day in the United States. On the day of the operation, I arrived at the hospital at five in the morning to find a transistor on and prayers being recited. About an hour or so after I reached the hospital, Dr Cooley came to see the President and asked him if he was ready. There used to be a joke that Giani responded with 'I am Zail Singh, not Reddy!'

The Secret Service guys who had been posted outside the room came over to meet me and asked if I'd like to observe the procedure in the operation theatre. I had absolutely no desire to do this and I said as much. So, I was given a space in the viewing gallery instead, from where I had a bird's-eye view of the entire operation. It was fascinating, in a squeamish kind of way. The doctors actually saw open your chest and ribcage, take out your heart and place it on some kind of machine. Then they take out the arteries from the side. That's what Cooley specialized in—the art of the bypass. The whole procedure was conducted with absolute precision, with Cooley coming in only at the end, to sew the heart back together. It was an incredible insight into how far medicine and science were advancing.

Giani was advised two weeks in hospital to rest and recover, and that meant an extended vacation for all of us. We had our different ways of coping with long hours in the hospital looking after the President. The young ADCs, for instance, made friends with the nurses on duty. Sardar Jagir Singh, also present every morning, watched the ADCs sauntering in and giving the nurses a little peck on the cheek as they arrived. The President's brother was most intrigued by this practice, and not a little indignant by the fact that he wasn't getting any pecks. After a day or two of watching the ADCs, he decided to take matters into his own hands, catching hold of one of these nurses and giving her a peck on the cheek himself! That seemed to satisfy Jagir Singh for the time being.

On yet another occasion, the entire family went shopping. I also joined them since I had some free time. In those days, everything in the United States was very cheap. You could get a white shirt for one dollar—which was then equivalent to eight and a half rupees. Jackets were $9.99. So, off I went to the nearby mall. After around half an hour I had finished shopping, but the family were not easily to be found in the large mall. Instead, I found Sardar Jagir Singh on the ground, snoring loudly. He had had enough walking around and had decided, quite simply, to lie down and rest.

The President's brother was the cause for some light-hearted moments during what would otherwise have been a rather tense trip, given Giani's health. One afternoon, Sardar Jagir Singh decided to take a nap. I have a feeling he may have had a bit too much vodka at lunch. Anyway, he ended up locking himself into the room—while being singularly unable to get himself out. After a while, I got a frantic telephone call to let me know that Jagir Singh had locked himself inside. I went down to the room, to find the ADCs outside, shouting, '*Sardar sahib! Taa nu chakko, aa nu chakko*! (Turn the handle up and down!)'

'*Main saare passe chak layi, khulda nahin* (I have turned it in all directions, but it is not opening!)' shouted Jagir Singh frantically. I had to go off to find the Secret Service guys, to let them know that the President's brother had locked himself inside his room. The point of these anecdotes is that it was lovely to see Sardar Jagir Singh not pretending to be anything other than who he was—a simple man from a simple village, who was in America just to be with his brother. He didn't care that his brother was the President of India, nor did he ever make a fuss about himself.

I was present when the doctors made Giani Zail Singh walk the day after his surgery, and I have to say, as I watched him, he had remarkable resilience for his age. He was a little wobbly with the medications, but he pushed through. In the meantime, Dr Chuttani had also undergone a heart bypass at around the same time as the President—a fact that he had omitted to tell us until the very end. His procedure was also successful, but his recovery was slow and somewhat worrying.

As the President recovered his strength, he naturally began to get somewhat restless. The doctors advised him kindly that while it was fine for him to shift back to the hotel and to move around, he wasn't ready to travel long distances just yet. But Giani had a mind of his own. One evening, after he had been shifted back to the hotel, he sent for me. He had decided, he told me, that he wanted to go out for a drive. It was around six in the evening, and the weather was perfectly pleasant. So, I went off to the Secret Service and informed them of the President's wishes. They looked as startled as trained agents can look.

'We don't have the arrangements in place for this,' they protested. 'We can't set this up so fast.'

'Well,' I retorted, 'the President cannot be denied. We don't need to worry. Surprise is the best security. I don't think any harm will come of this.'

In the end, of course, we did take Giani for that ride that he wanted so much.

Once he recovered fully from his surgery, the President began to take us further afield. He was always very nattily dressed. Like our first Prime Minister, Jawaharlal Nehru, Giani wore a boutonniere every day. He also loved his shoes. One day, on a trip into town, Giani decided that he wanted to buy himself a new pair of shoes from Bally's. On the way back, the presidential party began to plan the President's trip home and decided on a stopover in Manhattan.

We stayed at the Waldorf Astoria, one of the city's finest and most upmarket hotels. It was around seven in the evening, a perfect time for a drink. For those of us who had never been to or seen New York City, this was the experience of a lifetime, with brightly lit streets and bars and cabs and limousines lining up to ferry eager customers to their destinations. On this particular evening, about four of us were out and about, exploring the city. Along with us was a doctor—one Dr P.D. Nigam—from the President's entourage, who was thrilled in particular to see me. He announced, '*Dulat sahib, agar aap jaa rahe ho sheher ghoomne toh main bhi chalunga aapke saath.* (If you are going to the city, I too will come along.)'

With us was also one of the presidential ADCs, a young man by the name of Chakravarty, who was clearly looking for fun. He seemed to know that all the fun was on 42nd Street. That was, as he told us, the hub of New York's nightlife. It sounded great. So, we ordered the cabbie to take us there. The driver turned around in his seat, and eyed us doubtfully. 'If I were you,' he said, 'I wouldn't be going there. That's not the sort of place for you guys.' The ADC insisted, so the driver shrugged and drove on. For all his warnings, 42nd Street seemed harmless enough. We had a few drinks at one of the bars that lined the street and watched a few shows. Then, Chakravarty—as I say, he was young and resourceful—found himself a show within the show, and suddenly disappeared. We shrugged metaphorically and carried on having a good time.

After dinner, the doctor turned to me and asked, '*Ab kya karein?* (Now, what shall we do?)'

'*Chalte hain* (Let's go)' I said. 'Chakravarty will find his way home.'

We left the restaurant and found the same cabbie waiting at the curb. He eyed us again. 'Aren't you guys one short?' he asked.

'Yes,' we said, 'one of our guys has decided to stay back.'

Shaking his head speechlessly, the driver took us back to the hotel.

On our way home, in the aircraft, Giani—who was excellent with people, as I discovered—took the time to meet, one on one, with each of the people who had accompanied him, to express his thanks personally.

I had, for one, thoroughly enjoyed myself and I wondered if we would do it again. As it turned out, I accompanied Giani on every trip he took abroad, from 1982 to 1987. Our next trip was in 1983, to Doha. Tarlochan Singh had joined Giani's service by this time, as his press secretary—and what a superb job he did in this avatar! He had known Giani since the days of his chief ministership, and so he knew the President's foibles and quirks well. Tarlochan was also a past master at presenting an absolutely wonderful image of the President to the media.

For the trip to Doha, in the beginning, someone else was appointed to accompany Giani. Annoyed, he insisted that I return to accompany him on this trip. It was embarrassing for me, and more so for my colleague who had been appointed in my stead and whom the President had roundly rejected. As Giani told me: 'They wanted to change you, but security people should never be changed.' It was truly most kind of him, but my career had finally begun taking off. I could no longer travel as a security officer. In May 1984, I was transferred to Bhopal. When he heard the news, I got a telephone call from Hamid Ansari, chief of protocol (and later Vice President of India).

Hamid had also been travelling with the President on every trip, and in the course of time, as we did recces for presidential trips, we had become good friends. '*Partner, tum kahan jaa rahe ho?* (Where are you off to?),' Hamid demanded. 'There's a wonderful trip coming up. How can you miss it?' It really did sound wonderful, to be honest. It would start in Geneva, with a fuel halt in the Bahamas. From there, the President was to travel to Mexico City, thence to one of Mexico's many vibrant seaside resorts, and from there to Buenos Aires and Los Angeles. From Los Angeles, it would be Hawaii and from there to Hong Kong and back to Delhi.

When I heard this itinerary, my automatic reaction was—*Wow, this is really what you mean when you say seeing the world.*

It was too bad, as I told Hamid, that I was being transferred right now, particularly when this trip sounded so enjoyable. But I had reckoned without Giani insisting on my accompanying him. This had never happened: someone who had already been transferred to an outstation would be fished out and put back into service with the President. But Giani insisted that he wanted me to be there. So it was that, yet again, I found myself travelling to recce the places that Giani would visit.

Given the itinerary, Hamid and I crossed the world twice! Nearly every city has its own story. During our recce in Czechoslovakia, Hamid was in charge of the administrative side of things—the room arrangements, telling the hosts about the food habits of the President, that sort of thing. Now, it was winter in Prague. On the recce, Hamid mentioned that while the President certainly did eat chicken, there were vegetarians in the party. The Czechs were aghast. 'Vegetarians? What do you mean by vegetarians? All we have here in winter are potatoes and cabbage!' And that's exactly what was served during the presidential banquet. When the silver covers were lifted off the dishes that evening, the startled vegetarians were confronted by the unappetizing sight of large, steamed cabbages.

In many other ways, too, this was a momentous trip. During the course of 1984, a lot occurred that shook the foundations of Indian society and politics: Indira Gandhi was assassinated, riots broke out against the Sikhs in the north of the country and there was bitter discord between the Prime Minister and the President. Rajiv Gandhi didn't trust Giani or even the redoubtable R.K. Dhawan. While the Prime Minister never pointed an accusing finger at anybody, his reaction seemed to suggest that he held these people responsible for his mother's assassination. Now, of course, there are stories within stories at any point of time, and I could tell those stories forever.

Buenos Aires stands out for me. It was the end of the world if you know what I mean. Look at a map—Buenos Aires is quite literally the end of the world, with perhaps only New Zealand to compare with it. It's the only other city in South America—apart from Mexico—that I have visited, and there was, as I recall, something very English about the city. Maybe that had something to do with decades of British rule in Argentina, not to mention the Falklands War in more contemporary times. Call it what you want, but the Argentines are definitely the best polo players, with the best beef and wheat in the world. We made a memorable detour to visit the small Sikh community that lives in Salta, in the northern town of Jujuy, up in the mountains on the way to the Bolivian border.

How and when did the Sikhs settle there, in the remotest and most underdeveloped part of northern Argentina? History tells me that some of them came to work on the Bolivian railway lines, while others were contracted by local sugar plantation owners. Between 1908 and 1915, countries like the United States and Canada were putting walls of restrictions in place against their native Sikh communities, primarily because of the role that the Sikhs played in the Ghadar conspiracy. Turning to South America, Sikh communities felt that Argentina (which they sometimes called 'Tina') had better economic prospects. It was not always easy to get to, with groups of Sikhs who reached the shores of America being forced to travel further overland through Chile or Brazil.

With ownership of ranches, transport companies and retail shops, the Sikh community in South America is a highly respected one today. In those days, it was excellent optics for a Sikh President of India to visit and interact with this community of Sikhs. There were Sikhs who had settled there, from Moga and Ferozepur, in 1960. Gradually, they had adopted Spanish names, marrying the local women. During the President's visit, they all wore turbans for the first time, and set up a gurdwara which Giani himself inaugurated. The interaction itself was pure fun, since Giani enjoyed meeting people, and because the Sikhs went out of their way to speak in Punjabi with the President. In all, the omens for the visit were good, but sometimes, curveballs enter the picture in the most unexpected of ways.

Let me start at the beginning. As a rule, before the President left his hotel for the day's meetings, I used to check in on him about half an hour prior to departure. One morning, I was still getting ready, when someone burst into the room, exclaiming, '*Koi ADC nahin hai!* (No ADCs are around!)'

'What do you mean *koi ADC nahin hai*,' I demanded, baffled. 'There are two ADCs.'

'*Sir, ek toh off duty hai.* He's not even shaved and he's still in bed. The other one is not to be found.'

Obviously, there had been an error in communication between the ADCs on the question of who was to be on duty that morning. When we boarded the flight an hour later, there was still no ADC. I was caught off guard and ended up playing the role of the ADC myself. But I had reckoned without Hamid Ansari and his great habit of being a stickler for protocol.

No sooner had we boarded the flight than he came over to me. '*Bhai, ADC kahan hain* (Where is the ADC?)'

I pretended to be as surprised as he was at the absence of Chakravarty.

'*Haan, kahan hai?* (Yes, where is he?)' I said, in as astonished a tone as I could manage. '*Hai hi nahin idhar.* (He is not here.)'

'*Kaise nahin hai?* (How is it possible?)'

'I don't know. *Hona toh chahiye, par hai nahin.* (He should have been here, but he is missing.)'

Ansari was livid. 'I want an inquiry into this,' he said irritably, 'When we go back to Delhi, I want a full report on this.'

I was mildly tickled by this command. What inquiry did one hold when the facts were before us? I could tell you straight off whose duty it was, but what purpose did an inquiry serve? Now, it had never happened that the President was left alone to travel without an ADC, but there it was. But that wasn't the only unfortunate incident to have occurred on that trip.

After a smooth flight, we landed duly in Los Angeles. Between the landing of the flight and the banquet hosted that evening by the resident Indian community, there was a gap of only about four hours or so. So, of course, Murphy's Law dictated that it would have to be tonight of all nights that the US customs officials made the most unnecessary fuss, which usually doesn't happen on a presidential flight. Giani, his ADCs and secretaries were allowed to leave, but the rest of us had to keep sitting in the aircraft. Eventually, US immigration officials came around to check our passports and ask endless questions. The whole thing lasted for an hour or so, and by the time we were finally free to go back to the hotel, we were all exhausted. We also had only an hour to shower, shave and get down to the banquet.

We managed to make the deadline, but there were some elderly people in that entourage, such as Prem Bhatia, then the editor of *The Tribune*, who didn't come down in time. This became a huge embarrassment, because Prem tried to enter the room about fifteen minutes after the President. Now, normally, once the VIP (in this case, Giani) arrives, Secret Service protocol dictates that nobody else will be allowed to enter. So, Giani went up on to the dais, where he was introduced to several people waiting to meet him. Prem Bhatia chose this inauspicious moment to arrive. The Secret Service promptly barred his entry, and refused to let him in. Incensed, he snapped: 'How can I not go in? You don't know who I am! I'm a very senior journalist, part of the President's entourage. You cannot stop me.'

While Prem was arguing with the Secret Service, I was standing on the dais behind Giani sahib. At that moment, an American came up from behind us and stood on the dais. When the Secret Service began their regular frisking of people, a body search of this man revealed—much to our horror—a pistol.

There was instant uproar. I demanded to know how this had been allowed. The Secret Service's explanation was that a lot of people in America carried weapons as long as they held a valid licence. Nobody, they promised me, would be allowed to shoot the President.

'That's all very well,' I retorted, 'but I will have to put this in the official report and say that despite my presence, a pistol was brought on stage next to Giani Zail Singh.'

Now, if it hadn't been for Natwar Singh, I don't know what would have happened as a result of this chaos. But he stepped in gracefully: 'Dulat, I have seen all of this, and I will go and explain to the DIB. This is not your fault at all.' But that left another burning question—how did one deal with the livid Prem Bhatia? He was openly swearing in fluent Punjabi, and by the time we got around to dealing with him, he had already complained of his ill-treatment to Giani, who, in turn, was equally incensed. At that point, the ambassador in the United States was K. Shankar Bajpai, and the consul general was a man by the name of Deb Mukherjee. All of us—Giani, his ADC, Bajpai and myself—were in the lift travelling upwards, post the banquet. The President chose this unfortunate moment to cut loose at Bajpai. 'Mr Ambassador,' he snapped, 'you don't know how to run an embassy.' He was rather rude to poor Bajpai, and I felt quite sorry for the man. But there was nothing that I could do.

Before we left the United States, though, a special lunch had been thrown for the President by Dr Amarjit Singh Marwaha, on his huge ranch which was just outside Los Angeles. He laid it on really thick, with silver cutlery and an appearance (by helicopter) by the Mayor of Los Angeles. This was a fascinating visit, not least because of Marwaha's own personal connections to Kot Kapura, where Giani had been born. Yet another interesting character we met while we were in Los Angeles was Yogi Bhajan. Formerly Harbhajan Singh Puri, a customs inspector at the Delhi airport, he had come to Los Angeles, where he began teaching a new kind of yoga—kundalini yoga—in 1968 under the name of Yogi Bhajan. It was the year after the famous Summer of Love when the youth in the United States rebelled against conservative social norms, out of which the hippie movement was born. The country was on edge. Martin Luther King, Jr, was assassinated that year in Memphis; Robert Kennedy, Jr, was shot at Ambassador Hotel on Wilshire Boulevard and the Vietnam War was all that most people could talk about.

Yogi Bhajan cashed in on this ripe environment, setting up an ashram with its own Golden Temple (recognized by the Akal Takht) in Espanola, New Mexico. From here, he offered a cure for addiction that was a mix of yoga and meditation, which began to attract a wide spectrum of American women. He called it the '3HO' (healthy, happy, holy) way of life. In time, of course, corruption—moral and physical—crept in, and today, Yogi Bhajan stands accused of emotional, sexual and physical abuse.[2] But in the 1970s, he was a revered godman, bringing groups of women to India for cures.

In time, he grew close to Giani as well. The President patronized him quite openly, even going so far as to refuse to resign his post following Operation Blue Star on the advice of the Yogi. Their friendship earned Giani no small amount of criticism, and following his mother's assassination, Rajiv banned the entry of Yogi Bhajan into India. It was an association that had a lot of sticky connotations, particularly in later years, but at the time, I put it down to Giani's belief in matters to do with religion and spirituality.

From the United States, we travelled to Hong Kong. This was one of the longest trips that Giani had undertaken as President of India. Indeed, it was so long that instead of the usual one secretary, the trip was split between two secretaries—Romesh Bhandari and Natwar Singh. Romesh was a hard-working man, who loved life. Whenever we landed in a new country, if he was the secretary travelling with the President, he would tell me, 'The party's in my room.' He was senior to Natwar, though Natwar would eventually leave the IFS to join the Congress. Romesh would go on to become foreign secretary, and then governor in his later years. His specialization in the service

---

[2] See Stacie Stukin, 'Yogi Bhajan Turned an L.A. Yoga Studio into a Juggernaut, and Left Two Generations of Followers Reeling from Alleged Abuse', *L.A. Mag*, 25 July 2020. Available at: https://www.lamag.com/citythinkblog/yogi-bhajan/

was actually the Middle East, and he was popularly known as Sheikh Romesh, because his contacts were so excellent.

Travelling with Romesh was always a pleasure. Our families knew each other well and my father had been a colleague of Romesh's father, Chief Justice Amar Nath Bhandari, in the Punjab High Court. Old man Bhandari's wife, Padma, was quite a lady. She was charming, full of character and gutsy as hell. When our daughter, Priya, was getting married, we had taken a government bungalow for the wedding. Padma Bhandari was one of the first to arrive, driving herself in her own Fiat. She was all of ninety years old at the time, and she loved to drive herself about. I was a huge admirer then and even now the memory of her spunk can make me smile.

On the other hand, Natwar was—and is—a correct, cautious and a very fine man. If there was one thing I did learn from him, it was never to drink on a flight. 'I know you're young and you like your drink,' he once told me, 'but never drink on an international flight. It'll dehydrate you.' I stopped drinking on long flights almost immediately thereafter. Natwar was right—the alcohol drained you of energy and left you feeling heavy-headed and tired, on top of the jet lag.

The destinations the President travelled to sometimes were also equally far apart from one another, prompting all of us to dash off to seek relaxation anywhere we could find it. For instance, once we landed in Hong Kong from Honolulu on the 1984 trip, we were all so exhausted that the idea of a nice massage seemed heavenly. I asked the front desk at the hotel if there was a massage parlour nearby and was told that there was, in fact, one right around the corner. I would have to be quick though, they said, because we were fast approaching closing time. I lost no time in rushing off only to find that N.K.P. Salve, the minister-in-waiting and a fun guy himself, had got there before me!

The year was 1984, and these were the days right before Operation Blue Star. There was unrest among the Sikh community that lived in Hong Kong, and there was a distinct threat to the President of India's life. As a result, we were on the alert for any signs, or instincts of danger. But I found the time to take the President for a drive before the evening's schedule began. Everyone else was out, having saved up to shop as much as they could, and they would all only return much later. So, I went up to the President's room by myself.

'What are you doing here,' he said, surprised.

'Would you like to go for a drive?' I asked.

'But there's nobody here. My entire family's deserted me and gone off to shop. So why have you come?'

'I know nobody's here, but I felt that somebody should be here,' I said. 'So, would you like to go for a drive?'

'Fine.' Giani seemed rather touched. 'Let's go.'

We went around the city, driving through the leafy, tree-lined streets, up the Peak, from where one had a fabulous view of Hong Kong before we returned to the hotel. The President, with characteristic simplicity, took the time to thank me for the gesture and the drive—a trait that I have always respected in him. That evening, Giani was due to attend a dinner reception in the city and we undertook several rehearsals for it. Minor security adjustments had had to be made. For instance, we had to forgo a direct entry into a crowded room, much as Giani loved meeting people. It was decided to enter the room from a side door, so that the President could get safely to the dais. Any movements thereafter, we thought, could be controlled.

Everything went according to plan that night, until the very end, when the President decided to take matters into his own hands and leave the room directly through the gathered throng of people. I was appalled and not a little angry. 'Sir, I took you deliberately from the other way around. I requested you to listen to me today. You still decided to walk right through.' Giani's response was typical of the man and his character. 'I know you're doing your job,' he said. 'You're doing it very well too. But this is *my* job—I am a politician. Let me do my job.'

I was with Giani in Aden in south Yemen in 1984. The weather was hot and sticky, triggering a bad asthma attack. I had taken some medicines and was resting before I accompanied Giani to a function being held by the Indian community in Yemen. Half an hour before we were to leave, I got up and changed to go to Giani's room as I always did. But when the President came out of his suite, instead of walking directly to the banquet hall, he went straight to the bank of elevators.

This confused me so greatly that I asked, 'Sir, where are you going?'

Giani seemed astonished. 'What are you doing here? I was told you are unwell. I was coming up to see *you*.' It was, to my mind, a lovely example of how thoughtful the President was with those he worked with.

From Aden, we went to Sana'a. Tragedy struck when Indira Gandhi's Sikh bodyguards assassinated her on the morning of 31 October 1984. We were at the royal palace when the news came that the Prime Minister had been shot. We had to naturally cut our trip short, because the President insisted on leaving immediately. Soon after we were airborne, news came that she had died, which completely changed the whole atmosphere aboard the aircraft. Giani went into a huddle with the top bureaucrats accompanying him, which included Romesh Bhandari who was one of the secretaries in the MEA.

I remember that we arrived in Delhi at around five on the evening of 31 October 1984. Arun Nehru and R.K. Dhawan were waiting to receive the President. Arun's main concern at that moment was that Giani should have Rajiv sworn in as the Prime Minister immediately.

It was, after all, a well-known secret that the President didn't really like the young Gandhi scion. But Giani insisted on going to the All India Institute of Medical Sciences (AIIMS) first, to see Indira Gandhi's body. As the presidential cavalcade pulled through the gates of the hospital, stones were pelted by angry crowds.

An incident that happened during the presidential trip to Belgrade in 1986 is telling. Romesh Bhandari was the secretary travelling with us. There was a lunch scheduled for the President at which he was due to make a speech. We were sitting outside after lunch. After a while, Romesh Bhandari came in excitedly waving a newspaper. *'Dekho, Gianiji, dekho!'* The main paper's headline was that Farooq Abdullah had entered into an accord with Rajiv Gandhi. The President's remarks were stoic but prescient: 'This will be the beginning of the end of Farooq Abdullah. He will go the same way as Longowal.'

Farooq, according to Giani, was sunk. He believed that if you tied up with Delhi, as a regional leader, you were done for. In retrospect, that is an observation that has aged well. I was in Bhopal in 1987, when Giani's term as President was ending. I was a bit sad because his term was ending—not to mention that my trips abroad would also end. He came to Gwalior in 1987 and though it was none of my business to go to Gwalior for the President, I made it a point to go there, because I didn't know when I might get the chance to meet him again. I went back to Delhi soon after to find a city swirling with rumours.

When I went to headquarters, I sensed some kind of tension within the government, about how the President would behave while demitting office. Did he want a second term? There were damaging whispers that Giani would, as President, sack Rajiv Gandhi before he left office himself. The tension between them was palpable. Rajiv never trusted Giani fully, as I have said earlier in this chapter, nor did he trust R.K. Dhawan. Operation Blue Star deeply hurt Giani. Until it happened, he had been an ardent follower of Indira Gandhi. But the events that surrounded Operation Blue Star and the days thereafter had left Giani shaken. Indeed, in the aftermath of Operation Blue Star, the Prime Minister knew that her days were numbered and Giani was, apart from being deeply upset as a Sikh, extremely concerned about her personal safety.

Years later, that hurt seemed to have carried over into his attitude towards Rajiv. So, I decided to meet Giani again before I left Delhi. I made an appointment with his office to meet with the President. We talked of cabbages and kings as we usually did, but I came away from the meeting feeling that he had no such designs on Rajiv's position. In fact, I met him twice during that brief time in Delhi. The first time, before I could bring up the subject, he himself told me how Congress politicians including Arjun Singh and V.C. Shukla had met him suggesting that he form a new party. Giani looked at me and said: 'You have served in Madhya Pradesh. Would you trust either of these gentlemen?' And we both laughed together.

At one point, I was called at eight in the morning to the Rashtrapati Bhavan, I was admitted to his bedroom. The President was tying his turban before the mirror.

'*Ae, ki khabar le aaya?* (So, what news do you have for me?)'

I said I had just come to bid him farewell before returning to Bhopal. But the President was too crafty for that.

'*Main tennu gal sunanna.* (I have some news for you.)' He said: '*Tera home minister* [Buta Singh] *aaya si* (your home minister had come a little while ago) to ask whether I was forming a party.'

I was listening intently at this point.

'I told him: "If I am forming a party, why don't you join me?"' Giani continued, 'Buta Singh took off his turban and laid it at my feet. He said, "*Gianiji, ennu maaf kardeyo, badiyan galtiyan hogaye.* (Please forgive him. There have been many mistakes.) But Rajiv is like your son. Please forgive him." I told Buta, "There's no need for you to put your turban at my feet, you shameless swine!"'

Giani also said that Arjun Singh—then the chief minister of Madhya Pradesh—had come to see him about forming another party.

Since Giani had mentioned Arjun Singh and I knew Arjun Singh, I went to call on him. Before I could say anything, he inquired whether I knew K.C. Singh (who was deputy secretary to the President of India from 1983 to 1987). I said: 'Of course I know him, sir. But so would you. He is one of our prominent IFS officers and was in class with Rahul (Arjun Singh's son Ajay) in college.'

Little did I realize that Arjun Singh had already met KC and rumours were rife about backchannel talks between them. I, for one, was astonished, because as Tarlochan Singh told me, Giani never had the intention of dismissing Rajiv or forming any party. He just felt that he had been treated shabbily, and at the end, he had simply wanted to convey a message to Rajiv.

Much later, I visited Giani one more time—when our son Arjun was getting married. At the time, the former President was living in Chanakyapuri. He was, as always, delighted to see me and even more delighted to receive my box of mithai and the invitation card for Arjun's wedding.

'I'm told you're quite the bee's knees now, sir,' I told him appreciatively. 'Our Prime Minister (Narasimha Rao at the time) consults you all the time on Punjab!'

'*Karda te hai* (he does),' Giani said pensively, '*par luchcha bada hai!*' Now there's no equivalent of *luchcha* in the English language, but the closest meaning I can give you is—'crafty'. (But he is crafty.) Giani did attend my son Arjun's wedding reception, but this was the last time we had a conversation.

On 29 November 1994, his bulletproof car was hit head-on by a truck near Ropar in Punjab, when he was returning from a visit to Anandpur Sahib. There were some serious security lapses around his death. For one, the ambulance that was supposed to be accompanying him was, in fact, at the Ropar guest house where he was to halt en route to Chandigarh. As a result, the injured former President could not be taken to the hospital for nearly an hour and a half.

There were all kinds of rumours that swirled around his death, with state officials maintaining that Giani's family had not alerted them about the former President's travel plans, and others insisting that Singh's frequent journeys had weakened the security drill that normally was part of presidential protocol.[3] Nobody will ever know the truth behind Giani's death, just as I believe we still don't know the full truth behind Indira Gandhi's assassination. The truth may only be known when R.N. Kao's notes about her security, kept at the Nehru Memorial Museum and Library, are opened twenty-five years after his death.

To come back to Giani, it is altogether sad that, in the end, India lost a President who was—at his core—an honourable man, and an even more honourable Sikh. His puckish warmth and old-fashioned sartorial elegance embodied the personality of a bygone era.

---

3 Ramesh Vinayak, 'Lapses in Former President Zail Singh's security might prove fatal,' *India Today*, 31 December 1994. Available at: https://www.indiatoday.in/magazine/indiascope/story/19941231-lapses-in-zail-singh-security-may-prove-fatal-810092-1994-12-31

6
Bhopal

TROUBLE HAS FOLLOWED ME WHEREVER I HAVE GONE.
I laugh at this now—but in the thick of crisis, it didn't seem so funny. But then, in the summer of 1984, I hardly expected to find trouble in a placid city like Bhopal. The IB usually posts people to every state—not necessarily only the conflicted ones—and in these states, the job of those who are posted there is to liaise with the state governments. My designation at the time was deputy director. More senior officers are being posted to states like Madhya Pradesh now, but in those days, the head of the subsidiary bureau was the deputy director, and in this case, it was me. I would be dealing with Arjun Singh, the then chief minister of a Congress-ruled state.

It didn't take me long to realize that Singh was a canny, exceptional politician. He was also a damned good professional, not your run-of-the-mill politician who had irrational airs and graces. Arjun Singh gave me no problems like making me wait endlessly for appointments or playing hard to get if I asked to meet him.

However, it took me a little longer to realize that not everything about Arjun Singh was perfect. For instance, he liked playing some theatrical games. If I asked him for a meeting, I would inevitably be granted a 9 a.m. appointment. I would arrive punctually, and ask his secretary, '*Kab mulaqaat hogi?* (When will I get to meet him?)' After all, the chief minister was a busy man. But the answer I got from the secretary was always the same: '*Sahib, aapka toh ek number hai. Sabse pehle aapko bulaya hai.* (Sir, you are the first person in the list. He has called you ahead of others.)'

Initially, this was flattering to hear, but then I realized it was part of Singh's optics for anyone who might be watching. There were any number of hangers-on hovering about in his office, waiting to meet him. He wanted to show them all that the IB guy was his buddy. Quite often, I would find myself sitting silently in his office, while he glanced over the files on his desk. There would be little to no conversation—and Arjun Singh was a man of very few words—but he would keep me there for at least twenty minutes. The point being made to those waiting outside: *IB chief ke saath baat ho rahi hai.* (He is busy with the IB chief.) As we got to know each other better, a friendship beyond the professional began to bloom. He would often come home for dinner. He didn't drink, but he did love his food and, in those days, God bless him, Arjun Singh ate quite a bit!

That year was a troubled year for India and Indian politics. Punjab was teetering on the verge of secession; there was a distinct threat to the Prime Minister's life which culminated in her assassination in October and the world's worst industrial disaster left thousands dead in Bhopal in the winter of that year. Ramachandra Guha summed it up in his inimitable style in an essay for *Outlook* magazine in 2009, when he wrote: 'Marked by instability and conflict, by assassination and mass murder, it was in 1984 that the Republic of India came closest to being, as it were, a *non*-functioning anarchy.'[1]

A month after I arrived in Bhopal in June 1984, Indira Gandhi ordered the Indian army to launch an attack on the Golden Temple in Amritsar. Between 1982 and 1984, the complex had been occupied by armed Sikh radicals, led by the compelling, fiery Sikh preacher Sant Jarnail Singh Bhindranwale. Their demand was for a separate Sikh 'homeland'—Khalistan. With talks between the Government of India and Bhindranwale breaking down, the state of Punjab was in turmoil. Militants were running amok, killing anyone who appeared to be against what they stood for. Rumours were rife in Delhi that Khalistan would be declared a legitimate and independent state from inside the Golden Temple itself. There are, of course, debates about the timing of Indira Gandhi's decision. What followed was a six-day-long battle between the Indian army and the armed Sikhs. Blood was spilled by the gallons inside the Golden Temple, and the Akal Takht—the epicentre of Sikh authority—was reduced to rubble.

The trouble with the Sikhs would come to a head in the autumn of that year, but we were not to know that just yet. Tensions in the north of the country continued throughout the summer of 1984. The threat to Indira Gandhi's life was at its highest yet, and in recognition of that threat, R.N. Kao—who personally looked after her security—had removed Sikhs from her personal bodyguard contingent. Indira Gandhi refused to comply with this, however, insisting that such a move would only reinforce an already anti-Sikh image of herself in the public eye, not to mention handing her political opponents free fodder to strike at her. She ordered R.K. Dhawan that her Sikh bodyguards be brought back, including Beant Singh, who was

---

1   Ramachandra Guha, 'The Axis Year: When India was Closest to Being a Non-functioning Anarchy', *Outlook*, 21 August 2022, https://www.outlookindia.com/magazine/story/the-axis-year/262214

reported to be her favourite. The result of this impulsiveness would only be revealed to India and the world in the winter of that year.

Meanwhile, in Bhopal, I was doing my best to focus on learning the ropes in my new job. Bhopal was mostly deskwork for me, and as I've mentioned in an earlier chapter, deskwork is usually the best way to hone your analytical skills. Bhopal was also where I first encountered the question of the Muslims. Now, I am a native of Punjab, where Muslims were a rarity, post-Partition. Growing up, I hardly encountered Muslims, let alone heard of their problems.

But Bhopal was—and still is—a city with a considerable Muslim population. It was the place where I made plenty of Muslim friends and where I learned, for the first time, the workings of the 'Muslim mind'. During my tenure, there was also an occasion when there was Hindu–Muslim tension in the city, which gave me a further glimpse into the 'Muslim mind'.

I got the first whiff of togetherness in Bhopal in the Nagu household where one met more Muslims than Hindus, although Nagu sahib himself was a Kashmiri Pandit. Ram Narain Nagu was a large-hearted policeman better known as Jeewan, who had retired as the inspector general (IG) of police in Madhya Pradesh. Nagu kept an open house where one was always welcome. He liked his drink and chain-smoked, which ultimately got the better of him.

In those days, we were great friends with one of the branches of the erstwhile royal family of Bhopal. Shamla Kothi, where they lived, was a second home for us. Their little daughter had befriended our own daughter, Priya, and she came often to our home to play. But the understanding was very clear: she could and would only come to our home, because we were trusted—her family did not want her going to any other place at all. It was a strange insight into a way of thinking with which I was not at all familiar, but in many ways, Bhopal was also excellent training for my next posting: Kashmir.

A LIFE IN THE SHADOWS

In October 1984, the unthinkable happened. Indira Gandhi was walking the short distance from her residence on 1 Safdarjung Road to 1 Akbar Road, her office which was just next door. She had an early morning interview scheduled with the English actor Peter Ustinov, who was filming a documentary for Irish television. Clad in a saffron saree with a black border, and accompanied by constable Narayan Singh, personal security officer Rameshwar Dayal and personal secretary R.K. Dhawan, Indira Gandhi was just passing through the wicket gate between the two complexes, when Beant Singh and his colleague, Satwant Singh, opened fire.

Beant fired three rounds into her abdomen from his .38 revolver, followed by Satwant, who fired thirty rounds from his Sten, after Indira Gandhi had collapsed. Both men then flung down their arms. Beant is reported to have declared: 'I have done what I had to do. Now you must do what you want to do.' The rest of the story is, of course, a tragic and bloody part of Indian history, but when the news reached me I was no longer in Bhopal. I was, in fact, on special duty with President Giani Zail Singh in Sana'a, in Yemen. We were at the royal palace, where Giani was calling on Ali Abdullah Saleh, his presidential counterpart. It was, as I recall, nearly eleven in the morning. We were due to leave in a couple of hours anyway, but then the news arrived that Indira Gandhi had been shot. We had no idea whether she was alive or dead, but Giani insisted that we leave immediately. I ran to get the plane ready for departure and we took off for New Delhi as fast as we could. The sombre news of the Prime Minister's death was given to us shortly after the flight was airborne.

By 5 p.m. that day, we touched down at Palam airport, from where Giani rushed to AIIMS, where her body was being kept. At a loss, literally and metaphorically, I went to my mother's house in Tilak Marg. There was a hush in the air. Delhi had been shaken by this. An hour and a half later, there was still no word, either from the PMO or the IB. So I decided that I would only go in to work next morning. By this time, Doordarshan was broadcasting the news of the Prime Minister's death and its tragic circumstances. Vice President R. Venkataraman had made the announcement on television that Prime Minister Indira Gandhi was dead and a new government under her eldest son had been sworn in. I had also got wind of the fact that Giani's convoy had been stoned by angry crowds outside AIIMS. It was prudent, then, that I only go in to work the following day.

The next morning, as soon as I got into office, I was asked to stay back in Delhi. Many VIPs were scheduled to arrive in the capital for Indira Gandhi's funeral, and security protocols would be high. I was told that I would be on duty with one of the incoming VIPs. So I was still floating around in the office when R.K. Kapoor, then the DIB and an extremely good human being, called me to his office. He said urgently, '*Bhai, baat suno, tum phauren Bhopal jao. Yahan mat ruko. Yahan rioting shuru ho gayi. Tum wapas jao Bhopal aur sambhalo wahan.* (You better go to Bhopal immediately because rioting has begun here. You need to go back and take care of Madhya Pradesh.)'

Now, it's a fifty-minute flight from New Delhi to Bhopal. I should have taken that flight. To this day, I don't know what got into my head, but I decided to take the Tamil Nadu Express instead. This was a slow passenger train which left Delhi at 2 p.m. and chugged into Bhopal at around 9 p.m. that night. There was trouble on that train as soon as it left Delhi. First, it was pelted by stones, thrown by angry mobs, all the way from modern Gurgaon to Faridabad. The driver pushed on obstinately, but in Dholpur, he was forced to halt the train as protesters spread themselves across the tracks, shouting, '*Maaro saalon ko* (Kill the bastards)' and a number of other vile slogans. With the train at a dead halt, it didn't take long for them to swarm into the compartments. They were goons, armed with lathis and sticks, and they were clearly hunting for Sikhs.

I was terrified. I was sitting in a first-class compartment all by myself. The thoughts running through my head were jumbled. For one, I thought desperately that it was a damn good thing I was wearing a full-sleeved shirt. The cuffs hid my *kada*. If any of these hooligans saw that *kada*, it would be over for me. I thanked God that my father had, in his youth, cut his hair, and so neither of his sons had been compelled to wear a turban. Eventually, under cover of the commotion, I slipped out of the train and got on to the platform. Wild thoughts of fleeing the spot ran through my head. Then I pulled myself together. *Bewakoof*, I said to myself severely, *tu jayega kahan?* (You fool, where will you go?)

Finally, after what seemed like an endless passage of time, I re-entered the compartment and sat down. The train began to move, slowly, leaving the rioters behind. There was no one on board that train who was not deeply shaken and disturbed. Two Sikhs had been found on the train by the mob, and they had been murdered in cold blood. Halfway to Bhopal, the TT came to the compartment. '*Sahib*,' he asked anxiously, '*aap theek hain? Aapki fikr thi.* (Are you okay? I was worried about you.)' I assured him that I was all right, but I wasn't. The train pulled into Bhopal at midnight. It was running three hours late. I got off the train, shaken to my soul.

For nights afterwards, I couldn't sleep. I had nightmares of what I had been through. It was a time in my life that was personally harrowing. To be honest with you, I have often thought that this—the autumn of 1984—was the first time that I began truly thinking of myself in terms of my identity: as a Sikh. If I was anything first, I realized, I was a Sikh. Until all this had happened, I never thought of myself as anything but an Indian. Now, as I watched Sikhs across the north of India being murdered ruthlessly, I shared their fear and helpless anger.

As news of what was happening in Delhi and across Punjab reached Madhya Pradesh, there was tension in the air. There weren't, thank God, too many attacks on Sikhs in Bhopal, but there were certainly serious incidents in Indore, Jabalpur and Sagar. A delegation of Sikhs came to meet me one morning. They were worried and frank with regard to their anxieties, going so far as to warn me that if they perceived a threat to their lives and loved ones, they would have no compunction in taking up arms. There was little doubt that they meant what they were saying.

So, I went to meet Arjun Singh, shortly after I met with them, to convey their concerns. I suggested that as chief minister, he meet with the Sikhs in Bhopal to allay their worries. Now, I have to say, Arjun Singh's reaction in the face of rising tensions was not the best. He refused point-blank to meet with them. '*Yahan aisi koi baat nahin hai. Agar zaroorat hogi, toh aagey mil lenge.* (There is no problem right now. If there is any in the future, we will see.)' The message that he implicitly conveyed was that the state—and the Government of India—was making its point clear, and that the Sikhs were, if anything, supposed to feel insecure at this juncture.

Leaders from the Congress were marching through the streets, openly leading raging mobs with slogans like '*Khoon ka badla khoon*' (Blood for blood). I watched fellow Sikh officers in the IB shrink into themselves, afraid to speak the truth, afraid of what the consequences of speaking the truth might be. I was angry enough to tell Narayanan about it at a briefing in Delhi. 'I don't know how much of a Sikh you consider me, sir,' I said. 'But I am telling you, there is a lot of anger among the Sikhs. This will not heal in a hurry.'

I wish I hadn't been proved right about that—but it has been the case over the years. It will take a long, long time before the Sikhs of India forget the horrors of 1984.

Hardly had I recovered from my ordeal when, on the night of 2–3 December 1984, Paran and I were woken from our sleep by someone banging on our front door. Blearily, I looked at the clock. It was

4.30 a.m., not even dawn. We weren't expecting any early morning guests—nor was anyone scheduled to be making the trip down to Bhopal on the Grand Trunk Express (which passed through the city on its way to Madras from Delhi). Puzzled, I went to the door and opened it to find my neighbour, Sivaraman, on the doorstep. '*Bhai, utho!* (Get up!')', he said frantically. '*Sheher mein gas leak ho gaya. Log sheher chhodh rahe hain. Ham toh nikal rahe hain.* I would suggest *tum bhi niklo*. (There has been a gas leak in the city. People are leaving the city and we are also planning to go. I would suggest that you also leave.) It's not safe here.' He couldn't tell me what he meant by 'gas leak', or even what kind of gas might have leaked.

Anyone who lived in Bhopal, of course, knew of Union Carbide India Limited (UCIL)'s pesticide plant. It had been built in 1969, to produce Sevin, using methyl isocyanate (MIC) as an intermediate. An MIC production plant had been added to the UCIL site in 1979. The plant had continued production into the 1980s, despite a subsequent fall in the demand for pesticides. The UCIL plant was no stranger to controversy and danger, with complaints of pollution and earlier gas leaks, occurring throughout the late 1970s and early 1980s. By early December 1984, most of the plant's MIC-related safety systems were malfunctioning—something that we had no idea about at the time.

During the late evening hours of 2 December, water is believed to have entered one of the tanks containing MIC while attempts were being made to unclog it. The introduction of water into the tank created an extreme chemical reaction, prompting workers to look for gas leaks through the night. Though one minor leak was caught and stopped in time, the second (and much bigger) one was yet to occur. By 12.45 a.m., matters were spinning out of control. The reaction in the tank had reached a critical state, maxing out the temperatures, and bursting the emergency relief valve. About 30 tonnes of MIC escaped from the tank into the air within one hour. It would increase to 40 tonnes in two hours. With the gentle breezes of that calm December evening, the gases were being blown in a southerly direction over the city of Bhopal. I remember that the slums in the city were the worst affected, with hundreds—if not more—dying or ill in the face of these noxious winds.

The trouble was that nobody knew *which* gas and how dangerous it was. When I woke Paran, we were still puzzled and confused about what we should do. The fact that people were fleeing meant that the problem was a grave one indeed, but even if we fled too, where would we go? Also, even if we had decided to go, how could I have abandoned my post? Eventually, I decided that the best thing I could do was to go for a walk through my neighbourhood. Surely, if there was a gas leak, there would be some kind of smell in the air. In hindsight, I'm lucky we lived in the suburbs of the city, in a kind of geographical bowl called the Chauhatar Bangley (74 Bungalows), where the gas had not yet arrived. Nor did I know then that the SP had received panicky calls from the town inspector that residents of the neighbourhood of Chola (about 2 km away from the UCIL plant) were fleeing from a gas leak.

Calls between the UCIL plant management and the police between 1 and 2 a.m. that night led to a further delay, with false assurances of 'Everything is okay', and even, 'We don't know what has happened, sir', leading to a critical lag in the time between action that could have been taken.[2] Bhopal's Hamidia Hospital, for instance, was first told to expect patients suffering from the after-effects of inhaling ammonia, and then doctors were told it was phosgene and not ammonia. When the updated report—stating that the gas in question was actually

---

2 Ashay Chitre, 'The Bhopal Disaster', *India's Environment*, Centre for Science and Environment, Delhi, 1985, pp. 206–08. Available at: https://cdn.cseindia.org/userfiles/THE%20BHOPAL%20DISASTER.pdf

MIC—was received by the hospital, the staff had never heard of it, nor was there an antidote for it.[3]

Meanwhile, as dawn broke, I was walking aimlessly around the neighbourhood, until I bumped into Najeeb Jung, an IAS officer who lived close by and with whom we were good friends. He would much later become lieutenant governor of Delhi. He was obviously returning from the city. 'Najeeb,' I said, '*Kya ho raha hai?* (What's happening?)' He shook his head. 'City *se aa raha hoon. Halaat kharab hain. Kisi ko maloom nahin, par maine khud dekha hai. Log wahan ulti kar rahe hain, gir rahe hain...* (Things are not good. I am coming from the city. Nobody knows what's happening but I have seen people vomiting and falling down...)' Disturbed by this news, I went to knock at the door of Rajan Bakshi, a colleague and then the assistant director of the IB. He answered the door, half asleep.

'Rajan,' I said, '*Dilli ko phone karo, control room ko. Unko kaho ki yahan gadbad hai.* (Ring up Delhi. Tell them things are bad here.)'

'*Kya hua?* (What happened?)' he asked, confused.

I explained that I had just met Najeeb, and there was a gas leak in the city. Things were not going well. So both of us called the control room in Delhi, and told them of the situation. But at that hour of the morning, we both knew it was too early to personally speak to anyone senior. Given what I had just heard, I decided it was prudent to go home, get ready and dressed for what looked to be a strange, disturbing day. By eight o'clock, I rang up the chief minister's residence to ask for an urgent meeting with him. He asked me to come to see him immediately. As I arrived, I found his residence a hive of activity, with several cars gliding in and out.

---

3 *Seconds from Disaster: The Bhopal Nightmare.* Available on video at: https://web.archive.org/web/20190922182226/https://www.youtube.com/watch?v=gOIFK0E1Pgs&gl=US&hl=en

Bhopal

I went to his house, where I saw that his family was preparing to leave. '*Sir, kya ho raha hai? Reports hain ki sheher mein halaat bahut kharab hain. Teen chaar log mar bhi gaye?* (Sir, what's happening? There are reports that the situation in the city is very bad. Three–four people have already died?)'

'*Nahin, ussey bahut zyada log mar gaye hain. Union Carbide mein gas leak ho raha hai. Ham sab kuch kar rahe hain.* (No, a lot more people have died. There is a gas leakage from the Union Carbide factory. We are doing everything necessary),' he replied grimly.

But even he didn't know which gas it was. So about half an hour later, once I had finished talking to Singh, I drove to the office. To get to the IB office in Bhopal you had to drive through the city. The sights I saw on the way to the office that morning were unpleasant, to put it mildly. There was rampant devastation already. People were vomiting on the streets. Others were lying where they had obviously fallen, their eyes dull. Forcing myself to focus, I entered the office and found it packed. Nobody at the IB knew what was happening exactly. We just knew that those who lived closest to the site of the plant—on Hamidia Road, for instance—were dying.

At 11.30 a.m., there was a false alarm about another leak, prompting more people to flee. By this point, I could no longer stand the uncertainty and our complete ignorance of what this mysterious gas was. I felt I needed to *know*, even if I could do nothing actively to stop its spread. So I did what I could, and called one of my seniors, J.N. Roy.

'*Kya ho raha hai? Kaunsi gas leak hui hai?* (What is happening? What gas is leaking?)' he asked.

I said, 'Sir, *suna hai ki ammonia leak hua hai* (Sir, I've heard it is ammonia.)'

'*Pagal mat bano,*' he said sharply, '*Ammonia se kuch nuksaan nahin hota* (Don't be mad. Ammonia gas is not so harmful.) This must be something else.'

At a loss, I demanded of my senior colleagues at the Subsidiary Intelligence Bureau (SIB): '*Koi toh hoga jo hamein bata sakta hai ki kya ho raha hai.* (There must be someone who can tell us what is happening.)'

One of them advised me to go and see Nagu sahib, the former IG of Madhya Pradesh. If there was anyone who would know, it would be he. As it turned out, I was good friends with Nagu and his family. Nagu was a good man, who was unfortunately stricken with cancer of the lung.

The family took him to USA for treatment, but it was too late. When he returned, he looked frail and knew his days were numbered. When Paran and I went to visit him, his kind and gentle wife said, 'Nagu sahib is not receiving visitors.' Nonetheless he agreed to meet me.

When I was ushered in, I found him lying on a bed in the verandah, protected by a mosquito net, but smoking. He said to me there was nothing worse than smoking. '*Kuch bhi karna, yeh kambakhti mat karna*', he advised. (Whatever you do, don't smoke.)'

A couple of days later, he was gone.

But that was much later in Nagu sahib's life. During this particular day in 1984, there was none better to help in this situation, so I went immediately to see him. He seemed to know more than he was telling me, because he said: 'I am not a student of chemistry, but there is this lady who works at UCIL. Take my reference and ask her what happened. She will be able to tell you that the gas that leaked was MIC.'

I went to find this woman. She told me honestly: 'There has been a death earlier at this factory as well, along with an earlier gas leak. This is a heavy gas; it doesn't lift easily. It's like a cloud which goes whichever side the breeze takes it. If you can duck it, you're safe. But if you're in its path, you're in trouble. If that is the case, soak a towel in water and wrap it around your head. The water will soak up the gas.'

Over time, I learned that the workings at UCIL had been nothing short of shady. The MIC used to come from abroad in small cylinders. Somewhere along the line, whether UCIL got the permission to do so or not, they began manufacturing MIC in Bhopal, and that's when the first accidents began taking place. But at the end of that dreadful morning, I heard of bodies being taken out of Bhopal by the truckload. Only later would I discover the true figures—3,000 dead and over a lakh affected in the space of a few hours.

That evening, Warren Anderson, the chairman of UCIL, arrived in Bhopal, which was by then an empty ghost town. Now given that he arrived at such short notice, he could hardly have flown in from the United States, so it seems to me that he must have been somewhere in the neighbourhood of India. He had come to do the optics for UCIL, meet with the locals, let them know that UCIL would provide compensation. Arjun Singh, meanwhile, heard of his arrival and promptly panicked. I had no idea of what he had done until Swaraj Puri, the then senior superintendent of police (SSP), arrived to tell me frantically that Anderson had been arrested and locked into the UCIL guest house. No sooner had Puri burst in to tell me this than I got a call from Delhi. Delhi was not amused that a person of the stature of Warren Anderson had been whimsically arrested on the orders of the chief minister without any charges being levelled against him. He was, however, let off by the evening and flew off in a special plane.[4]

---

4 On 7 June 2010, a local court had convicted seven executives of UCIL to two years imprisonment in connection with the incident. The then Union Carbide Corporation (UCC) chairman, Warren Anderson, was the prime accused in the case but did not appear for the trial. On 1 February 1992, the Bhopal chief judicial magistrate (CJM) declared him an absconder. He died in the US in 2014.

In the wake of the tragedy, Bhopal took a few years to come back to some kind of normalcy. For those first weeks, it was a ghost city, with very few people around. From 74 Bangalows to my office would usually be a car ride of twenty minutes. But in the aftermath of the tragedy, it took five or seven minutes—simply because there was nobody on the roads. Human rights organizations arrived, as did documentary film-makers. But in all this, the chief minister didn't come across as someone who was capable of handling the crisis too well. There had been widespread panic in his city, and as chief minister, he had only fuelled that panic. Compensation remained a tricky issue, caught up as it was in tangles of red tape, but I remember being thankful that we did not have to apply for compensation.

Shortly thereafter, Rajiv Gandhi, India's new and youngest Prime Minister, arrived in the city to visit the victims in hospital. We were also gearing up for the 1984 elections, which Rajiv had called for in December that year. As deputy director of the IB in Bhopal, I used to meet Arjun Singh as often as possible, despite our guys on the ground writing in about what might happen. One day, I went to see him right before Madhya Pradesh went to the polls. It was our usual morning meeting, but today, the chief minister was inclined to talk.

'*Boliye, kya assessment hai aapka?* (So, what's your assessment?)'

Wondering what to say to such a question, I rattled off a figure somewhere around thirty-five seats (Madhya Pradesh had a total of forty seats in Parliament). Arjun Singh didn't seem too pleased at this. '*Forty kyun nahin?*', he demanded. '*Kahan haar rahe hain?* (Why not all forty? Where are we losing?)'

This stumped me even further, but I said gamely, '*Indore, Gwalior mein maamla tight lagta hai.* (It looks like a tight race in Indore and Gwalior.)'

'*Nahin, nahin,*' said Singh confidently, '*ham jeetenge.* (No, no! we will win.)'

Credits to Arjun Singh, the Congress certainly swept to victory in the 1984 general elections. This was in spite of certain trends that were unprecedented. For instance, in Gwalior, where Madhav Rao Scindia was standing from the Congress, it was a match between Scindia and Atal Bihari Vajpayee. I knew Scindia well by this time, and I had even gone to Gwalior to meet with him recently.

In 1984, his political star was on the rise and he succeeded in trouncing a stalwart like Vajpayee. I remember wondering how Vajpayee could have lost against someone infinitely less charismatic, albeit a good human being. So, I would definitely say that despite his little quirks, Arjun Singh definitely had his ear to the ground.

Now, there are some politicians who are clever, but people don't trust them. The Gandhis, as I discovered, had no trust in Arjun Singh. I saw it in his transfer to Punjab as governor. I don't know what he had done to provoke or deserve this, but Arjun Singh certainly wasn't happy with this decision. For three or four days after he heard the news, he did not step out of his house. By then, I was on rather friendly terms with his son, Ajay (fondly known as Rahul).

The sense that I was getting was that Arjun Singh was pondering quitting the party but I think better sense prevailed, and he dusted off his achkan (so to speak!) and went off to Punjab. Here, he made a success of his career, going on to become the architect of the Longowal Accord which brought peace to a disturbed state. For his hard work on the job, he was granted the post of vice president of the Congress party. Before leaving for Chandigarh though, he gave me a call. '*Tumhare wahan dost hongey. Main kisi ko nahin jaanta Chandigarh mein.* (You must be having friends there. I don't know anyone in Chandigarh.)' Typical of the man, so I gave him a couple of numbers and we stayed in touch through the years.

Arjun Singh never lost that need to play to the gallery wherever he went. I recall when Motilal Vohra became the new chief minister of Madhya Pradesh, he hosted a big lunch at the Bhopal Club. I was invited and so was Arjun Singh. I bumped into him just as he was entering the party. Seeing the chief minister watching him, Singh promptly put his arm jovially around me and took me to one side. The point was clear, even to Vohra. *Yeh mera banda hai* (He is my man). In actual fact, he merely took me to one side to tell me that the names I had given him when he left for Chandigarh had come in most useful!

He returned to Bhopal as chief minister in 1987, but by then I was preparing to leave Madhya Pradesh, moving on to a bigger posting in Kashmir. He remained keenly interested in politics until the end of his days. One of my last conversations with him happened in 2002, post the elections in Kashmir. He called me on my phone. '*Bhai, batao wahan kya ho raha hai.* (Tell me what is happening there.)' Now, the only other person I had briefed on Kashmir had been Dr Manmohan Singh, but I dutifully assured Arjun Singh that it would be a party victory, reminding him of the fact that the Congress had done well. Indeed, Singh stayed in touch with me throughout my time at the Vajpayee PMO, so much so that eventually I told Brajesh Mishra that he was very keen to stay connected.

Brajesh encouraged me to continue meeting and talking with him, and this connection became important in the aftermath of the National Conference's defeat in the elections. The Vajpayee PMO was upset that the National Conference (NC) and more particularly Omar Abdullah had lost the election. In those days there was an effective backchannel between Brajesh Mishra and Natwar Singh and possibly word was sent to Sonia Gandhi, via Natwar Singh, that the BJP would prefer a Congress government. But Sonia preferred Mufti as a buffer. So I was dispatched to talk to Arjun Singh, to say basically the same thing.

He knew what was in Sonia's mind already, so all he said was '*Hamaare banane mein kya fayda. Mufti hi theek hai.* (What do we gain by forming the government. Mufti is good enough for us.)' I tried to convince him otherwise, but he wouldn't hear of it, and eventually, a government was formed with Mufti at its head. Those were also the days when rumours were rife that, following my time at the PMO, I was due to be promoted to governor of Jammu and Kashmir.

It would have been a post I would have dearly loved to take up, and I was already incredulous that it had actually been suggested at the moment. I got a call from Arjun Singh a couple of days later: '*Maine toh khush khabri suni hai. Maine suna hai ki hamara dost jaa raha hai wahan, Kashmir?* (I have heard some good news. I have heard that my friend is going to Kashmir?)'

'Sir, there's no such news', I said, adding: 'I can make all the arrangements for you.'

He said, '*Mujhe toh rehna hai aapke saath jab aisa hoga.* (I will only visit Kashmir when you are there.)'

Arjun Singh refused to listen to me, saying he had heard it from reliable sources, and the thing is, I believed him because, even if I do say so myself, that was very much the word on the street in those days.

The last time I met Arjun Singh was in 2011, shortly before he passed away. He was unwell even then, and I encouraged him to consider Ajay (his son) as the new chief minister. Looking around at the other Congressmen present, he said to me sotto voce and with that spark of humour so typical of him: '*Yeh sab banne de tab na!* (If only they would permit him!)'

But one learnt a lot from Arjun Singh. He was a clever politician, and in the end, it is a pity that the cleverer the politician, the less likely they are to be trustworthy. In my opinion, he would have made a fine Union home minister. He was a man of few words and of swift decisive action. The events in Bhopal in 1984 sorely tested his mettle and I don't think it's unfair to say that he didn't really come out of either the aftermath of the Sikh riots or the UCIL gas tragedy smelling of roses.

My time in Bhopal came to an end in 1987. I was overdue to be posted out of Bhopal anyway by that time, and the news that I was to go to Srinagar was very welcome. At headquarters, you were just a cog in the machine. But in an outstation posting, I had more autonomy and a better sense that I was contributing towards something of value. I did ask the Bureau for a couple of days while I asked Paran: '*Srinagar chalna hai?* (Do you want to go to Srinagar?)' She was always game, of course.

In November 1987, I went off to Srinagar for a quick recce. A younger colleague of mine, Praveen Mahindroo, took me around and especially to Gulmarg, where it was snowing. I spent three or four days being shown around the Valley by Praveen. When I returned, I went to say goodbye to Arjun Singh, who had just returned to Madhya Pradesh as chief minister.

He said: '*Kyun, hamaare saath koi naraazgi hai kya?* (Are you unhappy with me?)'

I said: '*Aapke saath kya naraazgi hogi?* (How can there be any unhappiness with you?)'

He said: '*Jaise ham wapas aaye, aap jaa rahe ho* (Just when I have come back, you are going away). Should I ask for your transfer to be cancelled?'

'No, sir,' I said, smiling. 'I think I really should go.'

'Kashmir is an important position,' Arjun Singh agreed. 'Keep in touch with Farooq Abdullah. He's a good Indian.'

A very good Indian, as I was to find out in the years ahead!

The Congress was fortunate to have some of its best leaders from Madhya Pradesh in the 1980s. The master politician Arjun Singh apart, there was Madhavrao Scindia, Digvijay Singh, Kamal Nath, V.C. Shukla and Arjun Singh's son, the budding Ajay Singh. To my mind, each one was destined for bigger things. I have already written about Madhavrao earlier. Digvijay was the Provincial Congress Committee (PCC) president while I was in Bhopal, and following in

Arjun Singh's footsteps became chief minister twice. Diggy Raja, as he is referred to by his friends, is the perfect politician. I have never been greeted by him with anything but the most pleasant smile. He is also someone who after all these years is still available to meet, always.

Kamal Nath was the first of the Congressmen from Madhya Pradesh whom I met in Delhi before going to Bhopal. He was friendly immediately when we met at his residence in Friends Colony. Thereafter we remained in touch while I was in Bhopal. We were friends and then I was transferred to Srinagar and we temporarily lost contact. Kamal Nath, who had joined politics courtesy of his friend and classmate from Doon School, Sanjay Gandhi, has the distinction of being one of India's longest-serving parliamentarians with nine terms in the Lok Sabha. First elected from Chhindwara in 1980, Kamal remained in Parliament till 2018, except for a brief period in the late 1990s when he lost a by-election after his wife, Alka, had filled in for him and then resigned. Even in the worst of times for the Congress, Chhindwara has remained with it because of Kamal Nath's influence in the constituency. Who was to tell that one day we might be related?

Ajay Singh was a prominent visitor to Shamla Kothi during our days, and consequently became a friend. With his perfect political genes, I have always regarded him as a future chief minister. Unfortunately he lost the 2018 election, but age is on his side and he could still make it.

7
Doctor Sahib

'A*AP DOCTOR SAHIB SE MILENGE?* (WILL YOU MEET DOCTOR Sahib?)'

Five words, and yet I was expecting none of them. The call came in early 2020, some six months into a constitutional and political event that had made headlines across the country. On 5 August 2019, the Parliament of India had voted in favour of a resolution tabled by home minister Amit Shah to revoke the temporary special status—autonomy, to put it simply—granted to the state of Jammu and Kashmir under Article 370 of the Indian Constitution. Among the consequences of the abrogation was the cutting off of communication lines in the Kashmir Valley and the deployment of thousands of security forces to curb any uprising.

The political and popular reaction in the state was visceral. In a tweet on 4 August 2019, Mehbooba Mufti, the most recent chief minister of Jammu and Kashmir, said that the decision of the state's leadership to reject the two-nation theory in 1947, in order to align with India, had backfired. Omar Abdullah called the Government of India's move on Article 370 'a total betrayal of the trust that the people of Jammu and Kashmir had reposed in India, when the state acceded to it in 1947'. Asgar Ali Karbalai, the former chief executive councillor of Kargil's Hill Development Council, said that the people of Kargil considered the division of the state on any grounds—religious, linguistic or regional—to be undemocratic.

And what of Farooq Abdullah?

Not for nothing have I always considered Farooq to be one of the most intelligent politicians in the country. He is, to my mind, the tallest leader—certainly the tallest Muslim leader—that India has right now. There is no one who has been more closely entwined at the heart of both Kashmiri and Delhi politics than Doctor Sahib. Since April 2019, Farooq has been warning of an impending political crisis in Kashmir. 'If it (India) does not pay heed to the wishes of the people, the consequences will be grave,' he said. 'We will fight for the rights of people. This is a political problem that needs to be settled politically. It's not a developmental problem that you solve by making roads, hospitals or universities.'

Farooq's stand that Kashmir is a political problem has been evolving over the years. I would discover that early in my career, which really began in Kashmir in May 1988. In October 1987, I had received a call from my friend and former colleague M.K. Rathindran, who was at IB headquarters. Again, it was a call I was not expecting, but that—as I would discover—was part of the parcel at the IB.

'How would you react to a posting to Srinagar?'

It turned out that my predecessor, K.P. Singh—a future DIB himself—had been selected for training at the National Defence College (NDC). He had to join the NDC in November. Now, my mind was more or less made up. I had always hoped for a posting to Kashmir, but there were still a couple of things left to straighten out on my home front. First of all, I needed to talk to my wife, Paran, about the news. Next and rather importantly, my mother was in Delhi at that time. My father had died in 1982, and she was alone, and getting on in age. Further, I had to take into account the fact that I had a persistent bronchial problem. How would I bear the biting cold of Kashmir?

I took my concerns to M.K. Narayanan, my boss, with whom I shared a room in North Block when I joined the Bureau in March 1969. 'These are minor problems,' he said comfortingly. 'We'll take care of them. Take the posting.' And so it was that in November 1987, I found myself sitting on the balcony of K.P. Singh's residence on Gupkar Road, sipping pink gin and discussing the future of my proposed posting to Kashmir. Singh told me that only 'handpicked officers' made it to Srinagar. I have very few illusions about myself, and if this was the case, then I would need to find out as much as I could about the intricacies of Kashmiri politics and politicians.

The Abdullahs were the most important family that I would need to learn about before I got going, though, of course, the best kind of training comes from working on the job. For the most part of the last five decades, the NC headed by the influential Abdullah family has been synonymous with Indian politics in Jammu and Kashmir. Yet for years the same family has faced the wrath of Kashmir's local residents, as well as the separatists, for their loyalty to India. At the dawn of the armed rebellion that began three decades ago, an NC leader was the first political leader to be killed by the rebels, who, since my time in Kashmir, have killed several hundred NC party workers. Sheikh Abdullah himself had died in 1982, some six years before I arrived in Kashmir. I would, therefore, be dealing directly with his son, Farooq.

It would be the beginning of one of the most important associations of my life.

I formally took over in Srinagar in May 1988. My mandate was simple: *We need to keep Farooq on our right side.* This was a surprise to me. I had always thought that Farooq *was* on our right side. When I came out of Narayanan's room after my briefing, I dropped into the office of his special assistant Ratan Sahgal. He was also a friend.

'What's this I'm hearing about Farooq?' I asked. 'I thought he *was* on our side?'

'He is,' he replied. 'But Rajiv (Gandhi) has some concerns that we need to pay more attention to Farooq.'

From whatever I had heard of him, I knew that this was going to be easier said than done. Farooq's reputation preceded him by miles. He was known to be imperious in his manner, a man who rarely allowed anyone to get to him easily. Highly intelligent and quick-tempered, he was rumoured to be someone who could, should he wished to, cut you down to size immediately. Not surprisingly, then, I was a little nervous of meeting the big man. First of all, he was playing games with me—hard to get, if you'd like to put it that way. That was part of his style of dealing with people.

I had, upon assuming office, requested a meeting with him. He had been dodging me for nearly three or four weeks. Finally, a call came—summoning me to his official residence. Even more nervously, I asked my colleagues what I should address him as when I did meet him. Do I call him Farooq Sahib or Dr Abdullah?

The then home secretary and security adviser to the chief minister, O.P. Bhutani, told me: 'He's known as Doctor Sahib. That should be good enough.' Bhutani was the last of the gentlemen police officers who mentored me throughout my stay in Srinagar.

When I went to meet him, I don't know what I was expecting, but, as I was to learn, Farooq rarely had a pattern. He was on the move that day, brisk and brusque. 'Come on,' he said. 'Hop into the car with me.' He was on the way to the airport, and to Delhi.

'We'll talk on the way,' he said, taking the wheel. Farooq loved to drive in those days. He was rarely without the wheel in his hands if he could help it. I forget what we talked of on that day's drive, but as we neared the airport, Farooq told me: 'I'm coming back in a few days and we'll meet again.' When I got word that he had returned, I decided to try again, properly. I rang him up and said, rather formally, 'Sir, my wife and I would like to call on you at home.' Yet again, Farooq took me by surprise. 'What is this call on me business?' He ordered: 'Come and have a meal with us at home.'

So, Paran and I went for dinner on the appointed day. Farooq was at his most charming that evening. 'Would you like a drink?' I was a bit startled at the prospect of a chief minister offering me, the local head of the Intelligence Bureau, a drink, but I decided to go with the flow.

'If you're having a drink, I don't mind one.'

'Yes, of course, I'll have a drink.'

And so it was that Farooq and I had drinks and dinner and talked of many different things. His wife was also present that evening. From the start, I liked her. Mollie was warm and seemed to be an understanding, intelligent woman. There's this impression that Farooq can do what he likes, but she is very much the anchor in his domestic life. As I would discover during my time in Kashmir, there was a quiet serenity to their relationship. But this evening, one of the first of many in Kashmir, there seemed to be a certain chemistry developing—not just between Farooq and myself, but also between Mollie and Paran.

I remember one of the remarks he made to me that evening. 'Look,' he said, 'this is a very important job you've come to. So, don't be afraid to speak the truth to power. Don't tell lies.' After that first meeting, I realized that Farooq never required me to call on him formally every week. It was just implicitly understood that I would go to see him every two weeks or so. But God help me if I turned up any later than that. That's when Farooq would—and did—put me very firmly in my place. 'So,' he'd say coolly, 'you've finally found time to come to see me, have you? What is it you want?'

As time went on, I began to discover why Delhi found it so difficult to deal with Farooq. He was, quite simply, not what Delhi wanted. By the time I had met him, he had run the gauntlet of first being exactly what the PMO—then reigned over by Indira Gandhi—wanted, and then being exactly what she didn't want or like. In 1981–82, Sheikh Sahib was an old man, with rapidly fading health. Indira Gandhi, at the time, was very concerned. There was a lot of thought being given to what would happen after Sheikh passed away. The conclusion that she reached was that Farooq would be ideal. As a result, she pressed the old man to name Farooq as his political heir. He agreed, and Farooq entered active politics in October 1981.

At the time, in his first public and political speech he had said that he wanted to be the bridge between Delhi and Srinagar. Yet, two years after Farooq took the chief minister's office, Indira Gandhi sacked him. I can safely say that was a huge tragedy for not just Farooq, but for India. Those who watched him during those years say that this brief chief ministership was Farooq's best tenure. But the fact is that Farooq is not easy to handle. He never has been. His attitude has always been *'who the hell are you?'* He hated being taken for granted, and he despised anyone trying to tell him what to do. I learned that fairly early during my days in Kashmir. He was nothing like his father.

I recall Farooq telling me about Sheikh, and one maxim, in particular, has stayed with me all these years. While Sheikh was grooming Farooq to take over in Kashmir, he told his son: 'Remember one thing—politics is like jumping into the Jhelum and swimming against the tide.' As I was to discover, Farooq—in his own inimitable way—decided to go with the flow, instead of swimming against the tide. Not for him the constant pushing against the political current. He would do what it took to succeed in his political goals. Yet, even while he swam with the flow, he never forgot to remind you of who he was, and that he was not a man to be taken lightly.

In 1989, for instance, the IB was celebrating its centenary. Narayanan was still the DIB in those days, and he wanted the outstations to organize celebrations too. I was asked to arrange something in Srinagar, and I was to ensure that both the governor and the chief minister were present. Now this was far from easy to do. For one, Jagmohan was the governor and he and Farooq didn't get along. The chief minister resented Jagmohan who had been appointed as the governor earlier in 1984 as well and who had recommended Farooq's dismissal to Indira Gandhi in the summer of that year. Indeed, Farooq had earlier declared that he would resign if Jagmohan was made the governor. That was to follow soon, but at the time, I could hardly have foreseen the events that would lead to Farooq's exit from Kashmir.

On that morning, however, off I went to Jagmohan and explained the occasion. 'Don't worry,' he said, 'I'll come. Is the chief minister coming?' I had no idea. My meeting with Farooq was only after meeting Jagmohan. When I met Farooq and explained that this was an important occasion, which the governor would also be attending, he smiled. 'Why do you need me then?'

'Well, sir,' I said uncomfortably, 'without you, a function in Srinagar would be meaningless. It would also mean that I can't get the chief minister on board!'

Perhaps my honesty amused him. I'll never know. Anyway, Farooq nodded. 'I'll come,' he said. 'But I'm going off to Delhi today. What time is your function?'

I told him it was to be held the next day, at 10.30 in the morning.

'Right,' said Farooq, 'I'll take the morning flight back and be there.'

Now, I knew that this was deliberate—it's an example of how he plays hard to get. But it didn't stop me from feeling nervous as hell. There was nothing to do but take him at his word. The next morning, everything was ready. The audience had assembled.

Doctor Sahib

Even Jagmohan had arrived. In itself, this was a bad sign, because normally, a governor arrives after the chief minister. Of Farooq, there was no sign.

Feeling more and more nervous with each passing minute, I checked with colleagues. I was told that the chief minister was certainly back in town, but he had gone home first. Eventually, he arrived—a pointed ten or fifteen minutes late.

The two years that I was in Kashmir were years of tumult. Separatist militant violence had begun in the Valley two months after I took over in the summer of 1988. In July 1988, the JKLF began a separatist insurgency for independence of Kashmir from India. Before it exploded—literally and metaphorically—on to the political and public scene, there were, of course, whispers. But we could never pin it down. Nobody, it seemed, had any clue of what was happening. When I first heard of the JKLF boys, I met with one of our better informed deputy SPs on deputation from the Jammu and Kashmir Police, a man called Sapru, and I asked, '*Sapru sahib, yeh sab kya ho raha hai?* (Sapru sahib, what is happening?)' Even he was clueless. He said, '*Sir, yeh kuch nahin hai. Yeh sab aana jaana chalta rehta hai Kashmir mein. Aap mat ghabraiye.* (This is nothing really. All this going and coming is routine in Kashmir. Nothing for you to worry about.)'

Once the insurgency really took off, though, whatever intelligence we had, dried up. The situation changed yet again on the ground. Where nobody had a clue before, now nobody was willing to talk to us. Our officers were being openly targeted by the JKLF boys—in the space of three weeks, we lost four of our men. It was a terrible time. But I am willing to admit that the IB knew nothing of what was happening on the ground at the time. It was an intelligence failure at our end. As a young officer, very new to a potboiler theatre like Kashmir, I remember being out of my depth in an unfamiliar situation. Everything was happening far too fast, and far too quickly.

It was one of the hardest lessons I would learn out there in the field—that the loneliness one experiences during a crisis is absolute.

On 14 September 1989, the JKLF targeted a Kashmiri Pandit for the first time, when they killed Tika Lal Taploo, an advocate and a prominent leader of the BJP in Jammu and Kashmir, in front of several eyewitnesses. The killing petrified the Kashmiri Hindus, particularly since the killers were never caught. An even more gruesome killing—the assassination of Judge Neelkanth Ganjoo, who had sentenced Maqbool Bhat to death, in full public view in Hari Singh High Street—followed on 4 November 1989. Ganjoo lay there for hours, bleeding to death. Nobody came forward to help. The murder was the last straw. Feeling that they were unsafe and wouldn't be protected, the Kashmiri Pandits moved out of the state en masse. It was a milestone in Kashmir's political history and one for which Farooq received angry criticism.

There are still questions around the exodus, evidenced by the considerable controversy stoked by the recent release of a film titled *The Kashmir Files*. I don't have answers to those questions. I do remember that one of the questions was: How far was Jagmohan, the governor, responsible for it? I am no admirer of Jagmohan and he, quite frankly, hated my guts, but I will say that he had nothing to do with it. In the midst of all the bloodshed he witnessed when he returned, he didn't want the Kashmiri Pandits to be targeted—and hence, he was equally happy to see them leave. So yes, there was certainly a serious threat to the lives of the Kashmiri Pandits, and many of them still hold Farooq responsible for it, for losing control of a volatile situation. In relation to this, there are two incidents which—to me—prove that wrong.

On 15 August 1989, Farooq Abdullah made a speech at the Sher-e-Kashmir Stadium. Under regular circumstances, this would have been a normal event. But these were not normal times. The stadium was fairly deserted that morning, with only about a hundred people—including myself—present. Outside the stadium, bombs were exploding on the streets. The dull thuds of the bombs going off periodically shook the walls of the stadium. Yet Farooq seemed unruffled. His speech was a stirring one, nationalist and strongly pro-India. He was a fine orator, refusing the scripted speech and preferring to speak directly from his heart. This last quality was a cause for great alarm for his chief secretary, Moosa Raza. Raza was a Tamilian of the Gujarat cadre, posted in Kashmir. He was a nice guy, but at the end of the day it all came down to understanding how to deal with Farooq, who was, at the best of times, a man who liked to live on his own terms. This wasn't, of course, politically easy in 1989.

At the time, Delhi was agitated because they had heard that Farooq, at a public meeting in Anantnag, had said something to the effect of a hundred militants entering Kashmir. I received alarmed calls asking if this was true. I went off to Moosa to find out what Farooq had said in Anantnag, but he had no idea. Then I went to Farooq himself.

'Sir,' I said, 'in your speech in Anantnag, did you mention a hundred militants?'

'Did I?' Farooq inquired airily.

'Well, sir, that's what Delhi is saying.'

'Tell Delhi not to get so excited,' retorted Farooq. 'If there *are* a hundred militants in Kashmir, we'll deal with them.'

Farooq may have had the required sangfroid, but Moosa certainly didn't. He was alarmed enough to decide that the next time there was a public function where Farooq was scheduled to speak, he would give the chief minister written points. But when the next time came around, Farooq merely took the paper that Moosa gave him, and put it in his pocket. He never looked at it for the duration of his speech, despite Raza's frantic signalling to him. The message was quite clear—don't teach me about my own people or what is required to be done. Anyway, listening to Farooq speak—politically correct or not—was always a pleasure. I have rarely encountered such a fine orator in recent times, apart from Vajpayee. And, to bring my story back to the morning of 15 August 1989, if you had heard him that day, his words clear and eloquent, you would have felt truly proud to be an Indian.

After the ceremony was over, Farooq went to inspect the guard of honour. It was a question of walking about sixty or seventy yards. But because of the security threat at the time, the Jammu and Kashmir Police had lined up a special jeep for him, under the escort of the director general of police (DGP). Farooq went as far as the line-up, and then he jumped out of the jeep and did the slow march better than the DGP himself. He was excellent for theatre, in that sense.

In September 1989, Farooq gave—though I didn't know it at the time—what would be his last public speech as chief minister. Again, it was a strong speech, warning openly against the perils of succumbing to militancy. Kashmir and the Kashmiris would suffer for it, he declared. It would only bring the people of the state death, misery and destruction. By December 1989, Farooq was on his way out. He knew it as well as I did—Delhi's whole game had been to get him out. Once V.P. Singh came to power, the anti-Farooq coterie—Mufti Mohammad Sayeed, Arun Nehru and Jagmohan—began pushing to get him out of the chief minister's seat. Jagmohan was brought back into Kashmir as governor on 19 January 1990, and Farooq—who had made it clear to both VP and George Fernandes that if Jagmohan did come back, he would leave—decided that was the end of the matter.

The momentum to all this was stalled briefly by the kidnapping of Mufti's daughter, Rubaiyya, by the JKLF boys in December 1989. I use the word 'stalled', but as with most political events in Kashmir's modern history, that word, too, is a paradox. Because if anything, the momentum of the Centre's plans to have Farooq removed from power in Kashmir gained speed. From the Centre's point of view, here was a chief minister who was not even present during a time of crisis, leaving it to be handled by his chief secretary, the IB and Delhi. It all led up to the excuse that Farooq, as a leader, was useless and needed to go. That is a story that I have told in *The Vajpayee Years*, so it doesn't need retelling, but by January 1990, Farooq had resigned.

I would say that was the start of a void in Kashmir's politics. Farooq left Srinagar and went to Delhi, where he stayed for a few months, until April 1990. Then he went off to London. I was thrown out of Kashmir shortly after Farooq's departure. As I said, Jagmohan hated my guts! He asked Delhi to have me removed, saying that I was 'Farooq's man'. But Kashmir's politics have always been too volatile to permit any kind of stasis. In 1991, with Narasimha Rao becoming the Prime Minister, there was a realization that we needed to talk to the separatists. I was told: '*Ab tum toh Srinagar mein rahe ho.* (You have spent time in Srinagar.) You're more contemporary. Why don't you talk to these fellows?'

The main target at the time was a man called Shabir Shah, and it was around this time that we at the IB made Narasimha Rao believe that we could get Shabir to participate in the 1996 elections. In hindsight, I have to say that was far from the truth. We were working on him and we had given him prime importance, but it could never have happened in 1996. I do think, though, that if we had continued to work on him, it *may* have happened in 2002. But then, so many other things happened in between.

Now, on the matter of talking to people, I have to say—since I have talked to everyone from the separatists to the militants and to the National Conference guys—that talking to Farooq Abdullah is like talking to nobody else in Kashmir. Talking to Farooq is not—and never has been—easy. He doesn't make it easy. If you don't know him, he makes you feel uncomfortable because he takes a while to work the chemistry. He's a pretty good judge of people and looks beneath the façade they present. With nobody else did I have a problem, but even after so many years of knowing Farooq Abdullah, I never take him for granted. If anyone does so, God help them. But he did understand politics—the intricacies of it and the things you have to do sometimes to keep the ball rolling.

As I observed him over the years, I realized that there is within the man, an innate willingness to forgive, if not forget. Countless times has Delhi backtracked on its promises to Farooq—and countless times he has forgiven it all. In 1983, for example, when the NC turned down the Congress offer to ally with them in the upcoming elections, Indira Gandhi—thanks to the coterie that surrounded her—decided that Farooq simply wasn't what she had been looking for in a chief minister as far as Kashmir was concerned. His subsequent dismissal left a bitter taste in Farooq's mouth, and in the preface to the book *My Dismissal* (dictated to Sati Sahni),[1] he would go on to state publicly that Indira Gandhi was unwilling to live with rival centres of power in the states. In this notion, she was aided and abetted by many within the Congress, from Arun Nehru to Ghulam Nabi Azad, and from M.L. Fotedar to Arif Mohammad Khan, Mufti Mohammad Sayeed and G.M. Shah. Indeed, the transfer of the then governor, B.K. Nehru, and the appointment of Jagmohan was a clear red flag for Farooq. He knew then that his days were numbered. As he put it quoting *The Guardian*: 'The deed had to be done at the dead of night for fear that it might come unstuck.'[2]

Farooq was removed from power in July 1984, and though he always maintains that what Delhi did to him at that time was, in his words, 'not right', he has moved on. For him, the relationship with Delhi—given the length to which it stretches back in time—is

---

1 Farooq Abdullah (as told to Sati Sahni), *My Dismissal*, New Delhi: Vikas Publishing House, 1985.

2 Ibid., p. 8.

personal as well as political. But he warned then, as he does often today, that treating Kashmir as a colony would come with a heavy price for Delhi. That is what we are seeing today, in the aftermath of the abrogation of Article 370. And yet, to my constant wonder, Farooq has never closed the door for talks with Delhi. He has always been with Delhi and always will be; something sadly that Delhi has not understood all these years.

Maintaining this openness is a crucial quality in a politician who comes from a state as troubled as Kashmir. I recall, for instance, a time when the IB was talking to Shabir Shah of the People's League, to try to convince him that Delhi wanted him to participate in the elections of 1996. A stage was reached in our conversations when Shabir seemed persuaded of the fact. 'If Delhi is serious,' he said, 'then we need to talk to the politicians.' So we contacted Delhi and let the Prime Minister know that Shabir was ready to hold talks.

Surprisingly, because it was I who was leading the discussions with Shabir, I was sent to meet Dr Manmohan Singh, who was the finance minister at the time. This confused me for a moment. Why was I being sent to meet the finance minister, when Dr Singh wasn't remotely involved with Kashmir? Later, I realized that it was a measure of how much Rao trusted Manmohan Singh. That same trust was later shown by Sonia Gandhi. To me, it just displays what a special man he must be. Anyway, when I went to tell him, he kept his questions simple and brief. But one question struck me by its directness and relevance.

'Does Dr Farooq Abdullah know about this?' Dr Singh asked.

'No,' I replied, 'he doesn't.'

'Well, don't you think he should be informed?'

I laughed. 'Dr Farooq doesn't need to know everything, sir.'

We left it at that, but it highlighted Dr Manmohan Singh's consciousness that Farooq was the big leader in Kashmir and that we shouldn't have been bypassing him the way we were at the time. Now, obviously, Farooq did find out that we were talking to the separatists, but he has never known about Manmohan Singh's conversation with me. I don't think that he liked the fact that the separatists were now involved, but as I say, he is a man who understands that politics is a ball that must be kept rolling. His take on the matter has always been—*It's up to you guys. You can do your best, though I don't think it will work. Best of luck!*

Farooq has been proved right time and again, of course. It happened again in 2004, when Mufti was the chief minister, and Farooq was out of the political picture. Dr Manmohan Singh was the Prime Minister at the time, and he was keen to continue talking to the separatists, a move that the NDA had made in 2003. Advani had already had two rounds of talks with the separatists by 2004. Manmohan Singh was keen to push the NDA agenda forward. But he felt deeply uncomfortable in dealing with the BJP leadership. This is one of the ironies of our political system and one of the many times that Farooq was proved right. It was the right agenda to have pushed and yet Dr Singh kept looking over his shoulder, afraid of NDA criticism in case he did too much or too little. Through it all, Farooq's attitude remained—*Kar lo. Dekh lo.* (Try if you like. But nothing will happen.)

In 2015, two hardliner Hurriyat Conference leaders, part of a delegation sent by Syed Ali Geelani, met with Pakistan high commissioner Abdul Basit in Delhi, to tell him that Islamabad should maintain 'consistency and firmness' over its Kashmir policy, and that Pakistan should play an 'active role in highlighting the human rights violations' in Jammu and Kashmir at all international fora. The matter was a sensational media controversy in India, but it was not really so controversial, given the fact that—as Asad Durrani himself told me—Pakistan had given the separatists this political platform from which to negotiate. Through that controversy, Farooq remained

Doctor Sahib

unruffled. He rarely paid attention to what happened in the Pakistan high commission in Delhi anyway.

In that unflappable reaction, I noticed a palpable shift in the hot-headed man I had worked with in Srinagar in 1987. Back then, Farooq's line used to be: *These bloody Pakistanis need to be taught a lesson.* It was an aggressive reaction. But since Vajpayee's bus went to Lahore, and since that government made great attempts to forge peace with Pakistan, Farooq's line of thinking has changed too. Now, he feels it is important for India and Pakistan to be at peace because it is, at the end, the Kashmiri on the ground who suffers as a result.

To this day, though I always wonder why we have stopped the process of talking to the separatists. They are easier to talk to today than they ever have been. Why don't we mainstream them now that they are a broken movement? After all, isn't that what we have been trying to do in Kashmir since 1947?

The details of Doctor Sahib's political career aren't so much what I am trying to explain here. It is more about my own regret that, over the last two decades, Delhi has gone out of its way to misunderstand Farooq Abdullah. It is a sad tragedy because here is a tall, formidable leader, with considerable political clout and very openly willing to do what Delhi would like him to do. Yet, the very attributes that I talk of—the way he holds his political cards close to his chest, his idea of politics, his imperiousness—have been the ones that have put Delhi off from making use of Farooq.

In the first United Progressive Alliance (UPA) government, for instance, Farooq was left out in the cold. In the second UPA government, he was brought in as a Union minister. That meant he was in Delhi more frequently, and it was around this time that he gave a rather startling comment to Saeed Naqvi. Naqvi was going to Kashmir and he had rung me up to ask if there were any convivial souls with whom he could share an evening whisky. He also wanted to know if he could interview Farooq before he went to Srinagar. I called Farooq to ask him if Saeed Naqvi could speak with him.

'*Bhej do.* (Send him.)'

Now, at the end of the interview, Naqvi asked Farooq what he thought had gone wrong in Kashmir.

'What's gone wrong,' said Farooq Abdullah, Union minister in the UPA Government, 'is that we are not trusted by Delhi.' Now, as part of the IB, I would consider this to be an immensely revealing and significant statement, but it was never taken politically seriously here in Delhi. I do recall that whenever I asked him, during the second UPA regime, '*Aap toh ab idhar hain, toh baatcheet hoti hogi Kashmir ki?* (Now that you are in the government, they must be discussing Kashmir with you?)' The answer was always, '*Koi nahin karta.* (Nobody talks to me about Kashmir.)'

That's how it has always been. There might have been talks with Omar, since he was chief minister while his father was a Union minister in Delhi, and since P. Chidambaram—the home minister at the time—had a very good equation with Omar, even supporting his request for the repeal of the Armed Forces Special Powers Act (AFSPA). But with Farooq, there was little to no conversation. To my mind, this is the tragedy that has let Kashmir and its people down time and again—though, of course, there will be people who disagree with me. Omar Abdullah is seen to be the more pliant of the two Abdullah men, and yet it is Farooq who told me, as I was leaving Srinagar in 1990: 'I haven't got into politics to spend my life in jail. I'm not like my father. *Koi bhi Dilli mein hoga, main uske saath hoon. Ham Dilli ke saath rahenge.* (Whoever is in power in Delhi, I am with them. We will remain with Delhi.)'

The stature of Farooq becomes plain when you look at the respect that his political contemporaries—though I'd rather use the word 'adversaries'—have for him. They all have their differences, of course, but they are clear that Farooq is a deeply respected leader, the ilk of whom we aren't likely to see again soon. Whether it is the statesman in him or his importance in modern Kashmiri politics, particularly after the abrogation, he is lauded by all, from Sajjad Lone to Mehbooba Mufti. Indeed, the formation of the People's Alliance for Gupkar Declaration (PAGD) brought leaders from across the political spectrum together—all under the aegis of Farooq Abdullah. It was an initiative for the unity of Kashmir and for a political future on the state's own terms, and there was not a single leader in Kashmir who did not recognize this fact. In my years in Kashmir, and in dealing with Farooq, I have noticed this pattern of respect—trammelled sometimes by politics—persisting.

Take Mufti Mohammad Sayeed, for instance. He never trusted me to begin with, but over the course of time, our relationship improved. When he became chief minister (2002–05), he was very good to me, always making it a point to call when he was in Delhi and to stay in touch at all times otherwise. But his relationship with Farooq was an awkward one, because he had been—quite openly—part of the coterie that had wanted Farooq out, in the winter of 1989–90. In fact, Mufti had always known that as long as Farooq Abdullah was on the scene, he would never have a chance to be chief minister. That was what led to the formation of the The Jammu and Kashmir Peoples Democratic Party (PDP). And yet, when Farooq did leave in 1990, Mufti always maintained that there was only one solution to Kashmir—and that solution involved Farooq Abdullah.

Mufti's heyday was 2014, when two things happened. One was the BJP government coming to power. Mufti knew that with the BJP coming back, he also had a good chance of returning to power. In the Lok Sabha elections which were before the assembly elections, the NC lost all three seats it had held in the Valley. Farooq also lost his seat. Mufti was riding high. When I went to meet him, the elections were over but the results were not yet out. He said, 'I'm sorry, *tumhara dost haar raha hai elections mein, par Doctor Sahib ko log bhoolenge nahin.* (Your friend is losing in the polls, but the people won't forget Doctor Sahib.)'

After meeting Mufti, I went to meet Maulavi Iftikhar, the supreme among the Shia leaders. He and Farooq had been good friends until he became a minister in Farooq's government in 1996, but thereafter, there were some difficulties. When I went to see him, sadly, the relationship between the two men was not so good. But he did tell me, during the course of our conversation, '*Bhai, tumhara dost haar raha hain.* (Your friend is losing.)'

'*Woh toh aapke dost bhi hai*', (He is your friend too),' I quipped.

'*Bilkul hain,*' replied Iftikhar, '*Par maane tab na.* (Of course he is. But does he think so?)'

We laughed, but at one point, quite seriously, Iftikhar brought the conversation back to Farooq: 'He is God's gift to us,' he told me. '*Woh upar waale ki deyn hain.* What people here don't understand is that Farooq has been working for an arrangement between Delhi and Srinagar, because he suffers from no illusions that Kashmir can ever be permanently solved.' Looking back, it seems to me that nobody except Iftikhar has understood this about Farooq. And yet, in an oddly poignant twist of fate, the remark about God's gift is exactly what the great Khan Abdul Ghaffar Khan had said at one time about Sheikh Abdullah.[3]

In my time in Kashmir, I have watched Farooq evolve not only into a charismatic leader worth reckoning with, but also as a much loved popular face, capable of being both unconventional and appealing. I have watched him surrounded by local Kashmiris, listening attentively to their problems and women vying to kiss his hand. Once, in 1997, Farooq asked me to accompany him on a trip out into Doda, to attend a District Development Council meeting.

---

3 M.J. Akbar, *Kashmir: Behind the Vale*, New Delhi: Roli Books, 2002, p. 87.

Doctor Sahib

Now these were years when our chemistry was at its best, but even so, I was slightly startled by this request.

'*Sir, main wahan kya karunga?* (Sir, what will I do there?),' I asked.

'*Arey chalo na,*' Farooq said casually. '*Doda jayenge.* (Why don't you come? We will go to Doda.)'

So he swept me off to Doda. At the meeting, he told the leaders present, equally nonchalantly: 'I've brought the IB chief along. He'll brief you guys.' It was embarrassing and awkward, more so because I had had no idea that I might be asked to speak, much less be present at a local political meeting. I recall waffling a bit for a while, and then once the meeting was thankfully over, Farooq said: '*Chalo, ab mujhe sheher bhi jaana hai.* (Let's go, now I have to visit the city too.)' So we went to the city as well. By this time, it was around lunchtime. Suddenly, Farooq left my side and walked off into a nearby house. I was aghast. This was obviously a house known to Farooq, perhaps one of his party people, but I could hardly enter as well. So I remained standing outside. After about five minutes, someone came to summon me inside. I went in, not sure what to expect. I found Farooq seated on the floor, surrounded by the family, eating their lunch.

'What are you doing, standing outside?' demanded Farooq. 'Are you ashamed of sitting on the floor?'

'No, sir,' I said sheepishly.

'Then come and join us! Eat.'

That is precisely why Delhi should have taken Farooq much more seriously than it ever has. More than anyone else in Kashmir, Farooq has clearly understood that Kashmir is a political and popular problem, which needs to be resolved with politics, rather than brute force. Successive governments have failed to comprehend this. The current NDA government is no different. On 1 March 2014, I was invited to Jammu for the swearing in of Mufti sahib as the chief minister.

The BJP leadership had clearly shown its preference for Mufti's PDP. Why? I suspect the answer lies with my old friend Ajit Doval. The story dates back to 1996, when Farooq became chief minister. When the swearing in was taking place, we had a new DIB, Arun Bhagat, who had never worked in the IB before. So I suggested to him that he accompany me to the ceremony. Now it so happened that Doval had been posted in Srinagar too and he was to take over. I suggested that we take Doval along too.

From the airport, I took Ajit to Farooq's residence and introduced him as our new chief. They were polite, very polite. But there was no chemistry. That's how Ajit Doval became friendlier with Mufti sahib. This friendship also possibly gave rise to the story that the PDP was an eventual creation of the IB. It's surprising to me, considering that from Vajpayee's time there were strong reservations about Mufti. In 2002, the PMO having lost Omar clearly preferred the Congress to Mufti. Ironically, Ajit Doval, who had gone as additional director to Srinagar in 1996, had a better relationship with Mufti than with Farooq whereas his successor, K.M. Singh, got on quite famously with Farooq. Indeed, he got whatever he wanted done, with Farooq's help. KM often said that when it came to national security, Doctor Sahib was always on the side of Delhi. That is why I can't believe that nobody from the current NDA would have reached out to Farooq. He is too big a leader to ignore.

The story certainly goes that an attempt was made to call him, but he was ill and asked them to contact Omar instead. Omar refused to join the BJP. But if they had approached him properly and in time, I'm pretty sure Farooq might have given the idea serious thought.

So, on 1 March, I arrived in Jammu to find the who's who of the BJP and Rashtriya Swayamsevak Sangh (RSS) leadership present—from Prime Minister Narendra Modi to home minister Amit Shah to L.K. Advani among others. After the ceremony was over and the bigwigs had departed, the delighted Mufti gave a press conference,

Doctor Sahib

in which he publicly thanked Pakistan and the Hurriyat for allowing the 2014 elections to be held peacefully.

No sooner had we all arrived back in Delhi than I began getting agitated calls, demanding whether Mufti was leaning towards Pakistan. Again, to my mind, this story highlights the difference between the two men. Farooq is too much of a politician to have fallen into that trap. And yet, I find I cannot blame Mufti sahib either. After all, a chief minister in Kashmir has certain compulsions. The first inkling I got that the BJP was still trying to reach Farooq was in the winter of 2014, when he was lying in a London hospital, recovering after his kidney transplant. I was in Goa on holiday, when I got a call from Delhi, asking for Farooq's phone number.

'I'm on the beach, so I don't have it offhand, but you guys have woken up a bit late,' I couldn't help saying.

The man on the other end of the line protested, '*Aise kuch nahin hai*. (It's nothing like that.) We just wanted to inquire about his health.'

'Well,' I said, 'even if it's about his health, you guys have still left it a little too late.'

Too late, too cautious and too lacking in confidence is my diagnosis—that has never changed over the years, no matter how much Farooq himself has changed.

After the abrogation of Article 370 in 2019, it was Farooq who was the main player in bringing political parties together. He realized that Kashmiris needed to unite or perish. That was the motive behind the PAGD, an electoral alliance between the several regional political parties in the state of Jammu and Kashmir, with the aim of restoring special status, along with Article 35A of the state. Farooq is its president. In 2021, I went again to Kashmir, and this time of my own volition, I met with Mehbooba Mufti, the vice president of the PAGD. I wanted to meet her to further my own understanding of what was happening on the ground. I knew Mufti sahib better than I know his daughter, but to my mind, Mehbooba is a little more emotional, a little more Kashmiri in that sense—like Farooq, she, too, is the quintessential Kashmiri.

People say that the PDP is finished and that Mehbooba is finished too. But I have always felt that she is still relevant. Often, I told Farooq, '*Aap usko pakad ke rakhiye.* (Don't let go of her.)' On that point, I'm happy to report that he has always politically agreed with me. While I was there, her daughter Iltija was also present. She spoke little, but she impressed me immensely. The one significant thing she did tell me was that she was trying to learn politics from her mother. I asked Mehbooba what she thought of the PAGD. 'We are determined to stick together,' she told me. 'Everyone here recognizes that Doctor Sahib is the tallest leader. Everyone looks up to him.'

I met Farooq again shortly after that and said that I had met Mehbooba.

'She speaks highly of you,' I said.

He nodded. 'Yes, we will work together.'

The evolution of the PAGD had a remarkable impact on Farooq. My old friend, Sajjad Lone, told me—and this was back when he was still a member of the PAGD—that in his new avatar, Farooq was a man possessed, determined to fight for the dignity of Kashmir. I feel this, too. But Farooq had a much closer relationship with Sajjad's father, Abdul Ghani Lone. Even though they never appeared together in public after the 1987 elections, Farooq did warn Lone sahib against joining militancy, just as Lone warned Farooq not to stand in the 1996 elections—to which Farooq replied: 'I have already given Delhi my word.' In 1984, after his dismissal, Lone was the first person to warn Farooq of the dissidence within the party, and when G.M. Shah offered Lone the post of deputy chief minister after Farooq's dismissal, Lone turned it down. Indeed, so close were these two men, that the old Begum herself considered Abdul Ghani Lone to be her fourth son. This was, then, a complex history. The comments of the son, in 2019, only skim the surface of how much Farooq—and Kashmir—has changed since the days of his erstwhile friendship with Ghani Lone.

I have met Farooq several times since the abrogation of Article 370. He is far more emotional now, far more charged up, and deeply religious. When I went to meet him on 12 February 2020, he was sitting by himself in his study, a bank of telephones on one side of him and an open Quran on the other. That moment stands out clearly in my mind. It was the first time I was seeing Farooq after his detention. I noticed that he didn't let the phone ring more than once and he was eager to talk to whoever was calling. That's what loneliness does. He appeared happy to see me. When I inquired after his health, he said: 'I'm fine, you can see for yourself. The only thing I miss is golf.'

But I knew that more than just a desire to play golf was missing in the great man. He didn't look well—tired, haggard and certainly not his sartorial, confident self. He was attired in a simple kurta-pyjama with a cream jacket and chappals. Without his glasses, his eyes too looked tired. I didn't want to talk politics with him and so I avoided the subject altogether. Yet, as if to demonstrate his determination, Farooq said: 'We have this one fight, and we are all in this together.' Trying to change the subject, I said: 'Yes, but you need to look and think ahead,'

'Yes, of course, I am,' agreed Farooq. 'But we are Indians first and last. That's the way my father was and that's how we have been brought up and that's how we have brought up our children. The only thing is that it is difficult to explain to our grandchildren what Delhi has been doing in the last six months. If abrogation had to happen, then why did it happen like this?'

In the course of that two-hour conversation with him, he excused himself twice to pray. In July 2020, I witnessed yet another astonishing example of how deeply Farooq is taking refuge in faith. He was in Delhi, staying at his Tilak Marg residence. His wife was going to England, and he had come down with her to see her off. It was his first trip out of the Valley since his release from house arrest. While he was staying in Delhi for a while, he wanted to be among friends. I was asked to have lunch with him. Usually, our lunches have been private, one-to-one affairs, but this time, there were a few others there.

The conversation was full of history and old memories, much of which had to do with Sheikh sahib. While talking to his friends, I noted that Farooq was referring to Sheikh sahib as 'Papa'. It was a touching insight into how deeply Farooq was now immersed in his family and friends. We all sat down to an elaborate *wazwan*, but as lunch finished, Farooq rose and said grace. He thanked the Lord not only for what we had eaten, but prayed for the people of India and for Kashmir. After everyone had left, I stayed behind to chat with him for a bit longer. I was a little concerned, I must confess, because I recognized very few of the people who had come for lunch.

'Are you sure there were no moles?' I asked.

Farooq shook his head. 'No, no,' he said. 'They are friends.'

That moment highlighted for me the many ways in which Farooq has changed—and the many ways he had been broken—since the abrogation, as a man and as a politician. And yet, paradoxically, broken though he might be, the events following the abrogation had only made him doubly determined to fight for the rights of his state. As he told me recently, in the aftermath of the 2020 District Development Council elections: 'Accommodation doesn't matter to me any more. We must accommodate, but what matters is togetherness.'

It is a travesty that after my time in the state, nobody has maintained channels of communication, particularly when trust is hard to come by in Kashmir. In 1996, K. Padmanabhaiah—then the home secretary—gave Farooq a slip of paper with a name written on it. That was the name of an officer of the Maharashtra cadre, the same as that of Padmanabhaiah.

Farooq looked at the name and then handed the paper to me. 'Do you know who this is?'

'No,' I said, perplexed. 'But what's the issue?'

'Padmanabhaiah wants me to take this guy as chief secretary,'

'But you want Tony (Ashok Jaitly), don't you?' I asked.

'Yes,' he said.

'Well, then why should you compromise on it?'

And so, Farooq pushed for Tony to be brought on board as chief secretary, which he became. It was one of the rare times that Delhi actually let Farooq have his way. After 1996, he wasn't important because in 2002, they lost the elections. Channels were kept open with other players, but that regular mandate of keeping Farooq Abdullah on your right side has been lost. This is a tragedy because you cannot understand contemporary Kashmir without Farooq. Remove him from the political arena and all you will have left are pygmies. We might regret that one day.

Y.D. Gundevia (foreign secretary under Jawaharlal Nehru and Lal Bahadur Shastri) in his memoir, *Outside the Archives*,[4] says that no story of contemporary Kashmir can be complete without the Sher-i-Kashmir. I would say that is even more true now of Farooq. If there was a void of leadership after Sheikh, I fear there may be a gaping hole, a veritable crater, without Doctor Sahib.

At lunch with Doctor Sahib one misty cold afternoon in January 2022, we talked—as we often do—about Kashmir. It was a conversation tinged with history, politics, memories and sadness, winding its way across the years from 1953, when the first mischief-making rumours were carried to Nehru's ears. Like all great people, Jawaharlal Nehru was easy to carry tales to. He was always a friend

---

4 Y.D. Gundevia, *Outside the Archives*, New Delhi: Sangam Books, 1987.

of Sheikh Abdullah, but he was a lonely figure, unable to withstand the power of the coterie that was growing against Sheikh Abdullah. My conversation with Farooq in January reminded me of something his sister, Khalida, had told me on a visit to Srinagar in 2014, of how Sheikh Abdullah had repeatedly tried to convince Nehru—then hooked on to the idea of plebiscite—that it could be managed, and should be held while both of them were alive. Back then—Khalida had told me regretfully—Delhi never trusted Sheikh, and relations between the two men eventually began to sour. Things got so bad that Nehru once told Sheikh Abdullah: 'If you don't toe our line, we'll have to bind you with chains of gold.' 'If you do that,' Sheikh is said to have retorted, 'you'll lose Kashmir forever.'

The reality, of course, is that since 1947, India has been trying to mainstream Kashmir, but that sense of alienation and mistrust has gone past the point of no return now. With this new and crude muscular policy of state intervention, the feeling in Kashmir is now one of hatred. Historically, the old regret—that Sheikh Abdullah should have taken up Jinnah on his offer to accede to Pakistan—has flared up yet again. Talk to anyone in Kashmir who is prepared to talk to you, and he will tell you, '*Koi hamey own hi nahin karta. Ham na toh wahan ke hain, na toh yahan ke.* (We don't appear to belong anywhere. We are neither here nor there.)' I had asked Farooq about this when we met that January morning. He nodded. '*Haan, main jaanta hoon*', he said. 'But remember, *tab bhi inn Jamaatiyon ne ki thi baat* in 1947. (Yes, I know. But remember, even in 1947 the Jamaatis were the ones who did the talking.) They are the same people talking about it today.'

If history had any lesson, it is that Kashmir could only have been resolved while the two great men—Nehru and Sheikh—were still around. In January 1964, when Lord Mountbatten came as a special guest on Republic Day, he is said to have spent more than a day pleading with Nehru to engage with Pakistan and settle Kashmir.

Conscious of Nehru's failing health, Mountbatten told him if Kashmir was not settled in Nehru's lifetime, it would never be settled.

'But what do you feel about it?' I persisted with Farooq.

'Because of what India is doing in Kashmir now, that sentiment has flared up again. India is responsible for it.'

Yet, he remained oddly hopeful. 'Things will be all right,' he told me.

'Are you sure?'

'*Aur koi raasta hi nahin hai.* (There is no other option.)'

It is a peculiarly optimistic, oddly endearing quality in Farooq—his denial of any negative possibilities. I don't know, though, how far this will persist, with the darkness that has descended on Kashmir today. It brings to mind a remark of his that he made not long after the abrogation: 'Delhi doesn't want the PAGD to prevail,' he told me once. 'But the irony is that even if we did, we would not know what to do with a hostile Delhi.' To my mind, this was a revealing insight into Farooq the politician. Change, as Doctor Sahib knows well, does not come cheap.

No story of Doctor Sahib would be complete without 'King Kahlon', as Gurbachan Jagat, former DGP of Jammu and Kashmir and governor of Manipur refers to Group Captain Jagat Singh Kahlon, who revelled in pushing the limits of both man and machine. Jagat says that this reckless flying was allowed to continue for so long as the head of the Jammu and Kashmir Civil Aviation Department because his employer, Farooq Abdullah, was a risk-taker par excellence. I flew with Kahlon at least ten times and was amazed by his daredevilry myself. He crashed five times and survived each time.

Once, after I had retired from government service, we met at a party one night. Kahlon, drink in hand, walked up to me and inquired whether we would like to go to visit Mata Vaishno Devi in the morning. He was scheduled to ferry a minister from Delhi.

'No, thanks,' I said, 'but we'd be grateful if you could fly us to Amarnath.'

The 'King' who never said no, agreed, but warned us to be ready to fly at six the next morning. Paran and I flew to Amarnath at 6.15 a.m. as agreed. When we reached the cave, Kahlon left the engine running and stayed in the helicopter, while Paran and I had the *darshan* of the deity. We returned to Srinagar with the 'King' at 8 a.m. Sadly, a fortnight later, on a similar sortie from Amarnath, his luck ran out as the blades of his helicopter got entangled in wires as he was entering Srinagar. This time, he didn't survive—yet he was a larger than life figure, much like Farooq himself.

Delhi periodically remembers Farooq Abdullah in its machinations. Congress leader P. Chidambaram addressed Parliament on the subject of his house arrest in 2019, arguing that it was a monumental blunder, since there was no one in modern India more devoted to the cause of a united India than Farooq Abdullah. Opinions on the subject appeared in mainstream national dailies as well. An editorial in the *Indian Express* on 17 September 2019 argued that the detention of Farooq under the Public Safety Act 'beggars belief'. There was no need to detain a man 'who was the face of moderate politics in Kashmir, apart from being the standard bearer for India on the Kashmir issue'.[5]

It is somewhat ironic that when Delhi remembers Farooq, even today, it also remembers me. That is why when the call came to me in the winter of 2020, I was taken aback. From the brief conversation with the voice at the other end of the line, I gathered that Delhi was thinking of releasing Farooq from detention. They wanted someone to gauge his mood upon release, but at the same time, the obvious concern was that Farooq should not talk publicly either about the

---

5   Editorial, 'Public? Safety?' *The Indian Express,* 17 September 2019. Available at: https://indianexpress.com/article/opinion/editorials/farooq-abdullah-psa-detained-jammu-kashmir-6000960/

abrogation or about Pakistan. I certainly went to meet Farooq, but I never thought it necessary to even mention these matters.

I didn't have to.

My long association with him had given me the confidence that he was too canny a politician. As Arnold Toynbee once said: 'What we mean by greatness of any degree in a human being is the power in some measure and in some field to move other human beings.' Every time I have met Farooq since February 2020, I could not but be moved by him. When I met him in his beautiful garden in Gupkar, in June 2022, he was engrossed in understanding an interpretation of the Quran.

When the issue of the Prophet came up, he reminded me that there is no God but God, and the Prophet is his messenger. This is what he told his partymen even as he wept at a convention at Khanyar the previous day that faith, unity and honesty were paramount. Each meeting, and each incident, has only served to drive home the fact to me that if you don't like Farooq, it means you don't understand him, and if you don't understand Farooq, you will never understand Kashmir. He would never have openly jeopardized Kashmir's chances by going against Delhi's orders.

His daughter was there when I met him in February 2020. She and her aunt, Farooq's sister Suraiya, had been detained in Srinagar during the protests against the abrogation. She was plainly agitated. 'All this doesn't make us feel like we belong to India,' she told me. In contrast to his daughter, Farooq was quiet, lethargic—or what we Punjabis call *sust*. But in the course of our conversation, he said: 'Our family has always been with India. We will remain with India. But now, today, my grandchildren ask me—is this the India you want us to be with?'

When we met during the monsoon session of Parliament over lunch at Doctor Sahib's place on 8 August 2022, he was in his element, full of hope. Never, except once briefly in July 2020 when out of frustration he said to me he was not responsible forever for all Kashmiris, has Farooq sounded negative. This time he was more hopeful than in the past, repeatedly telling me: 'Wait and watch. Everything will be fine.' On his return to Srinagar in time for Muharram, he tested Covid positive for the second time but even that did not deter him from hoisting the national flag and distributing sweets on Independence Day in the presence of the family and more than fifty officers and men of the security forces to whom, in a sense, he was expressing his gratitude. Does that sound like someone who is anti-national?

Dr Farooq Abdullah still has a role to play in Kashmir and like Lord Alfred Tennyson's Ulysses, Farooq is determined to play it to the hilt.

8

Kashmiriyat: The Kashmiri and Delhi

I DON'T THINK A STORY OF MY LIFE—OR ON MY LIFE, HOWEVER you would like to think of it—would be complete without a chapter or two on Kashmir or the many Kashmiris—from the venerable Agha Ashraf Ali to Farooq Abdullah, from Shabir Shah to Yasin Malik and to the many Kashmiri boys who visit me to talk even today—I have interacted with over the course of my career. Then again, I don't think one lifetime is enough to understand the Kashmiri psyche.

As I have said quite often before, it took me a while to understand the state I found myself in during the summer of 1988. But once I began to talk to people, once I began to immerse myself in the political undercurrents that run through Kashmir, I began to understand better. Part of the answer lies—as it so often does—in the mists of history. During its existence, Kashmir has been ruled, at various points, by the Mughals, the Afghans, the Sikhs, the Dogras, and so on. There is, therefore, an exaggerated feeling of oppression.

Could you call it victimhood? I certainly would. It is not easy to see instantly, of course.

On the surface, the Kashmiri, if you can get to really know him, is a kind, gentle soul, but alongside that streak of victimhood runs a more practical streak of adaptability. History and its assorted cruelties have often forced the Kashmiri to adapt, to adjust himself to the vagaries of foreign rule and domination. If you threaten him, a Kashmiri will lie down—he might even play dead. But given a chance, he will rise again. Often I have observed this curious mix of aggrieved oppression and defiance: you might discriminate against them, you might not give them their due, but in the face of repression, they will get back on their feet again. Of necessity, the Kashmiri has learned over the years to be devious. It is, for them, the key to survival. They will not trust you easily, and they will trust each other not at all. As Brajesh Mishra often used to say, 'The only thing straight in Kashmir is the poplar tree!'

Not surprisingly, I've often told the Kashmiris I have interacted with: '*Tum log bahut harami ho, par pyaare ho bahut.* (You are all rascals but l very lovable human beings.)'

For the larger part of my career as an intelligence official, I have been associated with Kashmir and with the turbulence of its political process. I have spoken out publicly about the many facets of the political process and problems in Kashmir. Yet, if the political problems of Kashmir are multifaceted, so too are the Kashmiris I have met, some of whom I have been privileged to call friends. Vijay Dhar was one such man. Once part of Rajiv Gandhi's inner circle, Vijay and his wife Kiran have always been our good friends. Theirs is a family that has never left Kashmir, living through even the horrific exodus of the Kashmiri Pandits though they are Pandits themselves. They have never given up on Kashmir.

Vijay and Kiran lived right below our own home, on Gupkar Road. Neither husband nor wife drank, but in their home, you could always find the best of liquor, and as for the food, it was the best in town, beating even the delicious fare you might find at Farooq Abdullah's residence. One of Vijay's biggest contributions to the social landscape of Kashmir was the setting up of the Delhi Public School in Srinagar. Today, it is one of the finest schools in the country, but when Vijay began work on it, as he told a local Kashmiri newspaper, his family didn't speak to him for three months![1] None of them could understand why Vijay wanted to build a school here, rather than in Delhi. Vijay is a fine educationist today, with liberal, inclusive ideas of learning. In those days, he created a bit of a stir because he refused to discriminate between the average child and the child of a militant. For Vijay, there was just the idea of educating children—it mattered not a jot where his or her parents were from or what they did for a living!

Vijay continues to make the Delhi Public School a name to reckon with in Kashmir and across India today. In many ways, I think this endeavour of Vijay's is a prime example of Kashmiriyat, which is yet another facet of Kashmiri life and personality that I have often talked about publicly. I am, of course, not alone on the discussion of Kashmiriyat—that elusive but integral definition of Kashmir. Today, the term is widely accepted in the discourse on Kashmir, signifying a socio-cultural and secular Kashmiri identity. Over the years, it has been clad in all kinds of hues of nationalism, brushing aside any question of its evolution and original historical context.

Recent scholarship has challenged the idea of Kashmiriyat, of course. Nandita Haksar, author of *The Many Faces of Kashmiri*

---

1 Vijay Dhar, as told to Masood Hussain, for *Kashmir Life*, on 19 May 2017. Available at: https://kashmirlife.net/the-dhar-dictum-issue-07-vol-09-140950/

Nationalism,[2] and I were on a panel at a literature festival in Mumbai when this question came up. Nandita insisted that Kashmiriyat had been diluted and was not the same any more. '*Mahaul badal gaya hai* (The times have changed),' she said. To my mind, however, Kashmiriyat is beyond a concrete definition. The best way that I can think of describing it is 'togetherness', or 'unity'. In bringing students of myriad backgrounds together, without a thought of discrimination or segregation, Vijay's work in the Delhi Public School has been an example of the idea of Kashmiriyat. Another living example—sadly passed now—was the great Agha Ashraf Ali. Unfortunately, I never met him during his heyday. In fact, I only learned of his existence after I had left government service.

His son, Agha Shahid Ali, has the international name and fame as a poet, but in my opinion, Agha Ashraf Ali was an icon while he lived—the quintessential melding of Kashmiriyat and 'Ganga-Jamuni tehzeeb'. Born on 18 October 1922 into an illustrious and highly educated Kashmir family, Agha sahib was the youngest of three brothers. His older brothers would both go on to become civil servants—in a curious accident of history, one would choose India and the other Pakistan. As for himself, Agha sahib remained committed to the idea of educating society, going on to wear the hats of teacher, professor and commissioner of education with Sheikh Abdullah until he resigned. It was not such a leap of faith—academia veritably ran in his veins. His mother, Begum Zafar Ali, was an educationist and legislator herself, not to mention being the first female matriculate of Kashmir. Agha sahib's maternal grandfather, Agha Syed Hussain, was the first one in his family to pass his matriculation examination.

---

2 Nandita Haksar, *The Many Faces of Kashmiri Nationalism: From the Cold War to the Present Day*, New Delhi: Speaking Tiger, 2020.

Kashmiriyat: The Kashmiri and Delhi

I met Agha thanks to Nadir Ali, my young friend from the city and a member of the Agha household. '*Aap Agha sahib se miley ya nahin?* (Have you met Agha Sahib?)' he asked me on a visit in 2011, while I was in Kashmir researching *The Vajpayee Years*. I admit that I was slightly confused at first, but I agreed to go along and meet him at Sufia Nishan, Agha's residence on 4 Rajbagh Road. It was a delightful home, resembling an English country cottage, with roses thickly clustering the walls. The inside was a little darker and more austere. Gandhi's old books and photographs were scattered everywhere, with pride of place clearly occupied by Agha sahib's extensive and well-thumbed library. Later, I would learn that he only allowed a special and select handful into his library, even though he kept an open house, free of all kinds of discrimination.

It was, for me, an exhilarating first meeting, although I think Agha sahib seized the chance to exorcize his curiosity about just what a spook was and how crooked he could be! Here seemed to be a man who personified Kashmiriyat, but as I discovered when I tried to coax him to talk about his beloved land, he was also a man who refused to be baited. He just laughed and skirted the issue.

In 2012, a year later, Agha sahib was turning ninety years old. Even though I had no plans of being in Srinagar around that time, he insisted that I attend his birthday celebrations. Now it was pretty cold even then, and I detest the cold. I didn't want to go, but there was something so magnetic about the man that I couldn't refuse. For the first time I felt as though he had admitted me to a coveted inner circle. That implicit admission made it easier to be Agha sahib's friend, and finally, to learn of Agha sahib's colourful views on Kashmir's tallest political leaders.

For instance, he had much admiration for Sheikh Abdullah, respectfully calling him 'Sher-e-Kashmir'. Yet, as he told me bluntly, while Sheikh had certainly been a courageous man, he was sadly without any brains. Agha sahib found Sheikh Abdullah's reaction to

Partition in north India astonishing, in the light of what Jawaharlal Nehru as Prime Minister was trying to do to save Muslims in the rest of the country. Much later, I asked him curiously who he would vote for in the crucial 2014 elections. 'Farooq, of course,' he said. In his eyes, it was only Farooq who had the calibre and moral fibre to fight Narendra Modi. In those days, I recall that Agha was bitterly disappointed with the likes of Mufti Mohammad Sayeed who had thought nothing of tying up with the BJP, simply to make his political life less arduous. In his opinion, Mufti was an uneducated upstart, and when the deal with the BJP did come through, he shrugged when I asked him what he thought of it: '*Issey zyada kya ho sakta hai?* (Could anything worse have happened?)'

For someone like Agha, militancy was a world of scoundrels and scum. The only man, he told me, he had ever been taken in by was Yasin Malik and that was only because Malik had become Gandhian. However, Haji Altaf, the owner of a hardware shop in Maisuma, claims that Agha sahib had summoned him in 2018 to convey the message to the Abdullah family that it was Omar who was the future of Kashmir. The link with Maisuma possibly lay behind Agha's personal soft spot for Yasin and his so-called 'Gandhian path' until he realized that Yasin was going astray and lacked leadership qualities.

The great old man's philosophy was markedly unlike his son's. Shahid had once been quoted as saying: 'I don't have a philosophy; I have a temperament.' His father, on the other hand, had both, often asking questions and debating the answers. On 2 October 1941, Dr Zakir Husain delivered a lecture at the Jammu and Kashmir Students Federation Annual Conference, in SP College (Sri Pratap College), Srinagar. Agha sahib was deeply influenced by his speech. One of his favourite maxims by Zakir Husain that he remembered verbatim was: 'Youth is not an attainment, but an opportunity that should not be wasted.' As his library testified, Agha sahib himself was solidly Gandhian in philosophy and outlook. It was endearing to watch him imitate the Mahatma's notoriously squeaky voice when he talked of his beloved Bapu. That philosophy often emerged in his advice to the Kashmiri political leadership—*unite or perish,* words of wisdom to which nobody in recent Kashmiri times has paid attention, with the exception of perhaps Farooq himself.

For nearly two decades, as I discovered, Agha Ashraf Ali had lived alone, in that pretty house of his, after his wife's passing. Yet, you never found Agha sahib lonely or dwelling in the past. His was a curious mind, ever ready to learn, and he was never without a book in his hand. At every gathering—and in those days, there were quite a few—you'd find as many Kashmiri Pandits in attendance as there were Muslims. He was aware of his son's fame, but he only referred affectionately to 'Shahid bhaiyya' as Shahid was known, when we persuaded him to talk about him. Above all, he was a man of great integrity, wit and humility. He lived with his *'mulazims'*, who were his family in the absence of his children, and with whom he would share his meals every day. I remember Iqbal, his son, telling me about how *praja* was vital to Agha sahib's Sufia Nishan. In a beautiful kind of way, it made perfect sense.

In the monsoon of 2014, when many parts of Kashmir were affected by floods, Agha sahib was marooned in his home, trapped by rising waters. He had to be rescued by boat, from his first-floor window. Sufia Nishan was devastated by the floods, and his beautiful library was all but washed away. That day, the old man left Srinagar and came straight to Delhi. In those days, Paran and I lived in Friends Colony, and I was surprised to receive a telephone call from Agha sahib telling me that because of the floods, he had escaped to Delhi. If that was the case, I told him, he'd better come and have dinner at our home. I would invite my sister, for whom I knew meeting Agha sahib would be a joy. When Agha sahib arrived, he was visibly shaken. He lost no time in entering dramatically, exclaiming as he entered the living room, 'Dulat sahib, I escaped death by three minutes!'

The last time I saw Agha Ashraf Ali, he was living in a simple hut in Chashme Shahi in Srinagar. It was the summer of 2016, and he was growing older by the day. That year, I remember, I had none of my usual offering for Agha sahib—his favourite was whisky—with me. I was slightly shamefaced when I entered his house empty-handed, but he waved away my regrets, 'Don't worry,' he said humorously, 'I'm only ninety-four. You can bring me a bottle next year.'

But alas, there was to be no next year.

In the last two years of his life, Agha Ashraf Ali seemed to withdraw into himself. He was not particularly keen to communicate, and I was reduced to finding out what I could from his son, Iqbal, who visited his father from the United States every few months and, while he was in Delhi, was kind enough to call me. Agha Ashraf Ali died on 18 August 2020 as he had lived—quietly and smilingly. He was buried next to his beloved wife, Sufia, in Baba Mazar, the Shia graveyard in Zadibal, Srinagar. To the end, his youngest mulazim, Shaukat, was beside him and it was he who made the arrangements for the great man's final journey—a journey witnessed respectfully by hundreds of local residents despite the lockdown in the state.

Kashmiriyat is, therefore, something I find hard to define, especially since in my own lifetime I have seen it embodied so perfectly in those with whom I have interacted in Kashmir. I have often been asked, though, if that idea is changing now, particularly after the abrogation of Article 370 in August 2019.

Kashmir has never been a politically static place. The rise of militancy from the 1990s ensured that events like Rubaiyya's kidnapping (on 8 December 1989) or Burhan Wani's killing (8 July 2016) were simply milestones in a rapid downslide. In this change in the idea of Kashmiriyat, Delhi has played a central role, in machinations born of mistrust and political intrigue. In the winter of 1989, Vijay Dhar was the one who warned me, at the time of

Kashmiriyat: The Kashmiri and Delhi

Rubaiyya Sayeed's kidnapping, that Delhi was gunning for me and I would not survive long in Srinagar.

The day after Rubaiyya was released, I went to have coffee with Vijay to gather information that he may be privy to. He said: 'Between Mufti, Arun Nehru and Jagmohan, they want you out. You need to watch out.' That, of course, is exactly what happened. When Jagmohan returned to Srinagar as governor, he recommended to Delhi that I be transferred. I was seen to be too close to Farooq. When the news was made official, I can't say I was shocked. I was mentally prepared, thanks to Vijay's candour. Indeed, during those crucial five days when Rubaiyya was missing, I had spoken to Mufti sahib several times. His line of questioning about Farooq—critical always—had struck a note of warning. I had known for some time that something would have to give, but Vijay's news came as a kind of subconscious confirmation.

Delhi's constant stonewalling and backtracking has led to a change in Kashmiriyat on the ground—and of that, I think there can be no doubt, irrespective of whom you speak to in Kashmir. I have still held on to hope. If you had asked me, in 2016 like Nandita Haksar did at the Bombay Literature Festival, whether Kashmiriyat was over, I would have argued with you—as I did with her. Nandita herself is an acclaimed scholar on the subject, though her argument centres around the fact that Kashmiriyat is a concept, artificially constructed by the state for its own political ends in Kashmir. In 2016, she insisted to me that *mahaul badal gaya hai*. For myself, I kept asking her, 'How can Kashmiriyat be over?'

But the truth of it is that 2016 was the beginning of the end of Kashmir as we knew it. That was the year Burhan Wani was killed by Indian security forces. Wani's death sparked massive protests across the Valley, in what became the worst span of unrest in the region after 2010. Huge crowds turned out to attend his funeral as his body, wrapped in the flag of Pakistan, was buried next to his brother

Khalid, in Tral. Militants present at the funeral offered Wani a three-volley salute. The unrest and tensions across the state were immense, with separatist leaders calling for a state-wide shutdown and police and security forces repeatedly attacked by mobs. Stone pelting was reported across the Valley, with Kashmiri Pandits fleeing again. The internet was shut down and the national highway was closed off. Thousands—civilians and military personnel alike—were injured and nearly a hundred people lost their lives. D.S. Hooda of the Northern Command, appealed for peace. 'What can the army possibly do?' he said in a statement on 16 June 2016. 'We are helpless when entire villages come out in support of militancy and against us.'

I don't know the circumstances of Wani's death, but I was certainly in Srinagar that fateful summer when he was killed. I had stayed a longer time than I usually do, and on the surface of things, Kashmir was humming. Tourists had thronged to the Valley that year and the hotels and flights were all full. On sunny days, the Boulevard was packed to the point where driving a car was impossible. There seemed to be no better place than Kashmir. But if you stopped for a moment, and if you spoke to the local Kashmiris, you would discover that all was not well.

In my casual conversations, I sensed that something was in the air, waiting to happen. *Ramzan aane wala hai. Aap dekhna Eid ke baad kya hoga.* (Ramzan is approaching. See what happens after Eid.) That was the word on the streets. But as it turned out, Burhan was killed before Eid. So, in that sense, perhaps Nandita is right: *mahaul badal gaya hai*. It changed the day Burhan Wani was shot dead. Kashmir has never been the same since.

And yet, despite all this, there are stories that still make you—or at least, me—want to believe in Kashmiriyat's continued existence. There are stories from history: that of the secular, fundamentally peaceful Ghiyas-ud-Din Zain-ul-Abidin, the eighth sultan of Kashmir. Known by his subjects as Bud Shah, the Sultan was tolerant, humane

Kashmiriyat: The Kashmiri and Delhi

and a great lover of knowledge and art. He was not, by any means, a good fighter nor a good strategist, but he was a wise diplomat, with the humility to learn and understand where he could. The legend of Zain-ul-Abidin lives on today, even in a land so fraught with religious and communal dissension. His spirit can be seen in modern times, such as in the wake of the Pulwama shootout, when journalists zeroed in on the father of the boy who was alleged to have been the main culprit. 'I totally condemn what my son has done,' said this father bravely, 'but I want to say something. Since I am the father, I don't know whether I should say it or not, but I feel very sad for the families of those who have been killed and I would like to convey my apologies and condolences to them. I know because I am a Kashmiri they won't believe me but I would still like to tell them this.' To me, these are all the flavours of Kashmiriyat, present and strong as ever.

I haven't, as yet, mentioned the exodus of Kashmiri Pandits, and in this context, I feel I must, for no recollections of changing Kashmiriyat can exclude that. I must go back to Zain-ul-Abidin again. His is the prime example, I think, of the kind of ruler that Kashmir and Kashmiriyat needs today. In fact, if Kashmir cannot produce a modern Bud Shah (king of the Bhats, or the Pandits), then the present Kashmiri leadership—mainstream and separatist, as well as the likes of Kashmiri Pandit and trade unionist Sampat Prakash—must get together to appeal for the return of the Pandits, just as Bud Shah had done in his time. Without the Pandits, there may not be much hope for Kashmiriyat to survive.

In the wake of Vivek Agnihotri's film (I am on record as having said this, so I have no qualms in repeating it here), *The Kashmir Files,* there has been much debate about what happened during the terrible year of 1990. Why were the Pandits being killed? Why were they being hounded out of their homes? I have no real or right answer to this day, even though I am quite sure that the instructions to do this came from Pakistan. But despite my certainty, I have been told by all these JKLF boys that it was their own people who decided to target the Pandits. It was not, in fact, just the Pandits but IB officials as well.

The first IB officer to be killed was just outside Anantnag in a place called Botengo by a JKLF boy called Mansoor ul Islam, also known as Darzee. When he was asked why he had done this, he responded: '*Upar se hukm aaya hai ki agency waalon ko bhi maaro aur Panditon ko bhi maaro.* (Orders have come from above to kill Pandits as well as IB officers.)'

Some years ago, one of the JKLF boys who had been across the border for training in early 1989 told me that Muslims who migrated from Jammu at the time of Partition had extreme hatred for Kashmiri Pandits and Dogras. Some of them had joined the Pakistan army and then the ISI, who may have been behind the move to kill Pandits. He admitted that some JKLF boys were also anti-Pandit. The bigger villains, however, were the so-called ideologues of the movement who were in direct contact with the ISI and actively aided and abetted militancy in Kashmir.

The trouble with untangling all of this is that militancy in Kashmir is an inherently corrupt process. Today, the discontented murmurs on the street attest that Sheikh Abdullah made a grievous error in 1947, when he chose to support India. Jinnah's two-nation theory, feel many in Kashmir, was right in the long run. When I met with Farooq in January 2022, I brought the subject up. To my surprise, he said: 'I am aware of it, but it's the same people, those bloody *jamaatis*.'

It was, I have to admit, an epiphany of sorts for me. Farooq's remark took me back to the worst and first period of militancy, between 1990 and 1996. That period saw a rise in the rhetoric of aiding and abetting militancy. This was a time when people never took up arms wholesale. It was just a killing here and there. But there were many people who were actively aiding militancy, in helping these boys go and come across the border. Many of these people

Kashmiriyat: The Kashmiri and Delhi

already had links with Pakistan, yet others developed those links very fast. They provided guides to boys wanting to cross over. It was a secretive, deeply camouflaged, process. It was not one guide who took you across. There was a guide, for example, from Srinagar to Baramullah, who handed you over to somebody else who took you to Uri or towards Kupwara and there would be the real guy who helped you to cross the border, so that nobody knew who the other person was, and nobody knew where to point fingers.

These were the people who not only had links with Pakistan but were historically unhappy with Sheikh's decision to stay with India. So when Farooq told me it was the same people, that's who he meant at the time. People have benefited hugely off militancy. Although it was started with the idealistic goal of getting a better deal for Kashmir, it has devolved into a moneymaking machine.

So today, when there is anger about the militants who killed the Pandits, I often think to myself—why would you want to hang someone after thirty-five years? Why not after three years? What retribution are you going to get now? Why did Delhi reach out to them in the first place? So you see, we took a lot of credit for getting people to surrender back in the day, which they did. But the people who brought corruption into militancy and made a business of it had links with Pakistan.

We've drifted away from Kashmir and Delhi. Let us come back to that. Let me take you to the Hurriyat in Delhi which began to talk to the Government of India in 2002, a move which was officially announced by the NDA government in 2003. How was it that the Hurriyat, which was set up and controlled by Pakistan, came to talk to Delhi? It did so because of the new idea of India which they found in Vajpayee. This was the real thing, because he was talking of *insaniyat*, of Kashmiriyat, of *Jamhooriyat*, not of killing or murder. It was the same when Sushilkumar Shinde, Union home minister in 2012, decided to visit the forward areas of Jammu and Kashmir, amid ongoing tensions along the India–Pakistan border. The first Union minister to visit Kashmir in years, Shinde was due to visit border security posts and, in Srinagar, have meetings with Chief Minister Omar Abdullah and top security officials to take stock of the situation on the border.

It was on this visit that the home minister surprised everyone—including me. Driven in a private car, with Omar Abdullah at the wheel, Shinde had shopped at the posh Polo View Market, and was driven through Lal Chowk, the city centre, with minimal security. He thought nothing of jumping out to buy himself some Kashmiri suits, fruits and even stopping to buy and eat some ice cream. Of course, there was an agenda here too—to show that the situation in the Valley was not as grim as it seemed to be. But his manner was easy and informal, and his sheer openness (though it got him into trouble in Delhi) agreeably surprised the locals. Here, they felt, was a man who was not afraid of getting down from his high horse and mingling with them. More importantly, Shinde was a representative of Delhi, and for him to make this gesture meant a lot to the local residents who witnessed this moment of public diplomacy.

The local Kashmiri has always had mixed feelings—coated with distrust—about Delhi. Time and again, Delhi has misunderstood, not followed through on promises, or simply let them down. Time and again, the Kashmiri has been left betrayed. But there was—in those days—still a sense of hope, a sense that the situation could be salvaged. Even after I left active service, I still received visits from boys who talked to me hopefully of the need for young Congress leaders like Rahul and Priyanka Gandhi to come back to Kashmir. It would, they told me, have meant so much. For my part, I have often suggested that someone from the Congress—whether it is Sachin Pilot or one of the Gandhi siblings—make that gesture to a state that is, technically, their home.

Kashmiriyat: The Kashmiri and Delhi

Nothing has happened, of course, and in many ways the same sad story of distrust, suspicion and hostility continues to play out between Kashmiris and Delhi. In his memoir *Outside the Archives*, Y.D. Gundevia wonders why it was ever necessary to put up the tamasha of democracy in Kashmir. After all, if we had not put so much emphasis on democracy, we may never have had the intensity of these problems in Kashmir. In Gundevia's opinion, Kashmir went downhill the day that Sheikh Abdullah was arrested in 1953. Yet, decades into the future, it says much of how deeply interested the locals are in public diplomacy with Delhi that comparisons are still being drawn between Shinde's visit in 2012 to Amit Shah's trip in June 2019.

As Srinagar groaned under traffic curbs imposed for Shah's trip that week, Sheikh Gowhar Ali, joint secretary of the Kashmir Chamber of Commerce and Industry, the Valley's top industrial body, recalled Shinde's visit and its visible ease and informality and compared it with this visit which, he said, interfered not just with daily life but with tourism as well. *The Telegraph* spoke to Abdul Hamid Wangnoo, chairperson of the Houseboat Owners' Association too. He said that local people and tourists alike had suffered because of the restrictions, the likes of which he hadn't seen in a long time.[3] In addition, pro-India political parties were miffed to not have received any invite to meet Amit Shah, with local politicians wondering why the Centre had seen fit not to meet with leaders of political parties this time.

After the abrogation of Article 370 happened in 2019, I had written in a newspaper opinion piece that Vajpayee—like Banquo's

---

3 Ali and Wangnoo are quoted in Muzaffar Raina, 'Valley Contrasts Amit Shah Heat with Sushil Shinde Ice Cream', *The Telegraph*, 27 June 2019. Available at: https://www.telegraphindia.com/india/valley-contrasts-amit-shah-heat-with-sushil-shinde-ice-cream/cid/1693266

ghost—will haunt the BJP for a long time.[4] India is gradually forgetting the likes of Shinde and Vajpayee but in Kashmir, they have not been forgotten. These were the kind of men, the kind of political leaders, who held out hope to the Kashmiri. The Kashmiri has, from time to time, lived with hopelessness. Vajpayee gave them hope. Shinde gave them hope. Even Dr Manmohan Singh—who believed in peace more than anyone I know—tried to continue that process but as the Kashmiri observed, nothing he did could fructify in the end and nothing came of his best intentions.

Across the border, I can safely say that Pervez Musharraf was one of the more reasonable leaders that Pakistan has had in modern times. I remember one summer I was in Srinagar, at a time when the people on both sides of the border wanted peace too. In those days, there were two names in the air: Manmohan Singh and Musharraf. It is one of Kashmir and India's greatest collective tragedies that despite the leadership of men like Singh, Vajpayee and Musharraf, no political solution has emerged for the people of the Valley.

In 2022, then, I return to Nandita's old question—*Is Kashmiriyat over*. Two people can best illustrate some kind of answer to this. One response comes from Sampat Prakash, the hardcore communist and trade unionist, who came to see me while I was writing this book. I had always wanted to meet him and ask him this question, and that day, I did.

'Kashmiriyat is badly wounded, there's no doubt about that,' he said thoughtfully, 'but we have to resurrect it. We can't give up on it. After all, Kashmir *is* Kashmiriyat.'

Yet another perspective comes from a boy I often chat with, a Kashmiri boy who has often been thrashed by the army for no fault

---

4 'Compassion only door to hope in the Valley', *The Asian Age*, 24 February 2020. Available at: https://www.asianage.com/opinion/columnists/240220/compassion-only-door-to-hope-in-the-valley.html

Kashmiriyat: The Kashmiri and Delhi

of his and who, for obvious reasons, shall remain anonymous. This boy has often talked to me about the pride he used to feel in being an Indian, how he used to go with the Indian flag to school, and how now, without any provocation, boys like him are thrashed or, worse, simply because they are Kashmiris. The abrogation has been a sad and unfortunate thing, though here, I differ from my old friend Vijay Dhar. For myself, I did not think abrogation was necessary and I have said this quite publicly too. In Parliament, home minister Amit Shah said that the erosion (of Article 370) was something that was happening for such a long time that Narendra Modi's BJP government was merely completing the process. In this respect, he is right.

The erosion was certainly taking place: I think this chapter and everything I have ever written or spoken about Kashmir establishes this certainty. Abdul Ghani Lone, who was a realist and the true politician in the Hurriyat, had once remarked that Article 370 was never a big deal, and that it could go. But my question has always been: why deprive Kashmir—and the Kashmiris—of their lone fig leaf of dignity. Force, whenever applied, will always lead to increased separatism and radicalism. That is a fact of life and it has been proven in insurgencies across India, time and again, from the Naxals to the Northeast.

Today, the nightmare in the Kashmiri mind has changed. What the collective Kashmiri psyche fears most is chaos. Hence, it is always pleading for Indo-Pakistan peace. What it most dreams of is stability, and what it dreads most is the unknown. I hear it in the conversations that I have with the boys who come to meet me, with those in the Kashmiri political leadership that I still am in touch with. It is no longer a dream of *azaadi*; no longer even a dream to go to Pakistan. It is the nightmare of being reduced to a minority in their own land. It's not something that is openly said, but it is a fear that hangs over the Valley like a shadow.

If you know them well enough to sit down and share their meals with them, the Kashmiris will tell you this too. During my recent visits to Kashmir, I noticed a steady increase in the inflow of tourists—crossing over a lakh, I was told. No doubt this has made the Kashmiri businessman happy, but in the common Kashmiri, there is acute despondency. In my conversations with people, there is a dully resigned air, '*Ab kya baaki hai!* (What is left now!)'

Article 370 is done and dusted. Rhetoric aside, the Kashmiris are by and large reconciled to it so long as they don't feel a sense of defeat. In a manner, this is the ideal time to move forward politically. When Omar Abdullah expresses frustration with the Opposition, then all options appear to be on the table. Though Farooq Abdullah, no doubt, is the tallest leader in Kashmir, Omar still holds the key to chief ministership. Elections, if held, and the sooner the better, may be the way forward.

Sadly, we ourselves might be defeating not only Kashmiriyat, but more vitally, the idea of India in Kashmir. Kashmir has, after all, never succumbed to force. So even though the muscular policy, adopted by Delhi after the abrogation of Article 370 in 2019, has succeeded by and large, what it holds for Kashmir in the future, no one can tell. Peace is after all a state of fragile and fluid equilibrium, and as Kissinger warns, the global order is being shaken by the unravelling of entire regions and the intensifying antagonism of great powers with conflicting legitimacy. Has not our own Prime Minister reminded the world that 'this was not an era of war'?

9

Spooks as Friends: A Tale of Two Spymasters

I FIRST MET AJIT DOVAL A LITTLE OVER THREE DECADES AGO, IN the parking lot of the IB office in North Block. He was very young then and three years junior to me, but equally bright, and under the aegis of M.K. Narayanan, he was a rising star. I don't remember much of our conversation, but I do remember Ajit telling me enthusiastically of what a privilege it was to work with a boss like Narayanan. Hero worship aside, what struck me—and has stayed with me since—is the ambition that lies behind such a declaration.

His focus, even then, was on the chief. It was natural, of course, and it was important in a field such as ours. If you are on the right side of the chief, you stand a much better chance. That's not to say that I was ever on Narayanan's wrong side, but I don't think anyone was as much on his right side as Ajit Doval in those days. He had the determination to go places.

Ajit's legendary career is a well-known one, although it didn't really take off until he was sent to the Northeast, to Mizoram, where he served as the head of the Subsidiary Intelligence Bureau (SIB), the local unit of the IB. Doval arrived in Aizawl in 1972. It was a tricky time to be in the Northeast.

Half a decade earlier, in 1966, rebellion had broken out across the hills, then still a part of Assam. The Mizo National Front (MNF), headed by Laldenga, a former army havaldar, established a separatist insurgency. By the time Doval arrived in the region, the violence had waned, though the atmosphere was still palpably tense and the tide was turning against the MNF.

Following the creation of Bangladesh in 1971, the MNF rebels were left without a place to seek refuge. There was no option, it seemed, but to seek a settlement with India. As is so often the case, this was easier said than done, with talks foundering time and again.

Matters had been complicated by the recognition of Mizoram as a union territory in 1972, and the corresponding emergence of factions within the Front. But talks persisted secretly, between Laldenga and Indira Gandhi. Indeed, when the IB organized an emergency convention of the MNF in Calcutta in March 1976, it was said (certainly by J.F.R. Jacob, the Chief of Staff for the Eastern Army Command, in his memoir) that Doval had paved the way for the hostile leaders to attend.[1] The resulting agreement that came about in 1976 was the foundation for the Mizo Peace Accord that was signed a decade later, under Rajiv Gandhi, after which full statehood was granted to Mizoram.

In Praveen Donthi's remarkable profile of Doval for *Caravan*, he quotes V.K. Duggal, the district magistrate in Aizawl in the 1970s, as saying: 'The approval and directions came from the Prime Minister and the role was performed by the Lieutenant Governor and the

---

1   Quoted in Praveen Donthi, 'Ajit Doval in Theory and Practice', *Caravan*, 1 September 2017. Available at: https://caravanmagazine.in/reportage/ajit-doval-theory-practice

Spooks as Friends: A Tale of Two Spymasters

IB. The IB did the underground negotiations ... Doval was the field man in Mizoram. He had good connections with the underground.'[2] In yet another profile for NDTV, journalist Nitin Gokhale wrote about Doval's brilliance in infiltrating the underground MNF, weaning away half a dozen of its commanders and thus breaking the back of the insurgency where it stood.[3] The whole operation was an astounding success, proving Doval's merit as a true intelligence officer. He was already showing signs of being willing to do the unconventional in order to succeed, a maxim I myself subscribe to.

Many years later, in 2006, I appreciatively read an interview given by Ajit to *The Times of India* in which he narrates how he invited a band of armed men to the Doval homestead in Aizawl.[4] Doval told his wife, Anu, that they were all part of the same operation. In reality, these boys were the commanders of Laldenga's MNF. 'They were all heavily armed, but I had given my word that they would be safe. My wife cooked pork for them, even though she was not used to cooking pork,' Doval said with a chuckle in the interview.[5] When Anu realized just whom she had been cooking for, years later, she was understandably quite miffed! As anecdotes go, it is a gem, speaking volumes of Doval's ability to break away from protocol, if the situation calls for it.

---

2   Ibid.

3   Nitin Gokhale, 'Ajit Doval: The Spy Who Came in from the Cold', NDTV, 30 May 2014. Available at: https://www.ndtv.com/people/ajit-doval-the-spy-who-came-in-from-the-cold-564734

4   'Old men and their Official secrets', *The Times of India*, 3 September 2006. Available at: http://timesofindia.indiatimes.com/articleshow/msid-1951335,prtpage-1.cms. Also available on Ajit Doval's official blog, at: http://ajitdoval.blogspot.com/2008/11/old-men-and-their-official-secrets.html

5   'Old men and their Official secrets', *The Times of India*, 3 September 2006.

In this sense, our styles are similar. I, too, have no hesitation in dispensing with convention, if it gets me the results I need. I have often had boys—from separatists to locals—coming over to my house in Delhi, to have some tea and share some information. In places that are as troubled as Kashmir and the Northeast are, convention has very little place or, at times, necessity. So, I give him full marks because in the same way that I didn't go according to the book, neither did Ajit Doval. He went, truth be told, much more his own way than I did.

Ajit's career continued to rise after his success in the Northeast. Next came reports of his time in Islamabad, where he was posted to the Indian high commission. The cover story for his post varies, depending on whom you read—from 'information officer' (according to Donthi) to 'head of the commercial section' at a time when there wasn't that much commerce between India and Pakistan (according to Shekhar Gupta). But G. Parthasarathy, the Indian consul in Karachi from 1982 to 1985, remembers a young man with an astute sense of political acumen. Doval was, according to Parthasarathy, the first man to contact Nawaz Sharif, then a young and rising politician himself. When the Indian cricket team reached Lahore on a tour of Pakistan in 1982, Sharif welcomed them with a huge party at his residence. That party, says Parthasarathy, was facilitated by Doval.[6]

Word travelled swiftly and soon the whisper on the spooks' grapevine was that here was an officer to reckon with. Ajit's role in Operation Black Thunder II in 1988 cemented his reputation—an already extraordinary one for such a young officer—as a man ready to take risks and employ the art of the gamble. That year, his biographers say, Ajit was at the Golden Temple, in Amritsar, after Khalistani militants barricaded themselves inside the temple complex. It was a moment when the Sikh community relived its collective

---

6   Anecdote from Donthi, *Caravan*, 1 September 2017.

Spooks as Friends: A Tale of Two Spymasters

trauma of 1984, and there was no doubt that the government needed a better resolution this time. Under the command of K.P.S. Gill, the DG (Punjab), government security forces besieged the complex on 9 May 1988. Snipers were in position and water and electricity were cut off.

In a profile in *The New Indian Express,* journalist Yatish Yadav recounts: 'Sometime in 1988. Residents of Amritsar around the Golden Temple ... and Khalistani militants spotted a rickshaw puller plying his trade ... The rickshaw puller convinced the militants that he was an ISI operative, who had been sent by his Pakistani masters to help the Khalistan cause. Two days before Operation Black Thunder, the rickshaw-puller entered the Golden Temple and returned with crucial information, including the actual strength and positions of the terrorists inside the shrine. He was none other than Ajit Doval undercover. When the final assault came, the young police officer was inside Harmandir Sahib, streaming much needed information to security forces to carry out search-and-flush operations.'[7] Trapped and demoralized, the rebels surrendered on 18 May 1988, bringing Operation Black Thunder II to an end.

I won't go into the rest of Ajit's career, because there have been enough profiles and blogs written in an attempt to deconstruct and analyse the NSA's earlier achievements. But I have observed Ajit's rise for a long time. Much before he became the NSA, in the early 1990s, Ajit was facing some professional obstacles in Delhi, as all of us do. I was then chief of the Kashmir desk at headquarters. One day, I received a call from Arun Bhagat, then serving as the DIB. 'Ajit is not quite happy with his posting,' he said, 'but we do have openings in Kashmir. Would you be open to taking him with you?'

---

7   Yatish Yadav, 'Return of the Superspy', *The New Indian Express,* 8 June 2014. Available at: https://www.newindianexpress.com/magazine/2014/jun/08/Return-of-the-Superspy-622565.html

'Sir,' I said frankly, 'I would grab him.'

And so it was that Ajit Doval came to Srinagar, thus kicking off a pattern in our respective professional careers which kept us meeting at different points throughout and, consequently, forming a friendship which—I'd like to think—has persisted until this day. In an earlier chapter in this book I've mentioned that the popular rumour was that Doval had a hand to play in the future organization of the PDP, given his closeness and immediate rapport with Mufti Mohammad Sayeed. The more interesting rumour, in my opinion, was that Advani had also collaborated with the idea of the formation of the PDP. I somehow doubt, though, that Advani had the gumption to defy the likes of Atal Bihari Vajpayee. I don't know the details, of course, but there is something that doesn't quite fit in the story.

But I digress.

As far as Kashmir is concerned, I never intervened with the way in which Doval liked to function. I had heard enough of his success stories to know that he was a man who would get me results. How he got them was his business. As I observed him, I realized that Ajit's method of intelligence gathering was based on a dual process of trickery and a tough line. I had no problems with trickery. Every spook does it—at least, to some extent. But with Ajit, it was a more ruthless application. That is why, perhaps, he was the better spook of the both of us: he was able to be far more detached and, therefore, able to take colder, more calculated decisions.

Was that the right policy to adopt in Kashmir? The answer is for history and the Kashmiris of the present and the future to give. I do concede, though, that if you *are* ruthless in our line of work, it pays dividends. But for Ajit, there were still some rather difficult steps to take before he could wield the kind of power he has today.

On 24 December 1999, flight IC-814 with 178 passengers and eleven crew members left Kathmandu for Delhi. It entered Indian airspace at 5.30 p.m. According to interviews with the crew later, first a masked man stood up and threatened to blow up the plane. Four others in red masks got up and positioned themselves at different points in the aircraft. They directed the pilot, Captain Devi Sharan, to fly to Lahore, but Pakistan, clearly worried about the possible consequences of a hijacked Indian plane on its territory, refused permission for it to enter Pakistani airspace. Sharan then pleaded that there was insufficient fuel on board the flight and persuaded the hijackers to allow him to land the plane at Amritsar.

In less than an hour, the aircraft was suddenly airborne again. It went on to Lahore where it refuelled and was asked to immediately leave. Next, it flew to Dubai by which time one passenger had been stabbed to death and some others injured. Twenty-six passengers were released in Dubai. From there, the plane was taken to Kandahar in Afghanistan, under Taliban control at the time. Soon after the plane landed in Kandahar, we realized that we had fully lost control.

As a country, we had no dealings with the Taliban, which was in control in Afghanistan. India's relations with Pakistan, at the time, were also not great. It was, to say the least, a tough situation. One of the things that we—the Cabinet Committee on Security—decided at that point was that it would be best to send some people of ours to Kandahar.

The hijackers were demanding the release of Masood Azhar and someone was required there to negotiate. To me and Shyamal Datta, Brajesh said: '*Apne log bhej do.* (Send some of your men.)'

'The best on our side are C.D. Sahay and Anand Arni,' I said. 'They're both operational officers who know Afghanistan.'

It was Shyamal who said: 'The best in the IB are Ajit Doval and Nehchal Sandhu.'

The MEA separately tagged Joint Secretary Vivek Katju along. It was a time of high pressure and high stakes. The Government of India took a week to decide what to do, even as protests raged outside 7 Race Course Road. I can only imagine what must have been going through the minds of the hostages, their terrified families waiting here for some kind of news and our negotiators in Kandahar, among whom was Ajit. What I was surprised about was that it was Doval—rather than C.D. Sahay—who was calling me for advice on what to do. It's ironic that I came into play here, and it's possibly because I listen to what people say.

'*Jaldi faisla karwaiye*,' he urged me. '*Yahan bahut pressure hai. Pata nahin kya ho sakta hai idhar.* (Get the government to decide soon. There is a lot of pressure here. Don't know what may happen here.) They have started saying that if you cannot negotiate and cannot come to an agreement, then take the aircraft. We don't care where the hell you go.'

It's always difficult to imagine a man like Doval giving up hope. There are people who argue that we shouldn't ever negotiate, but in situations like this, even the Israelis—acknowledged to be among the toughest intelligence agencies—are known to negotiate. In crises like these, negotiating is sometimes the only option. Jaswant Singh, then minister of external affairs, addressed the issue in his book, *A Call to Honour*,[8] where he argued that national security decisions are always clad in multiple shades of grey. The decision to release terrorists, he argued, was no doubt a bad one, but it would have been worse to risk the lives of 160 innocent civilians. If given a choice, Singh argued, he would always lean towards saving lives.

In hindsight, it was a time of very different men holding very different opinions. L.K. Advani never openly said so, but he disapproved thoroughly of negotiating with terrorists. Doval, being Advani's man, possibly felt the same way, but because he was in a far more difficult situation, he wanted the earliest resolution. Yet

---

8 Jaswant Singh, *A Call to Honour: In Service of Emergent India*, Delhi: Rupa Publications, 2006. See also Jaswant Singh, *India at Risk: Misconceptions and Misadventures of Security Policy*, Delhi: Rupa Publications, 2013.

another opponent to the idea of releasing these prisoners—though not in Delhi—was, of course, Farooq Abdullah, but that is a story I have recounted in *The Vajpayee Years*.

It is a long story, and it has been told too often, but the sad truth is that the Government of India took too long to decide. As foreign minister, Jaswant Singh was a lonely man in those days. Nobody was responding to him, from the United States to Great Britain. At the bitter end, he even tried the Taliban foreign minister, to no avail. That is why when the decision to release the prisoners was taken, Jaswant Singh immediately raised his hand and asked: '*Atalji, main saath mein chala jaoon*? (Atalji, shall I go with them?)' He was a man, made despondent by the weight of the responsibility on his shoulders and I felt terrible for him.

Not surprisingly, then, negotiation is also an option that comes with great mental and emotional strain. Equally naturally, then, Ajit was under immense pressure. He kept me in the loop all through the negotiations. On the morning of 30 December 1999, before the meeting to release the prisoners was to take place, he called me. 'Sir,' he said, '*Yahan rehna bada mushkil hai*. (Sir, it's difficult to stay here.) They are threatening us now. They say if you cannot come to an agreement, get out. We don't know what will happen to either us or the hostages.'

We all know how the end of the hijacking of IC-814 turned out, and my point here is not to debate any of what we know already. To come back to Ajit, what I saw in him right from those days convinced me that here was a man who was going to rise to the very top of his career. He was everyone's friend and nobody's friend at the same time, a line that is vastly difficult for most of us to walk on an everyday basis. When Peter Jones of the University of Ottowa organized the first intelligence dialogues with retired officers from Indian and Pakistani agencies, Ajit Doval attended the first couple of sessions. At the very first session, Peter asked me to say a few introductory words. In the course of my speech, I said: 'Peter, this looks like a serious dialogue, because we have somebody in this very room who is soon going to go places.'

There was a moment of bewilderment, with everyone looking at each other, before the audience realized that I meant Doval. Since then, I have often been asked how I knew he would be the next NSA. My answer remains steadfastly the same—I have always known Ajit would go to the very top of the ladder, in terms of career. There was never anyone more suited for the job than Doval. A serious contender in those days was, of course, Hardeep Puri, but the only backing he had, sadly, was from Arun Jaitley. In fact, when I was leaving the PMO in 2004, M.K. Narayanan asked me: 'If you're leaving, who will look after Kashmir?'

'Doval,' I said without hesitation. 'Or K.M. Singh.'

'No, no, not Doval,' Narayanan replied quickly. 'He's going to be the DIB.'

As it turns out, since my time at the PMO, no other Prime Minister has followed suit by appointing a specialized post for a special state. Doval himself was destined for bigger things than just Kashmir, though Kashmir, of course, is where he has made his mark of late.

There was a slight lull in Doval's career, when he had more or less nothing to do in the aftermath of his posting as DIB. He was a little cut up about it, but he was always a smart and resourceful man. He founded the Vivekananda Foundation, which has become—over the years—one of the leading think tanks in the country. As Ajit's friend, I was always invited whenever the Foundation had an event, and the seminars and conferences that the Foundation held provided me with a somewhat startling ringside view of the evolution of Ajit's right-wing political orientation. In those days, when Ajit had a little more time to himself, we were having lunch one afternoon at the Gymkhana Club. I was then contesting the elections for president of the club and Ajit said to me: 'Don't worry. You'll never lose.'

Spooks as Friends: A Tale of Two Spymasters

More interestingly, he said: 'If you and I were to work together on Pakistan, we could achieve anything.' In a sense, this was what M.K. Narayanan repeatedly said when he talked about Dulat being the carrot and Doval being the stick as far as intelligence tactics were concerned.

When Ajit finally was appointed NSA in 2014, it came, as I have said, as no surprise to me. He and Prime Minister Narendra Modi are made for each other, another fact that I have often stated quite publicly. It's an awkward little part of the NSA's post, since he functions more or less like a second home minister. This almost never works—not between Narayanan and Chidambaram and not between Brajesh Mishra and L.K. Advani. It's an uneasy relationship at best. I have a feeling, even now, that it's not the best relationship—and if it's not great, then it makes it hard going for the DIB. Technically, the DIB reported to the home minister. But he also needed to keep the NSA updated and reported to him whenever the NSA wanted. Which way does he go? How does he walk the line between the NSA and the home minister?

In my time, when I was in the R&AW, I recall Doval suggesting that I meet Advani, who was then home minister. His way of thinking was that if I did, it would go a long way in sorting out our problems in Kashmir. He was not wrong, but in doing so, I would be in an immensely awkward position. It was well known that Brajesh Mishra and Advani didn't get along. My boss was Brajesh and if I suddenly began reporting to Advani too, there would be trouble. I had the same problem with Jaswant Singh, then the minister of external affairs, who also complained that I rarely briefed him. But again, the question always was—how could I suddenly desert my boss and start reporting to someone else? Yet, when Yashwant Sinha was appointed to the post of minister of external affairs, Brajesh Mishra had asked me to go and brief Sinha on various subjects.

To come back to Doval, then, as NSA, he lost no time in doing what he does best—putting out information that would go a long way in building a legacy. In his case, it is what is called the 'Doval Doctrine'. There's been so much discussion on the Doval Doctrine that it's sure to become part of the legend that is Ajit Doval. In short, Doval believes the enemy (Pakistan in this case) should be engaged at three levels:

- Defensive
- Defensive–offensive and
- Offensive

In themselves, the words don't mean much—until you listen to Doval speaking about them. In his opinion, India no longer needs to be defensive about its geopolitical stand. Instead, it must have the ability to tackle the problem where it originates. In the case of terrorism, India must be able to use high technology and intelligence-driven covert operations in order to infiltrate and—where possible—buy organizations out with money, weapons and manpower.

In all these concepts, morality takes a back seat and military might and muscularity are in the driver's seat. I never used weapons myself, but when the Hurriyat split, we grabbed the opportunity and fed whatever money was required into the system to mainstream the more moderate groups in Kashmir, which then began a dialogue with the Government of India. On the other hand, Doval has discussed his policies quite openly, but to me, the first inkling of it came in a question during a conversation between the two of us.

He asked me one day: 'What is your advice on Kashmir?'

'You know my advice,' I replied. 'It has always been to talk.'

'No,' Doval said. 'There's been enough talking. Now, we are no longer going to talk.'

And that is why Kashmir is the biggest theatre, so far, where Doval's ideas of muscular power are playing out. It is also why, following the abrogation of the special status in 2019, I often wonder to myself about which side Mehbooba is on. We will only know for sure once elections are held again in Kashmir some day.

The Doval Doctrine has, over the years, received much attention in the media as part of the building of a more muscular image for India. No less a person than home minister Amit Shah has said that since his appointment as NSA, militancy in the Valley has been controlled. So, Doval was obviously doing some things right. But given my own more accommodating style in Kashmir, it's perhaps no wonder that our approaches are often compared (as David Devadas did rather flatteringly for the Quint).[9]

In 2017, I had a flicker of hope that Doval might be reconsidering his ways when Dineshwar Sharma was appointed by the Centre to talk to any and all Kashmiris. I was delighted when Dineshwar was appointed. He and I had worked together, and he was one of the nicest and most honest men I had met. What I truly appreciated about him was his honesty. You could say something and if he didn't agree with you, he would come back smiling and say, 'Sir, I don't agree with you.'

I loved this approach.

'*Baitho*,' I would say. '*Samjhao mujhe*. (Sit and tell me about it.)'

Dineshwar's methods were such that they made room for honesty and debate. Other times, I would send him a note. Half an hour later, he would appear in the doorway to my room, waving the paper. 'Sir, *yeh theek nahin hai*. (Sir, this is not right.)'

Dineshwar came to see me when the appointment was announced.

---

9 'Centre's New Approach to Kashmir is More Dulat Than Doval'. Available at: https://www.thequint.com/voices/opinion/dulat-hand-in-dineshwar-sharma-appointment-as-kashmir-negotiator#read-more

'Dinesh,' I said, '*tumhara mandate kya hai? Wahan jaake karoge kya?* (What's your mandate? What will you do there?)' After all, there have been many interlocutors in Kashmir's modern history, but Dineshwar was no ordinary man. He had been the DIB himself.

'*Home minister ne mujhe khuli chhoot di hai,*' he told me. '*Bola hai sab se baat karo.* (The home minister has given me full latitude. He has told me to talk to everybody.)'

This sounded most promising.

'*Baitho,*' I said, '*aur baat suno. Kab jaa rahe ho?* (Sit. And listen. When are you going?)'

'*Agle hafte.* (Next week.)'

'*Dinesh, ek kaam karo. Mera ek hi sujhaav hai. Jab Srinagar pahunchoge, airport se seedha Mirwaiz ke ghar jao.* Go without an appointment. Say, *main aapke saath chai ya qahwa peene aaya hoon. Bas yehi bolo.*(Dinesh, do one thing. When you reach Srinagar, go to the home of the Mirwaiz, straight from the airport. Tell him, I have come to have tea with you. Just say this.) The message will go right across Kashmir—that here is a man from Delhi who is open and wants to talk to us.'

'*Bilkul theek kehte ho, sir,*' Dinesh replied, '*Par iss baar nahin, agli baar jaunga.* (You are right, sir. But not this time; I will go the next time.)'

'*Dinesh, agar iss baar nahin jaoge,*' I warned, '*toh phir kabhi nahin hoga.* (If you don't go now, I warned, it won't happen, ever.)'

That, unfortunately, is exactly what happened with Dineshwar. I publicly endorsed his appointment and appealed to the Hurriyat not to miss the opportunity to talk to him. But Dinesh never went to meet the Mirwaiz. He did nothing—and so, the other side did nothing either. In the course of time, his mandate was spelt out by other people. He was too honest and too straight for this kind of a job. When it comes to Kashmir, a little *lachak* (craftiness) is necessary. Dinesh sadly didn't—or perhaps couldn't—go that route. In the end,

Spooks as Friends: A Tale of Two Spymasters

he was sent out of Kashmir as an administrator to Lakshadweep—and interlocution in Kashmir ended, as it so often has, with zero results. Sadly, Dineshwar Sharma passed away soon after that.

In 2018, *Spy Chronicles,* my book with my ISI counterpart Asad Durrani came out, followed by Track-II meetings. At one of these meetings of intelligence officers from India and Pakistan, after Doval had left the group, the Pakistanis complained that nothing was happening. There was, in their opinion, a complete stalemate.

'I see your point,' I said. 'Let me make a suggestion. Why don't you get Doval to come to Lahore?'

The Pakistani response—basically from General Ehsaan ul Haq, the closest to the establishment—was that it was a good idea, but what if an invitation was sent and he still didn't come?

'Well, K.M. Singh is here. As his batchmate, he can do a check.'

That's what KM did and at the next meeting, he reported: 'Ajit will not refuse. He would be happy to come to Lahore.'

That invitation never came. And so it is that Pakistan, which always blames us for not doing anything, has missed the bus on many occasions. But the fact is that the Doval who was once interested in some kind of engagement has gone for good. He wants nothing to do with talking, with accommodation. His focus is on toughness, on ruthlessness, on ensuring that targets are met. This leg of his career, as NSA, has only honed his adaptability, because the Doval I knew in the old days was never focused on Narendra Modi. His attention was on Advani, whose favourite he was.

His loyalty is not so much to the politician as it is to power. If Rahul Gandhi were ever to become the prime minister and ask a younger Doval to stay on as national security adviser, my bet would be that Doval would have stayed. This is despite the fact that Modi and Doval are actually a match made in heaven. They are each very individualistic, and have very similar personalities. Where they both take India—and Kashmir—together remains to be seen.

A LIFE IN THE SHADOWS

On 16 October 2021, Prime Minister Narendra Modi gave a long and glowing speech at an investiture ceremony for the R&AW—a ceremony which I had the privilege to attend. Speaking for much longer than prime ministers normally would, Modi said something towards the end of his speech which struck me. He was talking about how agencies function, and in this context, he praised the work of the R&AW, saying, '*Goodwill banana bahut zaroori hai.* (It's important to build goodwill.)' After the ceremony, we were all ushered into a room for tea and samosas. The Prime Minister had stayed back to shake hands with some of us, and for the first time, I found myself face to face with Narendra Modi.

'*Kaise hain aap, Dulat sahib?* (How are you, Dulat sahib?)', he asked pleasantly.

'*Mauj mein hain, sir. Aaj aapko sunke bahut kuch seekha.* (Fine, sir. Listening to you, I have learnt a lot, today),' I replied.

The Prime Minister laughed and moved on, but his comment has stayed with me. I have always thought along similar lines of '*goodwill banana zaruri hai*', and that is what I have always tried to do in Kashmir. Perhaps other people have noted this. At a function in Delhi on 7 April 2022, I met the former governor of Jammu and Kashmir, Satyapal Malik, for the first time. When I introduced myself, he said, 'I know of you, Dulat sahib. The first thing I heard of in Srinagar was the Dulat doctrine.'

'*Sir, aapko log bahut yaad karte hain.*' (Sir, people miss you.)' I said, smiling.

'*Aapko zyada yaad karte hain* (But they miss you more),' he said, leaving me quite speechless.

Now, I have many more stories about Ajit, mostly complimentary. But as far as I am concerned, my own story as a spook ended with my time in the Vajpayee PMO in 2004. Ajit Doval's story, on the other hand, was only just beginning.

But that's a tale for another day and—maybe—another spook.

Epilogue

> For oft, when on my couch I lie
> In vacant or in pensive mood,
> They flash upon that inward eye
> Which is the bliss of solitude
>
> —William Wordsworth, 'I Wandered Lonely as a Cloud'

PERHAPS IT WAS IN A SIMILAR MOMENT IN THE LOCKDOWN during the pandemic that I first thought of this book.

This is my story, told from the heart, in my own words. Not an autobiography but vignettes arbitrarily picked from the kind of life I have led. When I look back, I feel the beginning starts too late and the end comes rather prematurely. Nonetheless, my beliefs are what I believe in; not believing in what I believe would violate everything I believe in.

In a sense, to paraphrase Franz Kafka, I have followed my most intense obsessions mercilessly.

Epilogue

One thing that comes to the elderly is a heightened memory of the distant past which one puts aside in the busy middle of one's life. Memories of childhood are not very accurate; you don't know if you remember or have been told a story. What I do remember is that one of the first toys my mother bought me on my eighth birthday was a cricket bat. I thought it might make me a cricketer with the result that while wicket keeping in home cricket, I had my front tooth knocked out, which led to my acquaintance of Dr P.P. Sahni—a renowned dentist in post-Partition Delhi.

I also recall playing Monopoly and struggling with Meccano. So clumsy was I in building things that I knew very early in life that I was unfit to be an engineer. Hobbies are a part of childhood; later in life they keep one preoccupied. I began collecting stamps at the age of eight or nine, and still occasionally do. Books were my best companions during the pandemic. Every time I have been to London, I make it a point to visit Charing Cross Road to look for secondhand books, just as I visit College Street when in Kolkata.

The life we have is the only one we are going to get—keeping this in mind reminds us of the value of things. Mortality and old age are scary. If only one could remain young or middle aged or, like J.M. Barrie's Peter Pan, never grow old.

I have endeavoured throughout to retain my boyishness. My mother always complained that I was a sickly child constantly on Cibazol, a sulfa drug for cough and cold. My first doctor in Sialkot was Dr Gurbaksh Singh, veteran journalist Kuldip Nayar's father, a kind and gentle soul.

We were never a religious family, so I engrossed myself more in literature than the scriptures. Despite my master's in history, literature remained my first love, the Shakespearean tragedies and the Romantic poets most of all. Keats, renowned for his odes, was my favourite. His letters to Fanny Brawne remain possibly the best in the English language. Of the Victorians, Browning and Tennyson equally attracted my attention.

It is not that I don't believe in a Supreme Being, because I still visit the gurdwara every Sunday. Having shifted residences more than once in Delhi, I can say that each gurdwara has an attraction of its own and a special place in my heart. Thanks to my schooling, the only scripture that I read was the Bible.

I think my parents enjoyed a very loving marriage, just as Paran and I believe life has been wonderful. But what happens in life, nobody really knows. I worshipped my father but I loved my mother more than I ever knew till she passed away. Funerals provide us with a script of how to deal with death. Sorrow is a part of life—at some point, all of us have endured it or will. It is one of the costs of the beautiful human ability to love.

Ever since my first visit, Kashmir has remained with me. Everything I was to become must have begun there, prophesied for better or worse. We talk of change, but we cannot wipe away yesterday. I have learnt over time that the Kashmiris are the kindest and gentlest of souls who one cannot but love. Lord Curzon once supposedly said, 'If you think you know the Afghans, you need to have your head examined.' I could say the same of the Kashmiris. But love for them has remained unwavering with me.

Acknowledgements

It all began early in 2022 when almost out of the blue the well-known literary agent Kanishka Gupta dropped in and without preamble said, 'Dulat sahib, you need to write two books quickly. A memoir to begin with.' I thought *The Vajpayee Years* had been a memoir, but Kanishka insisted that I had much more to write about. Needless to add that this book would never have happened without Kanishka Gupta. Of course, he wanted it carried to the best buyer, HarperCollins, which was good enough for me and lucky too. Happily I found that my former publishers also lapped it up quickly. The bigwigs, both Ananth Padmanabhan and Udayan Mitra, were extremely supportive.

This book would also not have happened without Narayani Basu, whom Kanishka introduced me to. Apart from being a historian and foreign policy analyst, she is also the great-granddaughter of V.P. Menon, on whom she has written a brilliant biography. Narayani, without any mention of herself, painstakingly helped me to structure *A Life in the Shadows*.

Acknowledgements

Antony Thomas, senior editor at HarperCollins, has to be the last word on the English language considering the consummate ease with which he translated so many phrases from Punjabi and Hindi to English.

For the cover, I must thank Vivan Mehra, who has to be the ultimate professional photographer, and Saurav Das, who designed the cover to perfection.

Swati Chopra, of course, has been my perfect editor. Given her charm and patience, she tolerated my endless whims over hours and hours of rectifications and time spent together discussing the memoir.

Last but not least is Paran, my wife, my ultimate critic, who went over and over the text correcting me wherever I was going astray apart from bearing up with my idiosyncrasies and the 'mess' I always created while writing.

It is difficult to name individually all the wonderful people—friends and colleagues—whom I have had the privilege of knowing, and who have enriched my life. To all of them, particularly in the IB and the R&AW, I am deeply indebted for their constant support. It is amazing that despite being an 'outsider', I ended up being accepted in the R&AW, and I owe it all to the organization and the people I worked with. The IB was, of course, my home for thirty years where I made lifelong friends.

Index

Abdullah, Farooq, 42, 45, 70, 116, 117, 148, 170, 173–202, 203, 205, 208, 209, 211, 214, 215, 220, 229
Abdullah, Omar, 116, 168, 172, 188, 192, 208, 220
Abdullah, Sheikh, 44, 177, 190, 196–98, 206, 207, 214, 217
A Call to Honour (Jaswant Singh), 228
Aceh province, Indonesia, 67
actionable intelligence, 72
Aden, 147
Advani, L.K., 73, 186, 192, 226, 228, 231
adversary, 45, 46, 188
Afghanistan, 227
Afghans, 203
Agent Running in the Field (le Carré), 64
Aggarwal, Rajendra Nath, 7
aggressive surveillance, 63
Agnihotri, Vivek, 213
Agra, 73, 103
Agricultural University, Hissar, 6
Ahtisaari, Martti, 67, 70
Aizawl, 222
Akal Takht, 154
Alam, Shah (Emperor), 25
Ali, Agha Ashraf, 203, 206–10
Ali, Agha Shahid, 206, 208, 209
Ali, Begum Zafar, 206

Ali, Nadir, 207
Ali, Sadiq, 107
Ali, Sheikh Gowhar, 217
Al Jazeera, 102
Allahabad High Court, 7
All India Institute of Medical Sciences (AIIMS), 148, 156, 157
All Parties' Hurriyat Conference, 47
al Qaeda, 44
Altaf, Haji, 208
Amarnath, 200
Ambassador Hotel, Wilshire Boulevard, 143
Ammar, Abu, 102
Amritsar, 53, 103, 104, 124, 154, 224, 225, 227
Ananda Marga organization, 93
Anandpur Sahib, 150
Anantnag, 181
Anderson, Warren, 165
Angleton, James Jesus, 33, 34, 47
annexation, Sikkim, 86
Ansari, Hamid, 138, 139, 141
Arafat, Yasser, 100–03
Argentina, 139, 140
Arjun, 19, 85, 150
Armed Forces Special Powers Act (AFSPA), 188
Arni, Anand, 227
Arnold, Thomas, 14

INDEX

Article 370, Indian Constitution, 70, 75, 172, 173, 185, 193, 195, 210, 217, 219, 220
Ashoka Hotel, 113, 114
Asian Games, 4
A Spy for All Seasons: My Life in the CIA (Clarridge), 40
Assam, 68, 222
assassination, 46, 80, 82, 93, 139, 144, 151, 153, 180
Athens, 129
atomic bomb, 40
autocracy, 94
Awami Action Committee, 47
Azad, Ghulam Nabi, 184
Azadi, 71
Azhar, Masood, 227

Baba Mazar, 210
Babbar, Arun, 29, 30, 31
Bab-e-Ali Stadium, Bhopal, 19
Babur (Emperor), 24
badminton, 8
Bahamas, 138
Bahrain, 130
Bajpai, K. Shankar, 143
Bakshi, Rajan, 162
Bandyopadhyay, A.C., 131
Bangalore, 103
Bangkok, 4, 119
Bangladesh, 81, 88, 222
Bangladesh war, 86
Baral, K.J., 93, 94
Baramullah, 215
Basit, Abdul, 186
'Battling Begums,' 82
Baweja, Harinder, 68
Bay, Guantanamo, 66
BCCI, 121
Beijing, 58, 90
Belgrade, 148
Benares, 47
Bhagat, Arun, 48, 192, 225
Bhajan, Yogi, 143, 144
Bhandari, Amar Nath, 11, 145
Bhandari, Padma, 145
Bhandari, Romesh, 144, 145, 147, 148

Bharatiya Janata Party (BJP), 77, 122, 180, 186, 189, 192, 193, 208, 218, 219
Bharatpur, 103, 105
Bhat, Maqbool, 180
Bhatia, Prem, 13, 126, 142, 143
Bhindranwale, Sant Jarnail Singh, 154
Bhopal, 19, 109, 115, 120, 138, 148, 149, 152–71
  deskwork, 155
  MIC leak, UCIL pesticide plant, 159–66
  Muslim population, 155
Bhopal Club, 167
Bupa Gang, Saurashtra, 99
Bhutan, 71, 88
Bhutani, O.P., 175
Bikaner, 1, 2
Bindra, I.S., 128, 131, 132, 133
bin Laden, Osama, 46
Birendra, King, 87, 88, 89, 90, 94
Birla House complex, New Delhi, 14
Bishop Cotton School, Simla, 14–16, 18–20, 30, 31
BJP, 77, 122, 180, 186, 189, 192, 193, 208, 218, 219
black nationalist movement, 34
Board of Control for Cricket in India (BCCI), 121
Boga, Jal, 16
Bombay, 103, 106, 109
Bombay Literature Festival, 211
Border Security Force (BSF), 99
Bose, Subhas Chandra, 130
Botengo, 214
boxing, 16
Brazil, 140
Brexit, 64
Britain, 44, 65, 108
Britain's Labour Party, 65
Buenos Aires, 138, 139
Bullet for Bullet (Gill), 68
Bureau of Security, MEA, 84
Bush, George W., 50, 79

Cabinet Committee, Security meetings, 53
Calcutta, 14, 22, 23, 103, 107, 222

Index

Canada, 140
Caravan, 222
Cawthorne, Gordon, 109, 110, 111, 112
Central Intelligence Agency (CIA), 34, 40, 46, 50, 73, 78, 82
Chamber of Commerce, Bombay, 109
Chanakyapuri, 150
Chandigarh, 1, 8, 19, 20, 21, 24, 27, 28, 32, 84, 120, 127, 128, 151, 167, 168
Charles, Prince of Wales, 103–09
Chashme Shahi, 210
Chauhatar Bangley, 161
Chavan, S.B., 117
Chhindwara, 171
Chidambaram, P., 188, 200, 231
Chile, 140
China, 40, 53, 58, 59, 71, 72, 79, 119
Chumbi valley, 71
Chuttani, P.N., 132, 135
Civil Lines Police Station, 12
Clarridge, Duane R., 40
Clinton, Bill, 50
Colby, William, 34
Cold War, the, 40, 76
Coleman, Lizzie, 25
Colombo, 79, 88
Colombo Town Hall, 79, 80
Commonwealth Heads of Government Meeting (CHOGM), 110, 112, 113
communism, 36, 37
community shower, 18
Congress, the, 86, 120, 121, 122, 125, 127, 144, 159, 167, 168, 170, 184, 192, 216
Connaught Place, 14
constitutional monarchy, 87
Cooley, Denton, 133, 134
Cotton, George Edward Lynch (Bishop), 14
Council of Regency, 2
counter-intelligence, 39, 40, 45, 62, 98, 123, 124
counterterrorism, 40, 68, 75
cricket, 4, 8, 13, 16, 17, 19, 28, 86, 90, 121
Curzon, Lord, 25

cybercrime, 40
Czechoslovakia, 138

Dadwal, Yudhvir Singh, 62
Dalhousie, 10
Damascus, 63
Daryaganj, 13
Datta, Shyamal, 227
Dave, A.K., 35, 36
Davis Cup, 8, 23
DAV School, 3
Dayal, Rameshwar, 156
Dehra Dun, 2
Delhi, 8, 10, 11, 12, 13, 14, 16, 19, 20, 25, 39, 44, 47, 53, 54, 57, 60, 70, 76, 77, 84, 96, 100, 103, 108, 114, 116, 117, 121, 127, 128, 132, 138, 141, 147, 148, 154, 156–58, 162, 165, 171, 173–75, 177, 181–188, 190–201, 205, 209–11, 215–17, 220, 224, 225, 226, 229, 234, 236
Delhi Public School, Srinagar, 205, 206
Delhi University, 20, 22
democracy, 70, 71, 217
Desai, Morarji, 87, 92–94
Dev, Kapil, 19
Devi, Gayatri, 105
Dewars, Frank, 84, 85
Dhaka, 12
Dhar, Vijay, 204–06, 210, 211, 219
Dharamshala, 6
Dhawan, R.K., 139, 147, 148, 154, 156
Dholpur, 157
Dikshit, Sheila, 121
diplomacy, 89
director general of police (DGP), 53, 118, 182, 189, 225
Director of the Intelligence Bureau (DIB), 48, 49, 53, 54, 61, 132, 143, 157, 178, 192, 230, 234
District Development Council elections, 2020, 196
Doda, 190, 191
Dogras, 203
Doha, 137
Doklam, 71, 72
Donthi, Praveen, 222

245

INDEX

Doon School, 14, 171
Doordarshan, 157
double agents, 45, 46, 55, 56
Doval, Ajit, 51, 61, 75, 192, 221–33, 235, 236
Doval Doctrine, 232, 233
draftsmanship, 35–36
Drug Enforcement Agency, 73
Dubai, 73, 227
Duggal, V.K., 222
Dulat, Amarjit Singh, 21, 38, 105, 108, 143, 209
Dulat, Bahadur Gurdial Singh, 2, 3, 4
Dulat, Jugjeet Barnaby, 4, 5, 14
Dulat, Shamsher, 3, 4
Dulat model, 40
Durrani, Asad, 75, 83, 186, 235
Dutt, Barkha, 96
Dutta, Shyamal, 48, 49, 53, 55, 75

electoral alliance, 193
Emergency, 85, 87, 88, 125, 127, 128
Enforcement Directorate, 70
England, 3, 5, 26, 52, 109, 196
Ershad, Hussain Muhammad, 82
Espanola, 144
espionage, 33, 34, 38–40, 45, 62, 64, 65, 77, 78

Falklands War, 139
Falshaw, Donald, 7, 11
family planning initiative, 87
Faridabad, 157
Faridkot, 124
Farooq, Mirwaiz Umar, 47, 76
Fernandes, George, 73, 128, 182
Ferozepur, 140
Feroz Shah Kotla ground, 121
Finland, 67
Finnish Foreign Service, 67
Fisher, F.H., 17
Fisherman's Cove, 106
Fletcher, A.R., 6
foreign policy, 50, 71, 72, 73, 77, 79, 85, 241
foreign spies, 39
Fort Aguada, 110
Fotedar, M.L., 184

Friends Colony, 171, 209

Gaitskell, Hugh, 65
Gallantry Award, 99
Galwan Valley of Ladakh, 72
Gandhi, Indira, 31, 65, 86, 87, 88, 93, 101, 104, 109–11, 125, 128, 132, 139, 147, 148, 151, 154, 156, 157, 177, 178, 184, 222
Gandhi, Mahatma, 207, 209
Gandhi, Priyanka, 216
Gandhi, Rahul, 122, 216, 235
Gandhi, Rajiv, 39, 65, 77, 78, 116, 120, 139, 144, 147, 148, 149, 150, 166, 175, 204, 222
Gandhi, Sanjay, 87, 94, 171
Gandhi, Sonia, 118, 168, 185
Ganga, Indian Airlines aircraft, 78
Ganga-Jamuni tehzeeb, 206
Ganjoo, Neelkanth, 180
Gareebi Hatao (eradicate poverty), 86
Geelani, Syed Ali Shah, 77, 186
Geneva, 131, 132, 138
geopolitical affairs, 79
geopolitics, 55
Germany, 40
Ghadar conspiracy, 140
Gill, Kanwar Pal Singh (K.P.S.), 68, 69, 70, 118, 119, 225
Gill, Mahinder Singh, 127
Giri, Tulsi, 88
Goa, 110, 111, 193
Gokhale, Nitin, 223
Golden Temple, 68, 144, 154, 224, 225
Gorbachev, Mikhail, 131
Government College, Ludhiana, 5
Government of India, 2, 26, 57, 101, 154, 159, 172, 173, 215, 227, 229, 232
governments and militants, relationship, 65
Grand Trunk Express, 160
Great Britain, 229
Greece, 129
Grewal, Balbir Singh, 26, 28
Griffin, Lepel, 1
Group A civil services, 46

Index

Guardian, The, 184
Guha, Ramachandra, 153
Gulmarg, 170
Gulmohar Park, 11
Gundevia, Y.D., 197, 217
Gupkar Road, 174, 201, 204
gurdwara, 130, 140, 239
Gurgaon, 157
Gurkha Regiment, 30
Gwalior, 121, 148, 166, 167
Gyanendra, king, 96
Gymkhana Club, 9, 230

Habibullah, Wajahat, 39, 117
Hague, The, 63
Haksar, Nandita, 205, 206, 211, 212, 218
Haksar, P.N., 86
Halevy, Efraim, 44
Hamas, 44
Hamidia Hospital, Bhopal, 161
Harballabh festival, 100
Hari Singh High Street, 180
Harvard, 87
Haryana, 6, 26
Hasina, Sheikh, 81, 82
Hawaii, 138
Headley, David, 73, 75
Heinz, Karl, 12
Helms, Richard, 72
Hezbollah, 102
High Court, 7, 11, 18, 145
Hindu College, 121
Hindu-Muslim tension, 155
Hindus, 5, 11, 12, 124, 155, 180
Hindustan Times, 68
hippie movement, 143
Hissar, 6
hockey, 29, 99
honeytrap, 34–35
Hong Kong, 138, 144, 145, 146
Honolulu, 145
Hooda, D.S., 212
Hoover, J. Edgar, 39
Hoshiarpur, 6
Hotel California, Eagles' song, 83
Houston, 126, 130, 131, 133
Hughes, Clive, 23

Hughes, Thomas, 14
human intelligence (HUMINT), 40
human rights violations, 186
Hurriyat, 61, 75, 76, 186, 193, 215, 219, 232
Husain, Zakir, 208
Hussain, Agha Syed, 206
Hyderabad House, 111, 112, 125

IAS, 24, 162
IC-814 hijack, 53, 82, 91, 226–27, 229
Iftikhar, Maulavi, 190
Indian Administrative Service (IAS), 24, 162
Indian army, the, 69, 154
Indian Civil Service (ICS), 4, 5, 24
Indian Constitution, the, 76, 172
Indian Express, The, 200
Indian Foreign Service (IFS), 24, 85, 144, 150
Indian Hockey Federation, 99
Indian National Championships, 4
Indian National Congress, 87, 124
Indian Olympic Association, 3
Indian Police Service (IPS), 24, 51, 68, 94, 99
Indian politics, 86, 87, 153, 174
India-Pakistan border, 216
India–United States Civil Nuclear Agreement, 79
Indonesia, 67
Indore, 159, 166
insaniyat, 76, 215
inspector general (IG), 155
intelligence
  actionable, 72
  counter-intelligence, 34, 39, 40, 46, 98, 123, 124
  dynamics, 71
  failure, 43, 65, 74, 83, 179
  gathering, 33, 40, 48, 56, 63, 70, 75, 83, 226
  geopolitical dynamics, 79
  human, 40
  international, 48, 49
  moles, 46
  scientific, 40
  source report, 35

INDEX

technical, 39–40
Intelligence Bureau (IB), 32, 36, 40, 42, 43, 48, 49, 51, 56, 61, 63, 65, 77, 90, 93, 94, 98, 128, 152, 157, 159, 162, 163, 166, 173, 178, 179, 183, 185, 188, 192, 214, 221–23, 227
inter-caste marriage, 5
international conflict, 67
international intelligence, 48, 49
International Olympic Committee, 3, 99
interrogation, 40, 65, 66
Inter-Services Intelligence (ISI), 46, 47, 56, 63, 73, 78, 82, 83, 91, 214, 225
Irish Republican Army (IRA), 111
Irwin Hall, Bishop Cotton School, 15, 16
Islamabad, 54, 63, 84, 186, 224
Israel, 44

Jabalpur, 159
Jagat, Gurbachan, 199
Jagmohan, 178, 179, 180, 182, 184, 211
Jaipur, 103, 105
Jaitley, Arun, 230
Jaitly, Ashok, 117, 197
Jalandhar, 100
jamaatis, 198, 214
Jamhooriyat, 76, 215
Jammu, 47, 191, 214
Jammu and Kashmir, 169, 172–74, 180, 186, 193, 215, 236
Jammu and Kashmir Civil Aviation Department, 199
Jammu and Kashmir Police, 179, 182
Jammu and Kashmir Students Federation Annual Conference, 208
Jammu Kashmir Liberation Front (JKLF), 116, 179, 180, 182, 214
Jammu-Satwari airport, 78
Jammu's Panthers Party, 103
Jammu-Srinagar highway, 42
Janata Party, the, 87
Jatti, B.D., 87
Jayawardene, 115
Jind, state of, 24

Jones, J.W., 15
Jones, Peter, 75, 229, 230
Jones, Taffy, 15
Jujuy, 139
Jung, Najeeb, 162

Kahlon, Jagat Singh, 199
Kairon, Sardar Partap Singh, 3, 21, 99
Kandahar, 227, 228
Kao, R.N., 37, 51, 52, 151, 154
Kapoor, R.K., 157
Karachi, 54, 74, 224
Karbalai, Asgar Ali, 173
Kargil's Hill Development Council, 173
Kargil war, 72
Kasauli, 16
Kashmeri Gate, 13
Kashmir, 6, 39–45, 48, 54, 55, 57, 62, 64–66, 68, 71, 75–77, 97, 115–17, 119, 155, 168, 170, 173, 174, 176, 179, 181–90, 193–202
Kashmir Chamber of Commerce and Industry, 217
Kashmir Files, The movie, 180, 213
Kashmiri Dogras, 214
Kashmiri Hindus, 180
Kashmiri Pandits, 155, 180, 204, 209, 212–14
Kashmiriyat, 76
   Delhi, role of, 210–11
   educating children/society, 205, 206
   Indo-Pakistan peace, 219
   militancy, 208, 210, 214, 215
   peace, 220
   political problems, 204
   public diplomacy, 216
   victimhood, 204
   Wani's killing, 210–12
Kathmandu, 19, 47, 84–86, 88, 89, 91, 92, 94, 95, 99, 108, 114, 128, 226
Katju, Vivek, 73, 227
Kaur, Gurcharan, 25
Kaur, Jaswant, 3, 25
Kaur, Raj, 25
Kaur, Rajbir, 26
Kennedy, Robert Jr., 143

Index

KGB, 58, 59, 83
Khalistan, 154
Khalistani militants, 224, 225
Khalistani terrorism, 68
Khan, Arif Mohammad, 184
Khan, Humayun, 16
Khan, Khan Abdul Ghaffar, 190
Khan, Mohammad Nayeem, 42
Khan, Sikander Hayat, 2
Khandelwal, R.K., 38
Khanna, Brij, 7
Khanyar, 201
King, Martin Luther, 143
King's College, 4
Kipling, 17
Kiran Cinema, 21, 27
knighthood, 50
Kodaikanal, 2
Kolhapure, Padmini, 106
Kosovo, 67
Kothi, Shamla, 171
Kot Kapura, 143
Kremlin, 59
Kullu, 6
Kumar, Ashwini, 99–100
Kumaratunga, Chandrika Bandaranaike, 79, 81
kundalini yoga, 143
Kupwara, 215

Ladakh, 72
Lahore, 3, 6, 10, 11, 20, 99, 187, 224, 227
Lal, Bansi, 6, 26
Lal, Bhajan, 26
Lal, Devi, 26
Lal Chowk, 216
Laldenga, 31, 222, 223
Lall, Donald, 12, 13
Lashkar, 74
Lausanne, 103
Lawrence, Eileen Margaret, 4, 5
Lawrence School, Sanawar, 16
le Carré, John, 64, 83
Le Corbusier, 21
leukaemia, 7
Liberation Tigers of Tamil Eelam (LTTE), 81

Line of Control, 42
London, 33, 62, 84, 89, 108, 183, 193
Lone, Abdul Ghani, 194, 219
Lone, Sajjad, 189, 194, 195
Longowal, 2, 148
Longowal Accord, 167
Los Angeles, 138, 141, 143
LTTE, 81
Lucknow, 123
Lucknow Mail, 121, 123
Ludhiana, 5, 20

Madhya Pradesh, 31, 121, 149, 150, 152, 155, 158, 166, 168
Madras, 95, 103, 106
Magdalene College, 3
Maharashtra, 197
Mahatma, 14
Mahindroo, Praveen, 170
Maidens Hotel, 12
Maisuma, 208
Majithia, Surjit Singh, 13
Malik, Satyapal, 236
Malik, Yasin, 60, 203, 208
Manali, 6
Manhattan, 136
Manipur, 199
Manningham-Buller, Elizabeth, 44
Many Faces of Kashmiri Nationalism, The (Haksar), 205–06
Marlborough College, 14
Marwaha, Amarjit Singh, 143
Mata Vaishno Devi, 199
McLean, John, 104, 108, 109
Medhekar, K.P., 94, 95
meditation, 144
Menon, N.B., 91
Menon, Shivshankar, 80
methyl isocyanate (MIC), 160, 162, 164, 165
Metro Cinema, 23
Mexico City, 138, 139
MI5, 44, 52
MI6, 33, 50, 52
Middle East, the, 145
militancy, 41, 42, 65, 69, 116, 118, 179, 182, 194, 208, 210, 214, 215, 233

INDEX

Ministry of External Affairs (MEA), 63, 84, 147, 227
Mishra, Brajesh, 49, 50, 54, 55, 58, 59, 67, 73, 80, 168, 204, 227, 231
Misra, S.K., 26
Mizo National Front (MNF), 222, 223
Mizo Peace Accord, 31, 222
Mizoram, 31, 221, 222
Modi, Narendra, 75, 192, 208, 219, 231, 235, 236
Moga, 140
moles, 46, 47, 196
money laundering, 56
Monolescue, Olive, 25, 26
Moscow, 35, 58, 84
Mossad, Israel intelligence agency, 44
Moti Doongri, 105
Moti Mahal, 109
Mount Abu, 29, 30, 31, 93
Mountbatten, Lord, 198, 199
Mufti, Mehbooba, 172, 186, 189, 193, 194
Mughals, 203
Mukherjee, Deb, 143
Mullick, B.N., 38, 51
Mumbai, 73, 74, 206
muscular policy, 68, 70, 71, 75, 76
Musharraf, Pervez, 54, 73, 78, 218
Muslims, 6, 10, 11, 12, 13, 15, 51, 129, 155, 173, 208, 209, 214
Mussoorie, 25
My Dismissal (Farooq Abdullah), 184
My Years with Nerhru (Mullick), 38

Nabha, 2
Nagu, Ram Narain, 155, 164
Namibia, 67
Naqvi, Saeed, 187, 188
Narayan, Jayaprakash, 86
Narayanan, M.K., 35–39, 51, 77, 78, 98, 159, 174, 175, 221, 230, 231
Nath, Kamal, 170, 171
National Conference (NC), 168, 174, 183, 184
National Defence College (NDC), 173
National Democratic Alliance (NDA), 68, 186, 191, 215

National Investigation Agency (NIA), 56
national security adviser (NSA), 49, 54, 67, 225, 230–33, 235
NATO, 40
Naxalism, 70, 118
Naya Kashmir policy, 70
Nazis, 40
NDTV, 223
Neel Masjid, 13
negotiation, 228–29
Nehru, Arun, 77, 86, 147, 182, 184, 211
Nehru, B.K., 184
Nehru, Jawaharlal, 21, 23, 38, 99, 124, 125, 126, 136, 197–99, 208
Nehru Memorial Museum and Library, 151
Nepal, 47, 64, 84–97, 98, 99, 108, 123
  Desai and Vajpayee visit, 92–94
  diplomacy, 89
  monarchy, 94, 96, 97
  monarchy, abolishment of, 96–97
  money, need of, 90
  Ranas, 89–90
  royal family massacre, 96
  violence, 94
Nepal Bharat Maitreyi Sangh, 92, 93
Nepali Congress, 90
Nepal Police, 85, 93
New Delhi, 9, 14, 35, 63, 81, 87, 88, 97, 100, 102, 104, 156, 157
New Empire Cinema, 23
New Indian Express, The, 225
New Mexico, 144
New York City, 136
New York Times, The, 34
New Zealand, 139
Nigam, P.D., 136
Nigambodh Ghat, 14
9/11 attack, 82
Nobel Peace Prize, 67, 102
Non-Aligned Nations Summit Conference, Colombo, 88
Norway, 40

Oldfield, Maurice, 52
Olympic Council of Asia (OCA), 4

250

Index

Olympics security, 99
one-upmanship, 60
Operation Black Thunder, 68, 224, 225
Operation Blue Star, 68, 144, 146, 148, 149
Outlook magazine, 153
Outside the Archives (Gundevia, Y.D.), 197, 217

Padma Bhushan, 99
Padmanabhaiah, K., 196, 197
Pakistan, 6, 10, 12, 16, 42, 45, 52, 54, 55, 56, 63, 71, 72, 75–78, 84, 85, 91, 95, 102, 186, 187, 193, 201, 206, 211, 214, 215, 218, 224, 227, 231, 235
Pal, Satyabrata, 78
Palam airport, 156
Palestine Liberation Organisation (PLO), 100, 101, 102
Pant, K.C., 57, 58
Paran, 24–29, 31, 32, 85, 91, 109, 116, 119, 159, 161, 164, 170, 173, 176, 200, 209
Paras, 96
Parliament attack, 2001, 72, 73
Parthasarathy, G., 224
partition, 3, 6, 10, 11, 12, 15, 208, 214
Pataudi, Iftikhar Ali Khan, 13
Pataudi, Tiger, 13
Patiala, 2, 128
Patiala and East Punjab States Union (PEPSU), 3, 124
PDP, 189, 192, 194, 226
peace talks, Kosovo, 67
People's Alliance for Gupkar Declaration (PAGD), 189, 193, 194, 199
Peoples Democratic Party (PDP), 189, 192, 194, 226
People's Liberation Army (PLA), 71, 72
Peres, Shimon, 102
Pfaff, Anita, 130
Philby, Kim, 33
Pilot, Rajesh, 39, 98, 115–20
Pilot, Sachin, 119, 120, 122, 216

Poland, 130
political crisis, 82, 173
political instability, 69
politics, Nepal, 94
Polo View Market, 216
Powell, Jonathan, 65
Prabhakaran, V., 81
Prague, 139
Praja Mandal, Faridkot, 124
Prakash, Sampat, 213, 218
Prasad, K.N., 35, 36
press freedom, 88
Prime Minister's Office (PMO), 29, 55, 56, 59, 63, 67, 101, 157, 168, 169, 177, 192, 230, 236
Prince Philip, 105
privy purse, abolition of, 88
Priya, 19, 85, 145
Prophet, the, 201
Provincial Congress Committee (PCC), 170
public diplomacy, 216, 217
Public Safety Act, 200
Pulwama shootout, 213
Punjab, 1, 6, 7, 10, 11, 16, 18, 21, 41, 44, 53, 65, 68, 69, 89, 99, 118, 119, 125, 127, 130, 150, 153–55, 158, 167
Punjab High Court, 145
Punjab Police, 53, 69
Punjab University, 20
Puri, Devraj, 13
Puri, Harbhajan Singh, 143
Puri, Hardeep, 230
Puri, Swaraj, 165
Putin, Vladimir, 59

Qazi, Ashraf Jehangir, 73
Queen Aishwarya, Nepal, 96
Queen Elizabeth, 111
Quran, 129, 195, 201
Qureshi, Hashim, 78

Rabin, Yitzhak, 102
radicalization, Kashmir, 71
Rae Bareli, 87
Rajasthan, 30
Raj Bhavan, 29, 106, 107

INDEX

Rajeshwar, T.V., 132
Rajkamal Studios, Bombay, 106
Rajouri-Poonch sector, 42
Rajput, 1
Rajya Sabha, 124, 126
Ram, Jagjivan, 95
Rambagh, 105
Ramban, 42
Rana, Devyani, 96, 97
Rana, Pashupati Shamsher Jang Bahadur, 96
Rana, Sagar, 90
Rao, Krishna, 118, 119
Rao, Narasimha, 63, 77, 117, 183, 185
Rarewala, Sardar Gian Singh, 3
rascality, 46, 47, 56
Rashtrapati Bhavan, 114, 115, 125, 130, 131, 149, 150
Rashtriya Swayamsevak Sangh (RSS), 192
Rathindran, M.K., 173
R&AW, 46, 48, 49, 50, 51, 52, 53, 54, 55, 59, 63, 65, 71, 74, 75, 81, 82, 91, 118, 119, 231, 236
Rawalpindi, 6, 10, 11
Raza, Moosa, 181
Red Square, 59
Research and Analysis Service (RAS), 46, 51, 52
Ribeiro, Julio, 68, 69
Rivaz, Charles, 16
R.K. Puram, 123
Ropar, 150
Roshanara Club, old Delhi, 13
Roy, J.N., 163
Rugby School, 14
running agents, 45
Russia, 58, 59, 79
Russia–China–India cooperation, 58

Sabharwal, M.N., 119
Sachar, Rajinder, 7
Sagar, Mehmood, 47
Sahay, C.D., 227, 228
Sahgal, Ratan, 175
Saleh, Ali Abdullah, 156
Salta, 139
Salve, N.K.P., 145

Samrajya (General), 89
Sana'a, 147, 156
Sanawar, 16, 17, 27, 116
Sandhu, Nehchal, 227
Sandhwan, 124
Sangrur, 25
Sarkar, Prabhat Ranjan, 93
Sattar, Abdul, 73
Sawhney, Praneet, 41
Sawhney, Shiv Ram, 2
Sawhney, S.L.R., 8, 23
Sawhney, S.P.R., 10, 11
Sawhney home, Temple Road, 3
Saxena, Gary, 51
Sayeed, Mufti Mohammad, 42, 182, 184, 189–93, 208, 211, 226
Sayeed, Rubaiyya, 43, 62, 182, 210, 211
scientific intelligence, 40
Scindia, Jyotiraditya, 122
Scindia, Madhavrao, 97, 120–22, 167, 170
Scindia Villa, New Delhi, 97
Scotland, 62
Second World War, 40
secrecy, 78
Secret Service protocol, 142
security liaison officer, 98, 101
senior superintendent of police (SSP), 165
separatism, 42
separatists, 60, 61, 66, 68, 76, 179, 183, 186, 222
Servamus (we serve), 16
Sessions Judges' Bungalow, 5
Shah, Amit, 172, 192, 217, 219, 233
Shah, Bud, 212, 213
Shah, G.M., 184
Shah, Shabir, 42, 47, 56, 57, 58, 183, 185, 203
Shahid Sikh Missionary College, Amritsar, 124
Shamla Kothi, 155
Shamsher, Sharda, 89
Sharan, Devi (Captain), 227
Sharif, Nawaz, 54, 224
Sharma, Dineshwar, 233, 234
Sharma, Shankar Dayal, 80
Shekhar, Chandra, 26

Index

Sher-i-Kashmir Stadium, Srinagar, 19, 180
Shia graveyard, Zadibal, 210
Shinde, Sushilkumar, 215–18
Shukla, V.C., 149, 170
Sialkot, 5, 6
Sikhs, 5, 10, 11, 21, 25, 66, 124–26, 128, 130, 131, 139, 140, 146, 147, 149, 151, 154, 157–59, 169, 203, 224
Sikkim, 86, 88
Siliguri Corridor, 71
Simla, 14, 18, 21
Singapore, 113, 115
Singh, Ajay, 170
Singh, Arjun, 97, 121, 149, 150, 152, 153, 159, 165–71
Singh, Arun, 77
Singh, Beant, 154, 156
Singh, Bhagat, 124
Singh, Bhalindra, 3, 4
Singh, Bhim, 103
Singh, Bhupendra, 3
Singh, Buta, 149
Singh, Digvijay, 170, 171
Singh, Gajpat, 24, 25
Singh, Giani Zail, 124–51, 156, 157
Singh, Jarnail, 124
Singh, Jaswant, 67, 68, 228, 229
Singh, Karan, 121
Singh, K.C., 150
Singh, Khushwant, 126
Singh, K.M., 192, 230, 235
Singh, K.P., 174
Singh, Kulwant (General), 6
Singh, Manmohan, 77, 79, 168, 185, 186, 218
Singh, Narayan, 156
Singh, Natwar, 143–45, 168
Singh, Rabinder, 63, 64
Singh, Ranbir, 25, 26
Singh, Ranjit, 25
Singh, Ripudaman, 2
Singh, Sardar Jagir, 130, 134, 135
Singh, Satwant, 156
Singh, Sucha, 99
Singh, Tarlochan, 125, 126, 129, 137, 150
Singh, V.P., 48, 182
Singha Durbar (Rana), 90
Singh II, Sawai Man (Maharaja), 105
Sinha, Yashwant, 231
Sivaraman, 160
Sodhi, S.S., 7
Sood, Vikram, 75
South America, 139, 140
South Asia, 52, 86
South Asia Portal, 69
Soviet Union, the, 34, 67, 131
Special Protection Group (SPG), 93
spook to spook dialogue, 75
Spy Chronicles, 235
Sri Lanka, 79, 81, 88
Srinagar, 19, 39, 41, 43, 56, 62, 70, 76, 78, 115, 116, 121, 170, 171, 173–75, 177, 178, 183, 187, 188, 190, 192, 198, 200–202, 207–12, 215–18, 226, 234, 236
Srinagar airport, 76, 78
station house officer (SHO), 12
St. Stephen's College, Delhi, 20
Stuart, Louis, 2
Subsidiary Intelligence Bureau (SIB), 164, 222
Sufia Nishan, 207, 209
Sujan Singh Park, 126
Sultan, Begum Sajida, 13
Sundaram, K.V.K., 8
Super Cop, 69
superintendent of police (SP), 12, 13
Supreme Court, 11, 95
surveillance, 34, 40, 62–64, 77, 78
swallows, 34
Switzerland, 103

Taj, The, 74
Taliban, 227
Talking to Terrorists: How to End Armed Conflict (Powell), 65
Tamil Nadu, 107
Tamil Nadu Express, 157
Tandan, Subhash, 126
Taploo, Tika Lal, 180
technical intelligence (TECHINT), 39–40
Tel Aviv, 44

INDEX

Telegraph, The, 217
Tenet, George, 50, 78
tennis, 8, 13
Tennyson, Lord Alfred, 202
Teresa, Mother, 82
terrorism, 68, 69, 73, 75, 79, 232
terrorists, 65, 68, 69, 76, 78, 79, 100, 225, 228
Thatcher, Margaret, 109–112
Thimphu, 71
Thompson, John, 104
'3HO' (healthy, happy, holy) way of life, 144
Tilak Marg, New Delhi, 9, 156, 195
Times of India, The, 223
Tiwana, Jasbir Singh, 120
Tom Brown's School Days (Hughes), 14
Toynbee, Arnold, 201
Track-II business, 75
Tribune, The, 126, 142
Trubnikov, Vyacheslav Ivanovich, 58, 59
Tunbridge Wells, Kent, 19
Turkman Gate demolitions, 87
26/11 attack, 73, 74, 82
two-nation theory, Jinnah, 214
Tyabji, Hindal, 117

Ukraine, 40
ul Haq, Ehsaan, 235
ul Islam, Mansoor, 214
Ulysses (Tennyson), 202
Union Carbide India Limited (UCIL)'s pesticide plant, 160, 161, 164, 165, 169
Unionist Party, 2
Union Law Commission, 8
Union Public Service Commission (UPSC), 22, 24
United Progressive Alliance (UPA) government, 187, 188
United States, the, 79, 126, 131, 133, 140, 143, 144, 165, 210, 229
University of Cambridge, 3, 4, 14
University of Ottowa, 75, 229
University of Tokyo, 87
Uri, 215
Ustinov, Peter, 156

Vajpayee, Atal Bihari, 29, 59, 67, 76, 77, 79, 92, 121, 167, 182, 187, 192, 217, 218, 226
Vajpayee Years, The (Dulat), 56, 72, 73, 183, 207, 229
Vaudois University Hospital Centre (CHUV), 103
Venkataraman, R., 157
Viborg, 67
victimhood, 204
Vietnam War, the, 143
Vishwanath, 99
Vivekananda Foundation, 230
Vohra, Motilal, 167, 168
Vohra, N.N., 57
Volga restaurant, 13

Walauwa, Horagolla, 80
Waldorf Astoria, 136
walk-in, 55
Wangchuck, Jigme Singye, 71
Wangnoo, Abdul Hamid, 217
Wani, Burhan, 210, 211, 212
Warsaw, 130
Washington, 84
Watergate, 34
Westminster School, 14
Whitmarsh Knight, T.W., 17
Wickremesinghe, Ranil, 80
Wimbledon, 8
Winter Olympics, Vancouver, 100
Winter War, 1939-40, 67
women, IB/R&AW, 51

Yacht Club, 74
Yadav, Yatish, 225
Yemen, 147, 156
Yew, Lee Kuan, 112–115
yoga, 143, 144

Zadibal, 210
Zafar Ali Road, Lahore, 3
Zain-ul-Abidin, Ghiyas-ud-Din, 212, 213
Zaman, Nayyar, 91
Zia, Khaleda, 81, 82
Zia-ul-Haq, 102
Zimbabwe, 19

About the Author

Amarjit Singh Dulat is a former head of the Research and Analysis Wing (R&AW), India's external intelligence agency. After retirement, he was appointed adviser on Kashmir in the Prime Minister's Office and served there from January 2001 to May 2004. During this time he accumulated a vast reservoir of goodwill with Kashmiris of all shades. As *Jane's Intelligence Digest* put it in 2001, 'Well known for his social skills, Dulat preferred dialogue to clandestine maneouvers.' In his heyday, Dulat was referred to as 'Mr Kashmir'.

Dulat was born in Sialkot, Punjab, in December 1940. With India's partition, his father Justice Shamsher Singh Dulat relocated his family to Delhi. After schooling in Delhi, Simla and Chandigarh, Dulat joined the Indian Police Service (IPS) in 1965, and then the Intelligence Bureau (IB) in 1969, where he served for almost thirty years. At IB he headed the Kashmir Group during the turbulent 1990s till he joined and headed the R&AW.

Dulat's first book, *Kashmir: The Vajpayee Years*, was published in 2015, followed by *The Spy Chronicles: R&AW, ISI and the Illusion of Peace* in 2018, which he co-authored with General Asad Durrani, former director-general of Pakistan's Inter-Services Intelligence Directorate.

30 Years *of* HarperCollins *Publishers* India

At HarperCollins, we believe in telling the best stories and finding the widest possible readership for our books in every format possible. We started publishing 30 years ago; a great deal has changed since then, but what has remained constant is the passion with which our authors write their books, the love with which readers receive them, and the sheer joy and excitement that we as publishers feel in being a part of the publishing process.

Over the years, we've had the pleasure of publishing some of the finest writing from the subcontinent and around the world, and some of the biggest bestsellers in India's publishing history. Our books and authors have won a phenomenal range of awards, and we ourselves have been named Publisher of the Year the greatest number of times. But nothing has meant more to us than the fact that millions of people have read the books we published, and somewhere, a book of ours might have made a difference.

As we step into our fourth decade, we go back to that one word – a word which has been a driving force for us all these years.

Read.